Communication in Everyday Use

Communication in Everyday Use

THIRD EDITION

ELIZABETH G. ANDERSCH, Ph.D.
Professor Emerita
Ohio University

LORIN C. STAATS, Ph.D.
University of Dayton

ROBERT N. BOSTROM, Ph.D.
Ohio University

RINEHART PRESS
SAN FRANCISCO

Copyright 1950, © 1960, 1969 by Holt, Rinehart and Winston, Inc.
All rights reserved
Library of Congress Catalog Card Number: 69-16074
ISBN: 0-03-080980-0
Printed in the United States of America
56789 090 98

Preface

The latter half of the twentieth century has brought profound changes in American education. One of the most interesting and perhaps the most significant of these changes has been the appearance of a systematic study of communication in colleges and universities. This attention has resulted from a widespread recognition of the critical role which communication plays in all aspects of our society.

Much of the academic growth in the area of communication has taken place in departments of speech. Given the freedom to develop, the communication approach has exploded the traditional boundaries of "speech," with far-reaching consequences. The present trend seems to be that modern communicologists are less concerned with the history and tradition of public address and are now more concerned with the function of communication in the daily contacts of individuals with other individuals and individuals with groups. Moreover, the contemporary speech teacher is making a far greater effort to contribute to the ever-growing body of research in the area of communication, together with sociologists, psychologists, linguists, managers, engineers, and so on. With this emphasis on communication has inevitably come new courses, new majors, and new approaches to the teaching of speech.

The service course in speech is beginning to reflect these comparatively recent developments in departments of speech. While retaining many of the objectives of the traditional service course, new goals have been added and the traditional goals expanded. The over-all purpose of the first course in "speech" still remains to improve the student's abilities to communicate. However, the definition of "to communicate" appears to be much broader and more functional. No longer is the speech teacher concerned solely with the ability of the student to transmit a message successfully. Of equal concern now is the reception of an oral message by a receiver and the total environment as it affects and is affected by communication in *any form.*

The first and second editions of *Speech for Everyday Use* reflected what appears now to have been somewhat unsophisticated efforts on the part of the authors to provide beginning students with a text which recognized the current communication approach to the teaching of speech. Since the second edition was published in 1960, there have been significant developments in the field of communication, academically and scientifically. The third edition, retitled, the authors hope appropriately, *Communication in Everyday Use,* reflects this tremendous activity in the area of communication.

Believing that a thorough knowledge of all aspects of communication is fundamental to becoming a functional communicator, the authors have devoted the first chapter of this text to a comprehensive review of communication theory, terminating in an original model of the communicative process. The model also provides the organization for the balance of the text, with individual chapters devoted to in-depth discussion of each of the elements included in the model. Subsequent chapters, then, are devoted to the source of communication, structuring a message, language, values, and attitudes which affect the message, and the transmission elements employed by the communicator. The elements in listening are treated in a separate chapter which includes discussion of the receiver and the activities which affect his reception of the message and his feedback to the sender of the message. The final chapter of Part One of the book is devoted to an analysis of the responsibilities which are incumbent upon the speaker and listener.

While language and organization are treated in individual chapters, the authors view the combination of these two elements as inseparable parts of the process of structuring a message. Both of these elements are treated from two major points of view: first, as prescriptive recommendations that the students can use in achieving their goals in a communicative act; second, as background against which students can compare other communicative acts which they encounter in society.

The principle criterion for the selection of materials for inclusion in Part One of the text has been their relevancy for beginning students. Since, for many college students, the first course in oral communication is their initial experience with subject matter of this type, every effort has been made to relate concepts to experiences which are familiar to students. Also, the authors have made a special effort to link the material in various chapters in the book to the material presented in previous chapters, insuring continuity and alerting the students to the concept that, in the case of oral communication, the whole is greater than the sum of its parts.

While Part One of the text is devoted to a discussion of communication theory, Part Two challenges the student to put into practice and/or apply the theory presented in Part One. Included in this portion of the text are drills and projects which may be done by the student outside of class. These activities direct the student's attention to certain principles presented in Part One. In addition, a set of diagnostic performances are described. Finally, a series of communicative problems are provided. These are arranged, the authors believe, in a sequence which leads the student from a fairly simple communicative task through a series of increasingly more difficult communication problems.

In this sequence of communication problems, the student is directed to concentrate on obtaining a specific response from his listeners. Unlike most beginning texts in this field, the purposes of communication are defined in terms of audience response in place of the more usual speaker purposes such as "to inform," "to persuade or convince," "to entertain," and so on. Thus, the speaker must continuously evaluate his audience response as the most important measure of his success. It is the hope of the authors that as a result of this approach, the student will not assess his success in communication solely on the basis of how well he has adhered to the principles, but will be more concerned with his audience response as an indication of his abilities to transmit a particular message.

While the authors believe that a knowledge of communication theory is essential to the improvement of the communicative ability of any individual, they also firmly support the need for frequent opportunities to put into practice the theoretical bases of communicating. The ability to analyze a communication breakdown is not enough. If the communicator is to be successful he must not only perceive the nature of breakdowns, but he must anticipate problems and challenges in the communication situation and must find a way, based on his knowledge of communication, to achieve a particular goal with his audience. In other words, he must be able to convert his knowledge of communication theory to *action*.

In our complex society, communication development is too important to be studied in a single, beginning course and too critical to be ignored when the course is completed. It is the hope of the authors that the material presented in this text will be sufficiently stimulating so that a student will be motivated to continue a study of the communication process formally or informally and that the progress which he makes while enrolled in the course will be the beginning of a continuous effort to develop communication abilities which are appropriate to his intellectual maturity.

Athens, Ohio
January 1969

E. G. A.
L. C. S.
R. N. B.

Acknowledgments

It would be almost impossible to identify all of the people who have shaped or influenced this textbook. Over a long period of time, casual discussions with colleagues, graduate students, undergraduates, and friends have been most helpful and certainly have had a significant effect on the present revision.

There are some people who have made substantial contributions to the present text, however. In the first revision, Dr. Claude E. Kantner provided a challenging and perceptive chapter, "The Nature, Function, and Problems of Language," and Dr. Edward M. Penson wrote a penetrating chapter dealing with the speaker as a source of communication. Although these two chapters do not appear in their original form in this revision, large segments of this valuable material have been included and woven into the new chapters. The authors are indebted to Dr. Kantner and Dr. Penson for permitting us to continue to use their original contributions to our advantage.

Special thanks are due also to Dr. Robert S. Goyer, Dr. Jon K. Shallop, Mr. Ronald Williams, Mr. Ray E. Wagner, and Miss Helen Siegelin for their critical evaluations of materials contained in the 1960 edition and of the proposed materials for this publication.

The authors also wish to express their gratitude to the U.S.D.A. Soil Conservation Service, The Athens Soil and Water Conservation District, Mrs. Thomas H. Evans, and Dr. Harry M. Kaneshige for providing resource materials for the model speech included in Chapter 3.

Mrs. Robert N. Bostrom typed most of the manuscript; the authors appreciate her expert help in preparing the manuscript and that of Miss Jean E. Dawson who also contributed some typing to the project.

The authors are also indebted to the many publishers, authors, and speakers who have granted permission to quote a great variety of materials.

CONTENTS

Preface   v

Acknowledgments   ix

PART ONE: COMMUNICATION THEORY

1
THE PROCESS OF COMMUNICATION   3
Introduction   3
Why Study Communication?   9
    Communication and Cultural Diffusion   9
    Occupational Demands and Communication   10
    Communication and Interpersonal Relationships   11
    Communication Is Learned   12
What Is Communication?   13
    Some Definitions of Communication   14
    Communication Models   18
    The Function of Models and Definitions   20
    Criteria for Establishing a Model   21
A Model for Study   22
    Basic Processes   22
    Communicative Purposes—Different Forms of Communication   24
        Oral Communication—The Study of Speech   34

2
THE SOURCE—THE BEGINNING OF COMMUNICATION   48
    Becoming a Source   48
        Invention   49
        Situations and Sources   50
    Thinking   52
        Thinking Depends upon Adequate Exposure to Stimuli   54
        Thinking Involves Establishing Proper Relationships   58
        Thinking Assists You in the Process of Isolating General Topics   61

Creating | 62
Other Source Characteristics | 66
    Adjustment | 67
    Causes of Poor Adjustment | 67
The Source and Control | 70
The Source Responsibility | 75

3
STRUCTURING THE MESSAGE 76
Introduction | 76
Outlining | 81
    The Introduction | 81
    The Key Idea | 84
    The Body of the Speech | 85
    Developing the Body of the Speech | 89
    The Conclusion | 92
Steps in Preparing a Formal Communication—a Speech | 95
Expanding the Outline | 96
Application of Outlining Principles to a Specific Communication Task | 99

4
LANGUAGE 113
The Nature and Function of Language | 113
    Our World of Words | 113
    Our Casual Attitude toward Language | 114
    Four Indispensable Tools: Speaking, Listening, Writing, Reading | 114
    A Difficult and Complex Process | 115
    The Importance of Speech to the Individual | 115
Barriers to Understanding | 116
    The Crucial Importance of Understanding | 116
    Barriers Imposed by the Use of Words | 117
    Language—a Calculated Risk | 119
Language—Tool of Communication | 119
    Words and Their Meanings | 120
    Language and Attitude Change | 124
Choice and Arrangement of Words | 125
Positive Approach to Better Language Use | 128
    Be Exact | 128
    Avoid Overworked Words | 129
    Be Vivid | 130
    Adapt Your Language to the Situation | 134
    Always Use Language That Is in Good Taste | 134

CONTENTS xiii

Avoid Verbosity	135
Build a Vocabulary	135
Transitions	136

5
COMMUNICATING TO AFFECT ATTITUDES — 139

Evidence	144
What Makes Evidence Effective?	145
Evidence and the Communication Model	146
Types of Evidence	149
Logic	153
Toulmin's Model of Logical Relationships	154
How Attitudes Change—Balance	158
Basic Tenets of Balance Theory	159

6
THE TRANSMITTERS OF ORAL COMMUNICATION — 163

Introduction	163
The Vocal Mechanism	165
Vocal Characteristics	170
Pitch	170
Quality	174
Loudness	177
Articulation-Pronunciation	179
Articulation	180
Pronunciation	184
Rate and Rhythm	189
Conversational Style	192
The Use of the Body in Speech	194
Eye Contact	194
Facial Expression	195
Gestures	195
Movement	196
Visual Aids	197

7
LISTENING — 201

Introduction	201
The Listener	206
The Listener Hears and Restructures	207

    The Listener Evaluates   210
    The Listener Reacts   219

8
THE COMMUNICATOR'S RESPONSIBILITY   223
"Freedom of Speech"   223
    Limitations on Communication   225
Obligations of the Communicator   229

PART TWO: COMMUNICATION THEORY IN PRACTICE

Introduction   233
    Assignment Outline   235
Drills and Projects   237
Diagnostic Performances   247
Communicative Problems   252

APPENDIX

Model Speeches   271
    "The Life of a Diplomat"   271
    "Education for Leadership: Harder to Teach Men than to Teach a Subject"   280
    Introduction of Dag Hammarskjöld   284
    "For the League of Nations"   285

INDEX   299

PART ONE

COMMUNICATION THEORY

1 THE PROCESS OF COMMUNICATION

INTRODUCTION

In the last few years, paleontologists have identified many interesting species of manlike-apes—creatures that lived up to 500 million years ago and seem to be the precursors of humanity in this world. When examining the known characteristics of any one of these species, it is difficult to tell whether the fossil represents a man or an ape, because most fossils have features common to both groups and therefore pose an interesting question in the origin of humanity. Paleontologists usually hedge in classifying any given species, but on one point they seem to be in general agreement—one of the indicators of "man" in a primitive environment is the use of symbols and communicative activity.[1] Man, then, is the "communicating animal" and the main characteristic that separates him from the rest of the animals is his facility for using symbols and engaging in communicative activity.

When man is compared to the other animals, he seems a truly pitiful creature—he cannot run as well as the horse, climb as well as the ape, swim, fight, fly, or do any of the specialized skills that most animals have developed. Even given his marvelous brain and prehensile hand, man remained a distinctly second-rate species—until communication established cooperating groups of men and civilization as we know it was developed. The profound difference this ability makes in us led the philosopher John Locke to exclaim that "God, having designed man for a sociable creature, made him not only with an inclination, and under a necessity to have fellowship with those of his own kind,

[1] G. H. R. Koenigswald, *The Evolution of Man*, (Ann Arbor, Michigan, 1962), p. 132.

but furnished him also with language, which was to be the great instrument and common tie of society."[2] Locke reasoned that God created man; the principal difference between men and animals is communicative; therefore God must have created our communicative ability.

Locke's interpretation of the origins of speech is somewhat out of fashion now, but it illustrates how the communicative function dominates our idea of humanity. Few of us are accustomed to think of ourselves as communicating animals, but our involvement in this process is total. The extent of this involvement was well put by the great British communications engineer, Colin Cherry, when he stated:

> Of all man's functions, that of building up systems of communication of infinite variety and purpose is one of the most characteristic. Of all living creatures he has the most complex and adaptable systems of language; he is the most widely observant of his physical environment and most responsive in his adjustment to it. He has organized ethical, political, and economic systems of varied kinds; he has the greatest subtlety of expressing his feelings and emotions, sympathy, awe, humor, hate—all the thousand facets of his personality. He is self-conscious and responsible; he has evolved spiritual, moral, and aesthetic sensibilities.
>
> A man is not an isolated being in a void; he is essentially integrated into society. The various aspects of man's behavior—his means of livelihood, his language, and all forms of self expression, his systems of economics and law, his religious ritual, all of which involve him in acts of communication—are not discrete and independent but are inherently related.[3]

If it seems that our involvement in communication has been overstated here, let us look for a moment at a few of the effects communication has on our everyday lives. We begin the day awakened from our rest by a message—in the form of noise from an alarm clock—communicated from ourselves the night before. We get out of our bed, which was put together in a factory largely as the result of instructions relayed from a foreman to his workers. These instructions were based on communications this foreman received earlier from engineers and designers in the form of a blueprint. The store where the bed was purchased secured the bed from the factory by using a written communication—an "order," and the bed was paid for by the store by another written communication—a check which told a bank to pay the factory a certain sum of money. Our bedclothes and pajamas were probably fabricated and purchased in a similar fashion.

[2] John Locke, *An Essay Concerning Human Understanding*, (London, 1965), p. 229.
[3] Colin Cherry, *On Human Communication*, (New York, 1961), p. 29.

Upon rising, we brush our teeth with a tooth paste which has been the subject of an intense communication campaign by an advertising agency. The desire to keep our teeth clean is largely the result of communications of this type—we call them "commercials"—and messages from dentists and health agencies which warn us about dental cavities. We dress ourselves in a manner which will signal our status to the rest of the world, and then go to breakfast. The breakfast offerings are communicated to us by means of a message called a menu, and after all of this communication, we finally raise our voice for the first time in the day, ordering something to eat. In so doing, we signal more than "ham and eggs" to the waitress; we also imply that we will eat what she brings and subsequently pay for it. We might also be signaling what kind of a night it was the night before by our intonation and our actions.

This very small sample should serve to illustrate the central role communication plays in our affairs. Most of the time we communicate largely out of habit and without consciously considering the process; it has become part of our daily routine. From time to time, however, we have to make a conscious effort to communicate with someone—perhaps by writing a letter or arranging a conference. We then become very aware of the communicative process and have to do things consciously that we normally do without thinking. We may become awkward about it, much as a basketball player becomes awkward when he concentrates on the form of his free throw, forgetting the total unity of the movement. We are making an effort to be "communicative," sometimes successfully, and sometimes not—and seldom knowing how effective we are.

Many of us are involved with communication to a much greater degree than others, because there are professions that are primarily communicative. Teachers, ministers, salesmen, executives, psychiatrists, aircraft controllers, and many others operate wholly as manipulators of symbols rather than as manipulators of things. David Berlo has correctly observed that this kind of occupation is on the increase in our society—and may be its fastest growing element.[4] This trend is largely the result of the new electronic technology, and is well described by Marshall McLuhan in his provocative book, *Understanding Media:*

> In this electric age we see ourselves being translated more and more into the form of information, moving toward the technological extension of consciousness. That is what we mean when we say that we daily know more and more about man. We mean that we can translate more and more of ourselves into other forms of expression that exceed ourselves.

[4] David Berlo, *The Process of Communication,* (New York, 1960), p. 24.

> Man is a form of expression who is traditionally expected to repeat himself and to praise his creator.[5]

In other words, we are communicating more and more; the distances in our world become smaller and smaller—the only way we can shut out communication is to become hermits—and then we'd probably spend our days communicating with ourselves.

Many persons, overwhelmed by the tremendous influence modern communication has on our lives, are genuinely concerned that we seem to communicate too much. This could well be the case. But in considering such questions, we need to include two very important points: (1) man has a fundamentally deep-rooted need to communicate with other men, and (2) when individuals begin to communicate poorly, this is very often a sign of other problems in social and life adjustment.

The need to communicate has been hypothesized by Susanne Langer, one of the most interesting of the modern philosophers, as the beginning of all esthetic activity in man.[6] Miss Langer argues that when primitive man was not communicating with a purpose—telling other men where the buffalo were and how to clean tiger skins—he apparently communicated for fun, and the result was storytelling and primitive drama. This in turn led to primitive music and literature, and the arts as we know them. This argument is rendered more plausible when we conside the inexplicable pleasure we derive from poetry and painting. They certainly do not afford us the ordinary satisfactions derived from hamburgers and air conditioning since the source of the enjoyment seems to be in the symbolic nature of the activity. In other words, communication of this type seems to satisfy us in ways that we cannot explain. It is easy to explain our desires for food and other physical comforts. It is not so easy to explain the desire to read a good novel. Miss Langer argues that this desire must imply a need for symbolic activity that transcends the survival motives of humanity. This need is part of what makes us human, and makes each of us aware of ourselves. Communication seems to be very close to our sense of identity, and without it, our lives would be very poor indeed.

The results of poor communication on social adjustments have been well put by Carl Rogers, the author of *Counseling and Psychotherapy*:

> The whole task of psychotherapy is the task of dealing with a failure in communication. The emotionally maladjusted person, the "neurotic," is in difficulty first because communication within himself has broken down, and second because as a result of this his communication with others

---

[5] Marshall McLuhan, *Understanding Media*, (New York, 1965), p. 28.
[6] Susanne Langer, *Philosophy in a New Key*, (New York, 1951), p. 49.

has been damaged. . . . We may say then that pschotherapy is good communication, within, and between men.[7]

So communication is more than an important part of our daily lives—it contributes crucially to our social well being, and is basic to our sense of the esthetic. When we consider these things, it is hard to believe that communication has only recently come under systematic study in universities, and that the basic principles involved in communication are only beginning to be understood.

Part of the impetus for such study has come from the realization that communication is not always efficient and mistakes in communication are not always correctable. Let us look at just one example of the effects of a simple error in the transmission of a message.

The battle of Leyte Gulf took place October 23–26, 1944, and in this battle, the United States Navy sank twenty-eight ships of the Imperial Japanese Fleet, ending Japan's claim to modern sea power. It was a triumph of our Navy in a long and dangerous conflict. Few people know that this battle was marred by a gross mistake which arose from a communication error, which had been compounded by many communicators who should have known better.

The battle was really several battles in one, some occurring simultaneously in widely separated areas. The American units were the Third and Seventh fleets, and the Japanese were divided into three forces—the Southern, the Central, and the Northern. Admiral William F. Halsey was in command of the Third Fleet and had basically two missions: (1) to support and protect General MacArthur's landing in the Philippine Islands, and (2) to engage such units of the enemy fleet that it might encounter. While supporting MacArthur, Halsey's pilots spotted an expected enemy carrier force north of their position, and Halsey took his fast carriers and battleships up off the northernmost Philippine Island to meet what he considered a major Japanese threat. In doing this, he left the Seventh Fleet in a weakened condition off Leyte, under the command of Admiral Kinkaid. The force that was to move north was designated by Halsey as "Task Force 34." However, none of Halsey's superiors, notably Fleet Admiral Chester Nimitz, knew the exact composition of Task Force 34, and when Halsey steamed north, they really weren't sure what was under way. Halsey radioed "PROCEEDING NORTH WITH 3 GROUPS TO ATTACK CARRIER FORCE AT DAWN," and Nimitz apparently assumed that Task Force 34 was detached and was guarding the San Bernadino straits, protecting MacArthur and Kinkaid. At 3:00 A.M. Halsey started north with Task

---

[7] Carl Rogers "Communication: Its Blocking and Its Facilitation," *Etc.*, (Winter, 1947), p. 84.

Force 34 and an hour later Nimitz radioed him "IS TASK FORCE 34 GUARDING SAN BERNADINO STRAITS?" Halsey didn't receive this message until 6:30 A.M. Meantime he was also getting reports that Kinkaid's small force was under heavy attack. At the same time, Halsey's pilots had been attacking the Japanese Northern Force for over an hour inflicting heavy damage, and Task Force 34's cruisers and battleships were racing to close with the enemy and finish off the ships that had been damaged by aerial attack. Everyone in the task force was ready for battle, and at 10:00 A.M. the force was only forty-two miles distant from the enemy.

At this moment, four-star Admiral Halsey received a strange message from five-star Admiral Nimitz. It read "ALL THE WORLD WONDERS WHERE IS TASK FORCE 34?" It was one of the most unusual dispatches a commander could receive from his superior just before battle. The phrase "all the world wonders" seems to come directly out of a poem by Alfred Tennyson, "The Charge of the Light Brigade," which describes one of the worst military blunders in recorded history. The phrase "all the world wondered" had been rhymed with "someone had blundered" and referred to the public reaction to that disastrous charge, familiar to civilian and military alike, as one of the worst examples of a command decision ever recorded. Admiral Halsey's reaction was extreme. "I was stunned as if I had been struck in the face," he said. "The paper rattled in my hands. I snatched off my cap, threw it on the deck, and shouted something that I am ashamed to remember."[8] The tone of the message implied that Halsey had made a poor disposition of his forces and that he should be supporting Kinkaid's position, nearly four hundred miles away. So he obediently turned around and headed south with Task Force 34. In the whole battle, the unit spent twenty-four hours steaming 300 miles up the coast of Luzon and then 300 miles back again without firing a shot at the enemy.

Did Admiral Nimitz mean to imply the tone of the message that Halsey received? He did not. The message was a wierd combination of cryptographer's and radio operator's errors that changed the fate of the battle. The Tennysonian phrase "all the world wonders" was one of hundreds of phrases of poetry used as disguising elements in sending messages. The practice was to send a phrase of poetry, then the message, then another phrase of poetry, to confuse enemy listeners. A typical message would read "QUOTH THE RAVEN NEVERMORE PROCEED AT ONCE TO POSITION FIVE FOOTPRINTS ON THE SANDS

---

[8] Frederick L. Gwynn, "Tennyson at Leyte Gulf," *The Pacific Spectator*, (Spring, 1951), p. 149.

OF TIME." It was relatively easy most of the time to pick the message out of the poetry. But when a cryptographer at Pearl Harbor picked the Tennysonian phrase to accompany the message "Where is Task Force 34?" he picked without thinking and without considering the semantic compatibility of the two phrases. Halsey's radiomen read it as part of the message, and so did Halsey himself. The operator at Pearl Harbor should have checked his message, the operators in Halsey's flagship should have asked for a repeat of the message, and Halsey himself should have asked for another transmission of the message.

Each of these individuals should have known better—but at that time did not and the results came close to being disastrous. History is full of such cases of mistaken communications, and each time a situation like this occurs, it seems to the participants that the mistake is unique—a chance occurrence that could not have been avoided. Yet in the case of the message about Task Force 34, the mistake could have been avoided, not once, but many times. It illustrates, as well as any other example could, the vital importance of the study of communication at all levels.

WHY STUDY COMMUNICATION?

Most of us would agree by now that communication plays a central role in our daily lives. We might also agree that poor communication can have disastrous effects and should be guarded against. But these two points in and of themselves do not imply a need for the study of communication, especially as part of the college curriculum. Such need arises from further considerations. Generally, we study communication for four important reasons: (1) Communication is the central process in cultural diffusion. (2) Communication is the most important factor that operates in our interpersonal relations. (3) Communication has specific import for given occupational skills, and (4) Communication is a *learned* activity and hence is improvable. Let us examine each one of these points in turn.

Communication and Cultural Diffusion

A college student is at least nominally committed to the process of improving his society—this is the main reason why society is willing to invest so much of its tax and contribution dollars toward the maintenance of institutions of higher education. Our society seems to feel that college students are worth this expenditure because educated individuals will eventually improve the society. If a college student is an improver of society, we must then conclude that anything that contributes to this process should be an essential ingredient in the student's education.

Most of the improvements that are introduced into any society are rather slowly adopted. The name we give to this slow process is "cultural diffusion." It has long been recognized that this diffusion is primarily a communicative activity and is best studied as such.[9] Whether it is the introduction of hybrids in agriculture, or new drugs in the practice of internal medicine, the process is much the same. The new knowledge is diffused from some central point to the practitioners involved in a given process; some pick up the new behavior and gradually the new behavior is passed on to almost everyone in the work area. A good example of this occurred when hybrid corn was introduced in the Midwest prior to World War II. The most common transmitting agent was the agricultural extension worker at the county level. These agents visited farm after farm, trying to bring about the adoption of hybrid seed corn in order to increase the harvests. These county agents originally thought that all one had to do was demonstrate to a farmer that the new corn was good. They soon found that there was more to this process than they thought. They found that by studying principles of communication, they could increase their effectiveness a great deal. Today new practices are adopted by farmers much more quickly than they once were—a process that has been much accelerated by the increased knowledge of communication available to extension agents in agricultural counties, and to agricultural departments in universities.

The act of attending a university implies that an individual is interested in occupying a special position in this process of diffusion. The university is an important source of innovation; therefore the communicative needs and abilities of college students are of necessity much greater than the rest of society. The range of cultural diffusion is wide. It may take the form of a civil rights demonstration or the reproduction of a blueprint. It may be as important as a birth control pill or as minor as a hairstyle change. But there are important elements common to all the diffusion processes which courses in communication are designed to teach.

Occupational Demands and Communication

There are many occupations which demand that an individual have a high degree of communicative skill, ranging from television news broadcasting to advertising graphics layout. Many industries, desperately

---

[9] "Diffusion" is only one of the many terms used with the spread of culture.

seeking communicative skill among their executives, have sent their personnel back to school for intensive training in communication. This training takes many forms, from Dale Carnegie "courses" to what is now euphemistically called "sensitivity training." Most industries do recognize that the first function of an executive, as Chester I. Barnard put it, is "to develop and maintain systems of communication."[10]

There seems to be no question at all that communicative skill developed early in the college career can mean real advantages in the form of increased job opportunities and greater job facility upon leaving school. More and more employers are depending upon demonstrated communicative ability in an interview as one of the critical factors in placing young people in corporations. More and more school superintendents are depending upon proven communicative ability as a factor in hiring new teachers. In government service, communication is playing an ever-increasing role in new job descriptions. As popular New York Mayor John Lindsay put it, "the whole art of politics lies in communication."[11] In short, communication has become increasingly important in the business of making a living.

Communication and Interpersonal Relationships

As you read the example of the gross communication breakdown earlier in these pages, you may have considered this a rather remote case, far removed from your experience. After all, most of us are not Admirals and our day-to-day affairs have none of the vital consequences of a naval engagement in the Pacific! But that does not mean that communication breakdowns are of little importance in our daily lives. Consider a situation that might arise if you went to see your freshman English teacher—who has penciled something fairly cryptic in the margin of one of your themes. You think it concerns your sentence structure. In addition, your grade wasn't at all what you expected (after all, you *were* an honor student in high school, and this adds to the tendency we all have to overvalue our own utterances) and you are more than a little disturbed when the first thing your English teacher says is, "Yes, I did feel that that particular sentence was horrible."

This hasn't assuaged your feelings at all (your high school English teacher was very kind to you) and so you reply defensively, "What leads you to say that? I can understand it perfectly."

You seem to have implied that you do not respect his judgment, so he responds a little tartly that you have attempted to use

---

[10] Chester I. Barnard, *The Functions of the Executive*, (Cambridge, 1938), p. 226.
[11] "Interview with John Lindsay," *Playboy*, (November, 1967), p. 119.

parallel structures for emphasis and have merely become repetitive. No one has ever said your sentences were repetitive before, so you ask him once more what was wrong with the sentence. Now he is truly convinced that you are questioning his authority—he responds "Because I know what a good sentence is and you don't!" With an edge in your voice you respond, "How could anyone write a decent sentence with an assignment like that?" His answer is "That assignment was perfectly clear to the less backward members of the class." By now, anything that either of you might have gained from the interview has been irrevocably lost, and neither of you will ever be the same again.

Does this sound like an unusual happening? If you've never had an experience of this kind, you are either extremely lucky or simply have not been perceptive enough to recognize yourself in the situation. Most of us recognize that breakdowns of this type are not fanciful; they happen every day. Everyone who works with students knows that there are days when nothing goes right for the students and days when nothing can go right for the instructor. Some days even the most cooperative students seem obstreperous, and the same is undoubtedly true of teachers. Employers know that there are times when alienation seems to rise out of the slightest encounter. In the example above, the cost might be great, both to the teacher and the student. In the business world the cost can almost always be counted in wasted time, money, or dissatisfied customers.

But probably the most important area in which the cost of poor communication is felt is in our relationships with others in the world in which we live. Few of us would want to live without friends. Most of us want to live with the close interpersonal relationships that a wife or a husband and children provide. But most young people who enter relationships of this type have no real idea how much difficulty is involved in good communication, even between two people who love one another. Good friendships also do not just happen. They are the product of mutual effort. It takes a lot of work just to get along with others, let alone build a strong personal friendship. Most of this effort must be manifested in communication.

Communication Is Learned

The last point is extremely important. Many students fail to respond to efforts to teach them to communicate simply because they feel that they have an optimum level of performance which they have no chance of exceeding. Nothing could be farther from the real state of affairs. All of the communication skills that we now have were originally learned at an early age. They can all be unlearned and new ones substituted in their places. Our communicative habits—especially our modes of speech—seem to be well established and difficult to change. Students are almost always surprised, however, to discover how little effort and practice are actually involved in the changing of our communicative habits. Anything which can be learned is improvable; therefore we should study our communicative habits to see which of them we wish to improve. Having identified which habits we wish to change, it's a simple matter, with practice and effort, to change them.

WHAT IS COMMUNICATION?

Up to this point, we've been discussing communication in a way that assumes that we all agree what the process is. Unfortunately, most of us have been accustomed to using the word *communication* fairly loosely, and tend to include either too much or too little when we talk about it. If we are ready to begin the study of communication, we must first have an idea of the nature of the process that we're going to study. So let us define this word *communication* and see what it is that the study of this discipline includes.

One of the problems in defining communication is that the discipline is relatively new. Many traditional disciplines have contributed to the knowledge and study of communication—notably anthropology, sociology, journalism, speech, physiology, psychology, and linguistics. Academic disciplines are traditionally separated from one another by a particular methodology or an approach to knowledge. Sometimes a claim to a unique body of subject matter separates one discipline from another. It is very difficult in today's academic world to draw the distinctions that we once did. And so it's probably meaningless to approach the study of communication as an "area" of psychology, or a "subdivision" of speech, or indeed, of any particular academic discipline. Probably the best method in defining communication would be to examine the subject matter it studies, the process of communication itself, and see what it is that we are discussing.

There are many different kinds of human behavior that we could include in the process of communication. When a dictionary defines the word, the lexicographer has simply referred to the manner in which men in general tend to use the word in their intercourse with one another. Let's look at the word *communication* as it is defined by the Merriam-Webster's *Seventh New Collegiate Dictionary:*

1. An act or instance of transmitting
2. Information communicated

14 COMMUNICATION THEORY

    3. A verbal or written message
    4. An exchange of information
    5. A system (as of telephones) for communicating
    6. A system of routes for moving troops, supplies, and vehicles
    7. Personnel engaged in communicating
    8. A process by which meanings are exchanged between individuals through a common system of symbols
    9. A technique for expressing ideas effectively (as in speech)
    10. The technology of the transmission of information[12]

That's quite a list. Unfortunately, it is not too helpful, in that it does not specify very well the kinds of behaviors or the behavioral elements that are involved in communication.

For instance, what happens when we respond to a traffic signal? We drive up to the intersection; the light is red; we stop. Has something been communicated to us or are we merely responding to a set of external stimuli? Edward Hall, in his book, *The Silent Language*, contends that silence is communicative.[13] If a wife asks her husband "How do you like my new eye makeup?" and the response is silence, it may well be that some real communication has taken place. What about the referee's signals at the football game? An editorial in *The New York Times*? The book you are reading at this moment? Are these all communication in the sense that we wish to study it in this book?

Some Definitions of Communication

Let's try another attack by looking at some definitions of communication that have been proposed by scholars in the field. Experts are notorious for disagreement, but perhaps we can learn something from the points of disagreement.

First let us look at an interesting, but brief definition of communication by Frank Hartman: "Communication is control of behavior through descriptive and reinforcing stimuli."[14] Hartman apparently includes most of the examples that we mentioned earlier—the traffic light controls our behavior through a discriminative stimulus; the stop sign at the corner does the same thing. To a lesser degree, so does *The New York Times* and a recipe in the *Betty Crocker Cookbook*. Hartman's definition includes a good deal of human behavior.

---

[12] By permission. From Webster's *Seventh New Collegiate Dictionary*, © 1969 by G. & C. Merriam Co., Publishers of the Merriam–Webster Dictionaries.
[13] Edward Hall, *The Silent Language*, (New York, 1959).
[14] Frank Hartman, "Communication," paper in private file.

Let's look at another definition, this one by Robert Goyer. He defines communication as "any occurrence involving a minimum of four sequential ingredients: (1) a generator of a (2) sign-symbol system which is (3) projected to (4) at least one receiver who assigns meaning."[15] Goyer has added some limitations to Hartman's definition. The *stimuli* have been narrowed to *sign-symbol* systems. There is a *generator* mentioned and a *receiver*. The *generator*, of course, is not the machine that manufactures electric current, but anything that *generates* information. Goyer also specifies that the process be sequential, that is, that the four elements have a progression in time.

Before we proceed any further, let's look at one more definition, this one by Gerald Miller: "Communication," he says, "has as its central interest those behavioral situations in which a source transmits a message to (a) receiver(s) *with conscious intent to affect the latter's behaviors.*"[16] Miller has added a new dimension to that given by Goyer and Hartman —the intent of the communicator (or the generator, as Goyer put it). All of these elements are important, and it seems that they all ought to be utilized.

Let us therefore propose a definition of communication that utilizes the definitions given above. Communication will be defined in this book as a purposeful process, which involves *sources, messages, channels,* and *receivers*. Let us examine these elements one at a time. First of all, the word *purposeful*. In the sense that Miller intended, it is based on a notion of conscious intent, excluding the kind of communication which does not come from the original purpose of the communicator. For example, if a professor is uneasy in an interview with his dean, he may avoid meeting the dean's eyes. This behavior may be highly communicative to the dean, who may interpret it correctly as meaning that the professor is anxious about the interview. Similarly, an individual in a dentist's chair may communicate acute anxiety to the dentist by many unconscious responses, all of which are familiar to the dentist who interprets them correctly. A popular song some years ago asserted that "Your lips tell me 'no, no,' but there's 'yes, yes' in your eyes!" Which is the communication? However meaningful these "indicators" are, they are not communication as we will treat it here. They represent a form of behavior which must be studied from a point of view quite different from the subject matter of a basic course in communication.

The second element in our definition involves the notion of

[15] Robert Goyer, "Communication Process: An Operational Approach," Ohio University Center for Communication Studies, Special Report No. 16, November, 1967, p. 4.

[16] Gerald R. Miller, "On Defining Communication: Another Stab," *Journal of Communication* (Vol. XVI, 1966), p. 92.

process; an idea which was well articulated by David Berlo in his book *The Process of Communication.*[17] Berlo views communication as a "dynamic, ongoing, everchanging and continuous act." He goes on to say that the process does not have a "beginning, an end, a fixed sequence of events."[18] It is not static; it is moving. The ingredients within the process interact; each affects all the others. This means then that we cannot really freeze communication at any one point, but must consider it the byproduct of interacting individuals. A message from one individual creates a response from the other individual which then becomes the message for the first individual—a continuous process.

The third element in our definition is the *source.* This seems like a fairly simple idea, excluding communications which don't come from anyone. A red sky at night may communicate "sailor's delight" to us—that is, it may communicate that tomorrow will be a nice day—but this is not the kind of communication that we will study here. The red sky didn't come from a source (let us not include the Deity for the time being) and therefore this process is one of interaction with the environment. Another example may be helpful. A score that a freshman achieves on an entrance test given for university admission may "communicate" to his biology teacher that this freshman will never achieve a high level of competence in biology and that this freshman ought to take chemistry instead. Assuming that the relationship of the test score and the freshman's ability is a good one, we still cannot call this inference a communicative act. The score was achieved by the freshman upon the completion of a task entirely unrelated to the biology teacher. Even if the freshman wished to communicate a given message, he could not, since he is limited to his own abilities. *If* the freshman knew the answers to the test and what probable use would be made of the answers, we might call the process a communicative one. Some of the performances on the tests given for the draft indicate a kind of communication about the military service! But normally this kind of "message" is not conscious or purposeful and cannot be said to originate from a source.

The *message* as the fourth central ingredient in the communicative process can be defined in many ways. A physicist might define a message as "negative entropy." We can satisfactorily define "message" as some alteration or disturbance of the physical environment, which can be attended to and discriminated from the rest of the physical environment. If one examines Morse code as a message, the "disturbance of the physical environment" element becomes a little clearer. We can send Morse code by banging on the wall (disturbing the air waves),

[17] Berlo, p. 41–58.
[18] p. 69.

THE PROCESS OF COMMUNICATION 17

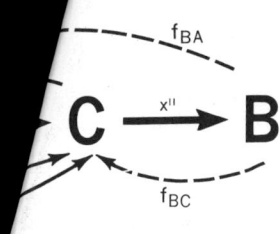

FIGURE 3

blinking a light (disturbing the light waves), or even by alternately turning a water hydrant on and off. Any disturbance of the physical environment can carry messages and become "messageful." Most commonly we disturb the air with sound waves produced by our larynx and modified by our lips, teeth, tongue, and palates and we call these disturbances "speech." But any kind of disturbance will do.

The fifth element of the definition, that of the *channel* helps define *message*. A channel is the medium in which the physical disturbance occurs. We have postulated some common channels, but they are certainly not all-inclusive. Normally, we use the channels of spoken sound which are listened to, or written symbols which are read. Some interesting research is now under way which uses the skin of individuals as perceptors, and the "tactile" channel has proved to be extremely useful in communication.

The last element in the definition is the *receiver*, the ultimate destination of the communicative attempt. Lord Byron once exclaimed poetically, "Roll on, thou deep and dark blue ocean! Roll!" and the ocean seems to be sensitive to the command, for it keeps on rolling along. Many of our verbalizations have no destination, since they are expressions of an inner state, or playful sounds for their own sake. Children exhibit more of this kind of speech than do adults, but it is clear that all utterances are not communicative in that all of them do not have an ultimate destination. Admittedly it may be rather difficult to contend that Lord Byron didn't have an ultimate destination, but at least we are sure that it wasn't the ocean. When Demosthenes spoke by the seashore, he too may have had an ultimate destination—but if he did, it was hidden in Demosthenes' mind. We can take a common sense point of view here and insist that the ultimate receiver be known to the communicator and that the communicator be aware of it, reserving the involutions of receiver definitions to more advanced study. However, one very important point must be made here. The receiver and the source are not static elements, but, as Berlo has pointed out, alternately shift around as the process goes on. First one is the source and then the other; the same is true with receivers.

As we look back through the elements of the definition we have posed, it is apparent that we have done more than simply define communication. We have set out a series of circumstances which we feel are necessary before communication can take place and a series of elements which we feel are necessary before communication happens. This is more than a definition in that it implies a more analytic approach to the process. When we become so specific about our definition, we find that we are doing more than defining—we are "modeling" the communication process as well.

Communication Models

Since we have now passed beyond definition in our study, we are ready to introduce the notion of models into our thinking about communication. Models are necessary for systematic study. Many of us are familiar with model airplanes; probably we also know that models of airplanes are used by aeronautical engineers in wind tunnels to look for defects before full scale airplanes are built. Many of us are also familiar with the models used by architects which help analyze the structure in mind before building begins. In communication, a model provides the structure—the relationships between the elements—which is lacking in simple definitions.

Many models of communication have been proposed, and we will examine only a few in these pages. The first model that has had real importance in the study of communication is the one proposed by Claude Shannon and Warren Weaver in their mathematical analysis[19] of the communication process. This model proposes a source, an encoder, a message, a decoder, and a receiver. They also hypothesized another element, a "noise" source, which interacts with the message and goes to the receiver. Figure 1 illustrates the structure of their model.

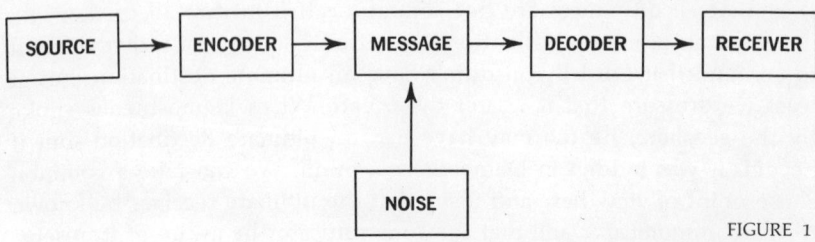

FIGURE 1

The encoder or decoder can be any device which translates information into some other form—a vacuum tube or a transistor, for example, can encode audio frequencies into radio frequencies. The human brain apparently has encoding systems which translate images and ideas into words and symbols which are capable of expression in speech or writing. The source of noise depends on the channel or message—it could be static in radio, irrelevant stimuli in reading or listening, or deliberate "jamming" by another communicator. The concept of noise illustrates graphically that there is a precarious relationship between the encoder and the decoder, and communicators should plan on overcoming noise.

Another way of looking at noise is the tendency for things to go

[19] Claude E. Shannon and Warren Weaver, *The Mathematical Theory of Communication*, (Urbana, 1949), p. 5.

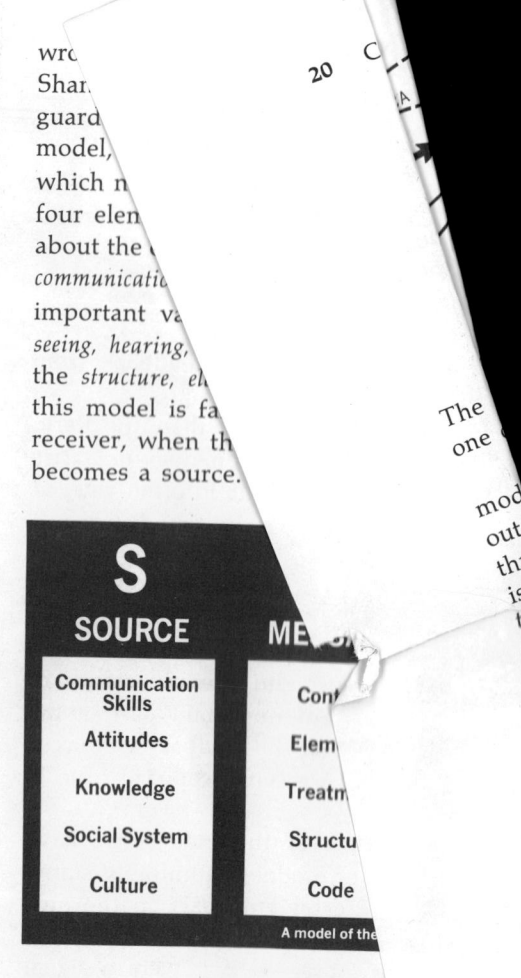

wr...
Shan...
guard...
model,...
which n...
four elem...
about the...
communicati...
important v...
seeing, hearing,...
the *structure, el*...
this model is fa...
receiver, when th...
becomes a source.

Bruce Westley and Malcol...
munication model slightly differ...
places greater emphasis on what...
explicates much better than Berl...
information. In Figure 3, p. 20, th...
sent events in the world which may...
The small "x_1, x_2s," and so on repr...
these events—since no one perceives...
The message x^1 is sent to C, who...
external world, represented by the x...
message x^{11} to B, who is the ultimate...

[20] Bruce Westley and Malcolm MacLean, "...
tions Research," *Journalism Quarterly*, (Winter, 1957...

"Girl number twenty unable to define a horse!" said Mr. Gradgrind, for the general behoof of all the little pitchers. "Girl number twenty possessed of no facts in reference to one of the commonest animals! Some boy's definition of a horse. Bitzer, yours!"

The square finger moving here and there alighted on Bitzer. "Quadruped, Gramnivorous. Forty teeth, namely twenty-four grinders, four eye-teeth, and twelve incisive. Sheds coat in the spring; in marshy countries, sheds hoofs, too. Hoofs hard, but requiring to be shod with iron. Age known by marks in mouth." Thus (and much more) from Bitzer.

"Now girl number twenty," said Mr. Gradgrind. "You know what a horse is."

It is obvious that a definition alone will not suffice to fill out our knowledge of communication.

Now that we have examined a few models and definitions, we can compare them and begin to assimilate them, but this assimilation ought to have a reasonable purpose related to the study of communication. As in every other discipline, we need to learn the terminology of the discipline before we can make sensible statements within it. In biology, one of the goals a teacher tries to achieve is to have his students use the word "platyhelminthes" instead of the phrase "that squiggly little thing with the thingamajigs on it." The first word may not imply much knowledge of flatworms, but it is the first step towards that knowledge and is infinitely better than the phrase.

Communications terminology is not quite as precise as the language of science, but nonetheless the acquisition of the terminology is important to the subsequent learning in the field. This terminology, as all other specialized language systems, exists only for the purpose of assisting students and scholars in understanding the processes involved. Generally it differs a good deal from lay usage. Students should expect that many of their current usages will have to be sharpened and improved before they can attain a good understanding of the process of communication.

Criteria for Establishing a Model

"Models provide a way of looking at and abstracting from the totality of communication,"[21] write Campbell and Hepler. If models are to do this, then some definite criteria for characteristics ought to be present in useful models. Let us list some characteristics a model ought to have:

---

[21] James H. Campbell and Hal W. Hepler, *Dimensions in Communication*, (Belmont, California, 1965), p. 9.

22 COMMUNICATION THEORY

1. A model should recognize the different types of mental processes important to communication.
2. A model ought to show what communication is not, as well as what is is.
3. A model ought to specify the different types of communication and lead to an understanding of why they are different.

In other words, a communication model helps define communication and helps specify what kinds of communication are present in human interaction—and should clarify the relationship between them. Since we have examined the definitions of communication and some previous attempts at modeling the process, we now need to examine the various types of communication and various processes we typically call the "internalizations" of human beings.

A MODEL FOR STUDY

Basic Processes

Let us begin with the individual who is going to be doing the communicating in our environment, and look at what is going on within his frame of reference. In the diagram presented in Figure 4, the individual is represented by a circle and the events of his environment are represented by the E_1, E_2, and so on. Some of these events are perceived by the individual and some are not. When one is perceived, it becomes a "percept," or an image. These data from the external environment, through experience and learning, are interpreted through language, together with the individual's emotions, feelings, and beliefs. None of the perceptions are "accurate," since a perception and an event are quite different. Consider the case of the church steeple that you see from a distance—it appears quite small, yet you are able to identify it as the steeple of the church you attend each week. Upon nearing the

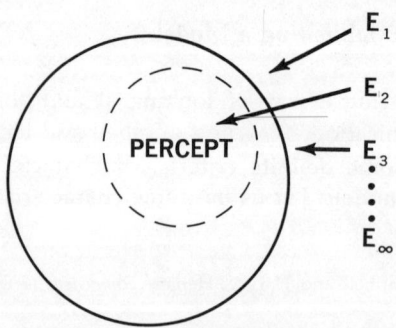

FIGURE 4

blinking a light (disturbing the light waves), or even by alternately turning a water hydrant on and off. Any disturbance of the physical environment can carry messages and become "messageful." Most commonly we disturb the air with sound waves produced by our larynx and modified by our lips, teeth, tongue, and palates and we call these disturbances "speech." But any kind of disturbance will do.

The fifth element of the definition, that of the *channel* helps define *message*. A channel is the medium in which the physical disturbance occurs. We have postulated some common channels, but they are certainly not all-inclusive. Normally, we use the channels of spoken sound which are listened to, or written symbols which are read. Some interesting research is now under way which uses the skin of individuals as perceptors, and the "tactile" channel has proved to be extremely useful in communication.

The last element in the definition is the *receiver*, the ultimate destination of the communicative attempt. Lord Byron once exclaimed poetically, "Roll on, thou deep and dark blue ocean! Roll!" and the ocean seems to be sensitive to the command, for it keeps on rolling along. Many of our verbalizations have no destination, since they are expressions of an inner state, or playful sounds for their own sake. Children exhibit more of this kind of speech than do adults, but it is clear that all utterances are not communicative in that all of them do not have an ultimate destination. Admittedly it may be rather difficult to contend that Lord Byron didn't have an ultimate destination, but at least we are sure that it wasn't the ocean. When Demosthenes spoke by the seashore, he too may have had an ultimate destination—but if he did, it was hidden in Demosthenes' mind. We can take a common sense point of view here and insist that the ultimate receiver be known to the communicator and that the communicator be aware of it, reserving the involutions of receiver definitions to more advanced study. However, one very important point must be made here. The receiver and the source are not static elements, but, as Berlo has pointed out, alternately shift around as the process goes on. First one is the source and then the other; the same is true with receivers.

As we look back through the elements of the definition we have posed, it is apparent that we have done more than simply define communication. We have set out a series of circumstances which we feel are necessary before communication can take place and a series of elements which we feel are necessary before communication happens. This is more than a definition in that it implies a more analytic approach to the process. When we become so specific about our definition, we find that we are doing more than defining—we are "modeling" the communication process as well.

Communication Models

Since we have now passed beyond definition in our study, we are ready to introduce the notion of models into our thinking about communication. Models are necessary for systematic study. Many of us are familiar with model airplanes; probably we also know that models of airplanes are used by aeronautical engineers in wind tunnels to look for defects before full scale airplanes are built. Many of us are also familiar with the models used by architects which help analyze the structure in mind before building begins. In communication, a model provides the structure—the relationships between the elements—which is lacking in simple definitions.

Many models of communication have been proposed, and we will examine only a few in these pages. The first model that has had real importance in the study of communication is the one proposed by Claude Shannon and Warren Weaver in their mathematical analysis[19] of the communication process. This model proposes a source, an encoder, a message, a decoder, and a receiver. They also hypothesized another element, a "noise" source, which interacts with the message and goes to the receiver. Figure 1 illustrates the structure of their model.

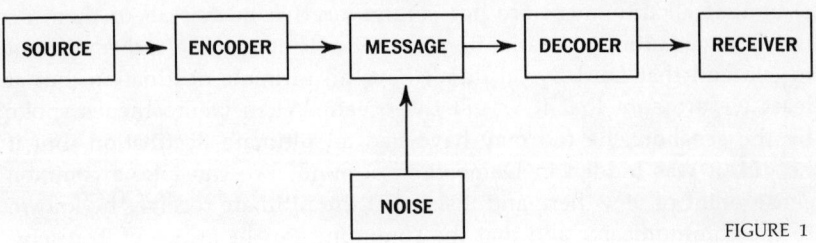

FIGURE 1

The encoder or decoder can be any device which translates information into some other form—a vacuum tube or a transistor, for example, can encode audio frequencies into radio frequencies. The human brain apparently has encoding systems which translate images and ideas into words and symbols which are capable of expression in speech or writing. The source of noise depends on the channel or message—it could be static in radio, irrelevant stimuli in reading or listening, or deliberate "jamming" by another communicator. The concept of noise illustrates graphically that there is a precarious relationship between the encoder and the decoder, and communicators should plan on overcoming noise.

Another way of looking at noise is the tendency for things to go

---

[19] Claude E. Shannon and Warren Weaver, *The Mathematical Theory of Communication*, (Urbana, 1949), p. 5.

wrong in a communication. When communication is one-way, as Shannon and Weaver seem to imply, noise must be planned for and guarded against before the communication takes place. In David Berlo's model, Figure 2, communication is seen as a continuous process in which noise is overcome by a process called "feedback." Berlo includes four elements—*source, message, channel,* and *receiver*—and is fairly explicit about the elements involved in each. In sources, we find that the source's *communication skills, attitudes, knowledge, social systems,* and *culture* are the important variables; the receiver has the same factors. Channels are *seeing, hearing, touching, smelling,* and *tasting,* and messages are varied in the *structure, elements, content, code,* and *treatment.* Berlo emphasizes that this model is far from static and needs feedback between source and receiver, when the source actually becomes a receiver and the receiver becomes a source.

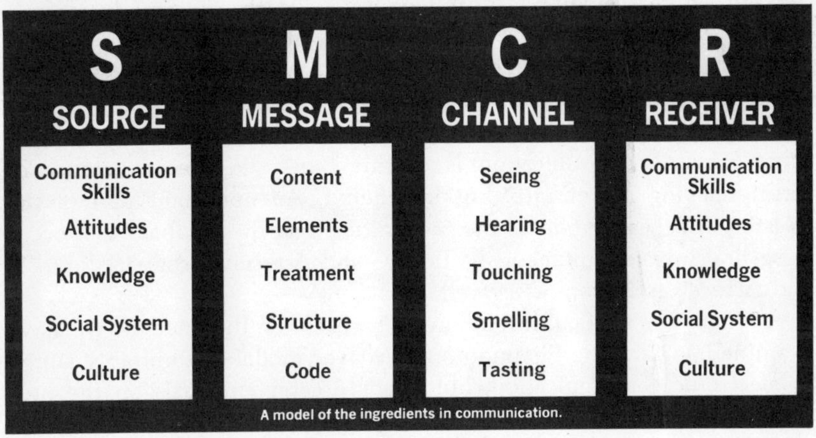

S SOURCE	M MESSAGE	C CHANNEL	R RECEIVER
Communication Skills	Content	Seeing	Communication Skills
Attitudes	Elements	Hearing	Attitudes
Knowledge	Treatment	Touching	Knowledge
Social System	Structure	Smelling	Social System
Culture	Code	Tasting	Culture

A model of the ingredients in communication.

FIGURE 2

Bruce Westley and Malcolm MacLean[20] have formulated a communication model slightly different from the previous ones in that it places greater emphasis on what goes into the communication—and explicates much better than Berlo how a source comes to generate information. In Figure 3, p. 20, the large "X_1, X_2" and so on represent events in the world which may or may not affect individual "A." The small "x_1, x_2s," and so on represent the perception that A has of these events—since no one perceives the external world exactly as it is. The message x^1 is sent to C, who also has some perception of the external world, represented by the x_{3c} and x_4. C then transmits a message x^{11} to B, who is the ultimate destination of the information.

[20] Bruce Westley and Malcolm MacLean, "A Conceptual Model for Communications Research," *Journalism Quarterly,* (Winter, 1957), p. 36.

COMMUNICATION THEORY

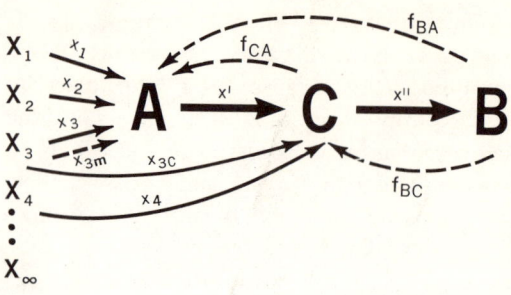

FIGURE 3

The dotted lines labeled "f_{CA}, f_{BC}, and f_{BA}" represent feedback from one communicator to another.

The Westley-MacLean model is more complete than the Berlo model because it recognizes that most communication does not arise out of simple perception of an outside stimulus but is often relayed through an intermediary (in the figure, C is the intermediary) and is therefore changed. For example, when your instructor informs you that there will be a departmental test on Friday morning, he is probably acting as C on the figure, and the primary source of the information is probably the departmental coordinator of the course you are taking. Most human communication is of this type, and the occurrence of direct relaying is not rare, but infrequent. An important part of the Westley-MacLean model is the recognition that the feedback can occur in several ways simultaneously. Both C and A receive feedback from B, and A receives it from C as well.

There are difficulties inherent in each of the models we have examined so far. The Shannon and Weaver model is admirably suited to electronic communication, but needs greater emphasis on the processes of feedback, the interaction of receiver and source. The Berlo model stresses feedback, but treats the source as if it were a signal generator by itself and not a reactor to other factors in the environment. The Westley-MacLean model recognizes the interaction of the communicator in the environment, but doesn't treat each of the individuals involved in the process as a complex organism. In addition, none of the models cited above imply different types of communicative activity; "communication" is treated as if it were a single type of process.

The Function of Models and Definitions

Students often assimilate material in textbooks out of habit, memorizing definitions in the fashion of Thomas Gradgrind in the Dickens story. In *Hard Times*, Dickens describes two pupils, one (Sissy Jupe) who has lived among horses all her life, and another (Bitzer) who has never seen a horse:

steeple, you find that you have an entirely different image, yet your "perception" remains the same—it is the same steeple, your perception tells you. What you know as a church steeple becomes a perception, which is not the same as the sense impression you had of it. All of the incoming data that we process are of this type. We can assign language to them and make evaluations from them. However, our language and our emotions do not have to be related to the perceptions and images before they can exist. Many terms in our language have no reference to perceptions or external events. Many attitudes and beliefs are the same. So the circles representing language and attitudes and beliefs are shown to have intersection, but also have important areas that are unrelated.

Let us look at an example to make the relationship more clear. It is quite possible for one to have an attitude about Negroes without ever having any perceptions about Negroes at all. Many other minority groups in our country have suffered from attitudinal structures which were learned separately from perceptions about the minority group. It is also quite possible to know the name of an object—like the "Horse's Head Nebula"—and never have had any perception of the object itself. It is also possible to have words for which referents are unknown or imaginary. Most of these words are metaphorical—like the phrase "hotter than the hinges of hell"—but a great many of them are used as if they referred to some object, when they actually do not. "Democracy" and "Communism" are two good examples.

Now that we have sketchily examined the relationships between some of these "mental" events and the outside environment, we can proceed to the description of the communicative process between two individuals. Figure 5 represents such an interaction. It must be remembered that to each individual the other is only another event in the

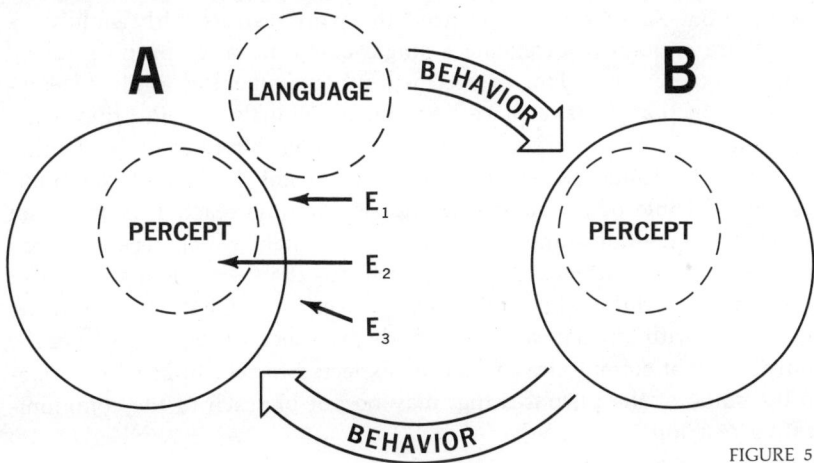

FIGURE 5

"outside" environment—that even if we do assume that others are like us and have similar thought processes, we do not communicate mind-to-mind but by disturbing the physical environment. In the diagram in Figure 5, individual A has a perception of event E_2 which individual A lacks. There may be no real reason for B to have missed event E_2, or event E_2 may be in a situation where B could not perceive it. Whatever the circumstances, one individual has perceived the event and the other has not, and therefore individual A has decided that he will "communicate" this event to individual B. His perception of E_2 first gets translated into language. This language then becomes an event by individual A behaving in some verbal way, represented by the heavy arrow "behavior" in the diagram. Individual B may now have a perception of E_2 that is somewhat similar to individual A's perception of it, depending on the communicative ability, the language system, and the behavioral choice of the two participants. As a result of the language event of E_2, B may respond, and this response becomes another stimulus for A. This is what we generally call "feedback" in communication. To say that these events may happen is, of course, no assurance that they will happen in any given communicative interaction. There are many kinds of interactions possible in this basic scheme of communication, and before we can look at them all, we are going to have to examine the purposes in communication.

Communicative Purposes—Different Forms of Communication

Earlier in this chapter communication was defined as a purposive interaction between sources and receivers, and the word purposive was used to distinguish communications with intent from those accidental interactions which are nonetheless similar to the process we call communication. At that point we used the word *purpose* fairly simply, as if it were enough to designate a single communicative purpose for all interactions present. However, when we examine the kinds of communication that do take place between individuals, we find that many of them are quite different and seem to follow different kinds of rules. It is hard to decide, for example, whether or not the goal of communication is visible or invisible—behavior is a visible reaction that we can perceive, and understanding is an invisible state which receivers may have without our knowing. It is also obvious that behavioral goals differ quite a bit in the quality and quantity of effort involved. So before we go farther with an analysis of our model, we need to set out some of the purposes that communication can be expected to accomplish, and hopefully, some of the purposes that may be out of reach of the communicative reaction.

THE PROCESS OF COMMUNICATION   25

What criteria should we use to distinguish the purposes of communication? One of the oldest methods is to simply ask the communicator about it—to simply say "What are you trying to do in this situation?" He may respond with statements like "I wanted to persuade the audience that we should abolish college football." Again, he may say "I wanted the audience to appreciate our public schools better." Or he may say simply "I wanted my wife to understand how a spark plug works." When we eliminate the specific audience descriptions and the subject matter designations from the statements, we find that we are left with words like "persuade," "inform," and others, which give a clue to the different kinds of tasks that were apparently involved. If we were to ask a large number of people this kind of question when we see them communicating, we would find great range and variety in the vocabulary they use. And if we were to make a list of all of these words, we might find that it turned out to be quite a long one. The following list contains only a few of the words that we generally use when we are describing communicative activity:

inform	demonstrate	plead
persuade	tell	reveal
convince	show	state
stimulate	point out	make aware of
illustrate	teach	express
exemplify	orate	suggest
prove	move	impress
define	enlighten	convey
argue	illuminate	relate
explain	sway	present
please	set forth	

Our list would be limited only by the vocabulary of the interviewees that we decided to study. The only way this approach could turn out to be productive would be if we could make general classifications into which these words would fit. Happily, some of them seem to fit into larger groupings. For example, "plead," "persuade," "convince," and "argue" all seem to have some similar elements that "inform," "define," "point out," and "show" lack. Historically, writers in communication have made arbitrary distinctions among these functions, usually based on the classical writers in communication such as Aristotle or Cicero. From this frame of reference, communication is usually defined as "persuasive," or "informative," and sometimes other terms are added to explain the main divisions. The definitions arrived at using this method are generally validated by the vocabularies of communication mentioned above, so if we classify this way, we are really making judgments about our language system and not the objective we are seeking to define.

Another problem with using the traditional divisions like "informing" and "persuading" is that laymen use these terms for many kinds of different communicative activity. The word "persuade" is used to describe almost everything from the selling of hair dryers to the advocacy of a new way of life from the pulpit. The same problem exists when we use a word like "inform." We say that we are informing when we tell someone how to use a new cake recipe, and we also say we are informing when we are detailing the reasons why we should withdraw from Vietnam.

Another way we might classify communicative purpose is to look at the form the message takes or the channel that seems to be appropriate. We usually acknowledge that we can put most any kind of message into any channel, but there might be differences in the kind of language or kind of utterance that is used. A statement that says "Only a fool would continue smoking in the light of the Surgeon General's report on smoking and lung cancer" is clearly different from the statement that says, "There seems to be some established statistical trends between smoking and the incidence of lung cancer." The messages we receive from day to day *do* differ a great deal, and these differences may furnish a key to the identification of communicative purpose.

A third way of classifying different kinds of communication lies in the differential effects communication can have on receivers. It is clear that the listener or receiver can ignore the communication, act on it at once, forget it, or even disagree violently and attack the communicator. The same communication may produce all kinds of differential responses in different receivers. Coming from a Sunday sermon, for example, you may say "Now I understand the life and letters of Paul," while your friend might respond "I don't know how you could after the miserable exposition we heard of it from the pulpit today." And it may be that neither of these responses was the one that the pastor had in mind when he planned the sermon.

What kind of responses are available to the receivers of a communication? Some writers have argued that only behavioral responses are of any interest in the study of communication, because only observable behavior can be studied and analyzed. For example, the result of a communication might be that you know that dinosaur eggs have been found in the Gobi desert—yet an observer might not know that you know it until you display the response by some behavior or another, such as saying, "Dinosaur eggs have been found in the Gobi desert."

It would be hard to imagine this knowledge affecting your behavior in any other way than that kind of verbalization. Clearly, if we decide that only behavioral goals are acceptable as the end products of communication, we are forced to eliminate a good deal of activity from our definition of communication.

To make the point a bit clearer, let us consider what happens when a stranger in town stops and asks for directions to the courthouse. We may present him with an elaborate set of directions, and after receiving them the stranger may say "I understand" and drive off. If I am only concerned about the behavior that resulted from my communication, I am still faced with the problem of deciding which behavior is the important one. It may be that I only wanted the stranger out of my hair because I don't want to deal with his presence any longer. If this is the case, his driving off is the response I really want and the rest is irrelevant. I may not be so callous, however, and might have some desire to see him arrive at the courthouse. If so, I will present a good set of directions, and when he drives off he will truly know how to get to his destination. But the only way I will know if my communication has been effective would be to leap on my motorcycle and follow him to the courthouse and see if he got there the way that I prescribed. This is pretty silly but at least possible. But what about the set of directions I give to a young boy scout who is concerned about how to handle a possible snake bite? I can give the directions, but I sincerely hope he will never have to use them. Many of us can recall the dire warnings given us in first-aid classes about artificial respiration; fortunately few of us have had to actually perform the behaviors specified in these kinds of directions.

If I say that communication has not taken place unless some behavior has been altered in the behavioral repertoire of the receiver, then I am leaving out a good deal of activity that seems to be fairly important. Clearly there is communication when we are given the directions about snake bite or artificial respiration—although there is no appreciable change in behavior. What has changed is the internal makeup of the receiver—tucked away somewhere in the receiver's repertoire of responses is the *potentiality* of responding a certain way. What you get in the first-aid class is not behavioral change, but the *potential* for a given behavior, which is not the same thing at all. When the directions were given for the route to the courthouse, the communicator instilled a response potential, and not an actual response. We could infer its presence by certain tests (Now tell me again, which way do you turn at the second stop light?) but we could only validate the communication if we actually observed the behavior which got the traveler to the courthouse. Since most of the time we cannot do this, we infer the response's potentiality on the basis of past performances by similar human beings in similar situations. We cannot observe these response potentials; we can only infer them.

Let us recapitulate a moment. While it might be easy to say that the goal of communication is a response on the part of the receiver, actually the situation is much more complex than that. What the communicator aims for is not behavior, but potential behavior. We can try to infer the presence of such potential responses by tests or questions, but most of the time, we simply infer from past validations of similar persons in similar situations. We have often distinguished between types of communication on the basis of whether or not the response desired was an observable, overt response, or whether it was simply a potential response. The former has traditionally been called "persuasive" and latter "informative," but these terms are poor ones in that much more is implied by these designations.

So if we sum up the discussion of communicative purposes, we find that we can classify any communicative act at least three ways: in terms of the stated intent of the source, the form the message takes, and the kind of result we observe in the receiver. We might add one further note here—the channel is sometimes an interesting way of distinguishing kinds of communication. When communication is transmitted by the mass media, or when a communication is from a single speaker to a crowd of 40,000 persons, certain very important differences begin to be made apparent. These kind of differences are usually considered the subject of more advanced study in communication, however, and will not be discussed here. Our original three methods of classifying communication purposes, source statements, message forms, and receiver effects have all been applied singly or in combination in one form or another to arrive at distinctions among types of communication. It seems obvious that not one of these could serve as a criterion by itself. All three must be utilized. It also should be obvious that no cogent system of classification should ignore the characteristics of the communication model—since the model exists only to explain communicative behavior, and considerations of purpose and classification are simply different elements which should interact in the model. Let us then attempt to look at the different kinds of communicative behavior, both from the point of view of the three modes of classification and from the standpoint of the functions described in the communications model.

Let us first look at one of the most simple communicative acts. This occurs when one individual attempts to describe for another individual the emotions, feelings, or beliefs present in his mental makeup. Figure 6 describes this kind of communication in terms of the characteristics of the communication model. Here the particular

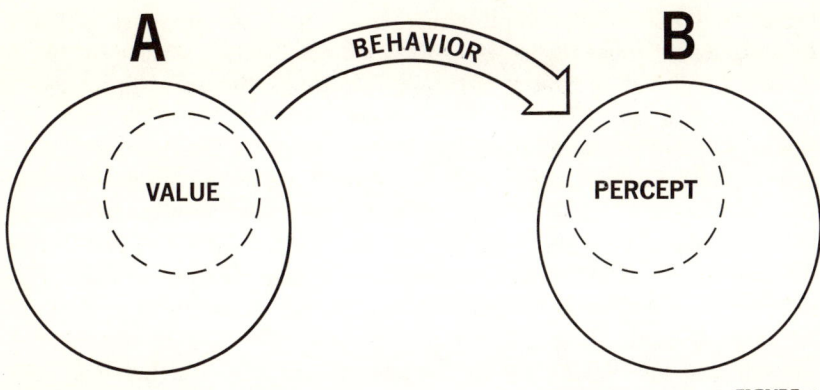

FIGURE 6

attitude or emotion is encoded into language and then put into externally observable behavior—visible speech, symbolic activity, or any other kind of signal that can be translated into a perception by B. A good term for this is "externalizing," since the communicator is externalizing his internal responses. The receiver, or B in Figure 6, responds appropriately. Notice, however, that the communicative behavior is shown "passing through" the emotional system. This is to represent the "filtering" effect such systems have on our behavior. This may or may not destroy the relevance the communication has for B, and if it does, we might say that the communication failed. If not, it was successful.

Let's look at an example of this kind of communication. Your roommate might tell you "I like pizza." This does not give you any information about pizza itself, or provide any value judgments about Italian food. Roomie has simply identified or externalized the internal attitude about pizza. For the communication to be successful, you must know what "I" means, what "like" means, and what "pizza" means. You may never have tasted pizza pie, but you know what it is, and can identify it as a food. Before you can understand the communication, you must have some comparable feeling that corresponds to the verb "like" that your roommate used. You have an idea about turkey dinners which you have described as "liking turkey" in the past, and so you can compare your roommate's use of "like" with your use of "like." If the only way you have used the word "like" is in connection with the opposite sex, then this particular communication is going to be highly analogous at best and probably a dismal failure. Therefore, while externalizing may seem a fairly simple communicative act, the truth is that it depends on a series of rather complex events for its success.

Externalizing is a fairly common communication form, and occurs a good deal in human interaction. "I feel sick," "I'm tired," and "To Hell with you" are some fairly simple examples of externalization.

Occasionally a more complex case of externalization arises when a communicator presents an exposition of his values or basic attitudes in a formal way. Some years ago, Edward R. Murrow produced a famous series for radio that was entitled simply "This I Believe." In this series, famous people were invited to express their personal philosophy and values in a short radio talk. Some of these short expositions of personal beliefs have become classics of communicative expression, and the simplicity of the communicative task in no way indicates the quality of the expression. Externalization can also be rather unproductive, in that it tends to center on the source rather than the receiver. We are all familiar with the individual who can talk of nothing but himself and his reactions to the world around him. But however irritating this form of communication can become, it is a fairly important form of communication which we engage in quite often.

Another simple form of communicative behavior takes place when we have the situation diagramed in Figure 5, our first diagram of the communicative process. In Figure 5, you recall that individual A had perceived external event E_2 which individual B had no perception of. A translated this perception into language which became externally observable behavior. B then "received" some sort of perception of E_2— different, of course, from A's because it had been modified by the language system common to them both and perhaps by A's and B's emotions, feelings, and beliefs. The "filtering" effect is not included in Figure 5, but is exactly the same as Figure 6.

If you have ever read a book to a blind person, you've engaged in a very simple form of this behavior. When you look out the window and say "it's snowing," you are engaging in this form of communication, which is called "relaying." The communicator acts as a surrogate stimulus for the receiver, who either cannot or has not perceived the original stimulus from the external world of events. The emotional system shown in Figure 6 should not influence ideal relaying, but in practice, it filters much the same as externalizing. Relaying takes place when we draw maps, transmit recipes, and diagram football plays. It is one of the most common forms of communicative activity, and, as in the case with externalizing, is often misused to give the illusion of communication.

A third kind of communicative activity has been named the "mand" by B. F. Skinner.[22] Skinner's "mand" is a communication that specifies its own reinforcement, which is to say that it describes a reinforcing contingency. "Give me a glass of water please," is a good example of a mand, since it specifies the action by the receiver which will reinforce the communication. Mands refer to behavior yet to be

[22] B. F. Skinner, *Verbal Behavior*, (New York, 1957), p. 35.

adopted by the receiver, and refer to an internal state of the communicator. "May I have a cigarette?" is a mand that refers to a behavior not yet performed (giving of a cigarette) which will be rewarding to the communicator. Very simply stated, we are using mands when we ask, order, or command anyone to do anything. Presumably there is a reinforcement structure involved with the command or the command would not have been given in the first place. Mands combine externalization (they imply an inner state of need) and expectation of future behavior on the part of the receiver.

Let us look at the simpler communicative acts together and see how they compare with one another:

COMMUNICATIVE TYPE	CHARACTERISTICS
Externalization	Expresses inner state only; may refer to attitudes or beliefs, or simple inner comfort or discomfort. No behavior or reply necessary.
Relaying	Communicator acts as surrogate stimulus, mediating events of outside world to receiver who is not able to perceive them. Best success comes when little of relayer's attitudes or emotions are involved.
Mand	Specifies a future behavior on the part of receiver that source will value, or find rewarding. Has some of the characteristics of externalizing.

Students will recognize at once that the intensity at which all of these take place may vary considerably, and that intensity may seem to create differences which are only apparent ones. For example, the mand "Hand me that ashtray" is seemingly quite different from the infantry officer's "Charge!" but in actuality, both are mands of different intensity referring to different behaviors. "The moon is full tonight" is a relaying communication which seems quite different from the precise observations of the moon made with the Hale telescope at Mount Palomar, yet both of these are relays that differ in precision and intensity. Students must be wary of confusing intensity with real differences in kind; such problems will not arise if the communicative form is analyzed thoroughly for its principal elements. One other problem—the different forms have been treated thus far as if they occurred separately. In actuality, externalizations, relays, and mands are interwoven through the communicative activity of man and occasionally cannot be distinguished.

At this point, most students might feel that, while externalizations, relays, and mands are certainly present in much of our communicative activity, there is much more happening in the communicative setting than these simple processes. What kind of communication is the formal political speech, the television commercial, or the newspaper editorial? Certainly these contain the simple elements discussed above, but they seem to have a good deal more emphasis on our society, much more concern with "right and wrong," and a great deal more general importance than the simple forms of communication discussed above. It should be immediately obvious that there is a level of communicative activity that is much more complex and challenging than the simple levels described above. Much of this communication is centered around the changing, building, or reinforcing of audience attitudes. This form of communication will be discussed in Chapter 4. It may seem that we have not exhausted the possibilities for the communicative interaction, but we have still another purpose that plays an important part in human interaction. This is the kind of communication that aims at an esthetic response.

Little is understood about the nature of the esthetic response, but almost everyone recognizes it when it occurs. When we listen to great music, read a great poem, or see a great painting, the emotional reaction elicited is commonly known as an esthetic response. Almost everyone is capable of esthetic responses, but they take place at different levels. Children experience esthetically at very simple levels, and the presence of beauty in simple things is a common occurrence in folk and primitive art. Many persons never get beyond the very simple level of esthetics—a glance at typical television programming is ample proof of this. Most of us respond esthetically at some level or another, and it is a rare human being who does not attempt to decorate or "prettify" his surroundings in some way or another.

Inexperienced communicators seldom recognize that a good deal of modern communication has no purpose other than an esthetic one. The old-fashioned "oratory" openly strived for esthetic effect, and the vulgarities of the oratory of the nineteenth century are only surpassed by the vulgarities of the romantic painters and the hideous Victorian houses that still detract from the beauty of many residential neighborhoods. The advent of cynicism in the reportage of public affairs has altered public utterance a great deal, but communication for esthetic effect still remains. That tired wheeze, the commencement address, has become largely decorative as has the sermon (following the mass, which has become an art form).[23] Few public utterances of today can match some of the beauty of the great speeches of the past. It is unlikely that Lincoln's second inaugural address will ever be surpassed—but occasionally communicators today do succeed in achieving a quality of utterance. Adlai Stevenson's acceptance speech at the Democratic National Conven-

---

[23] An important movement seems to be under way to reverse this trend.

tion in 1952 is a truly great speech, as is John Kennedy's inaugural address. To treat such speeches as esthetic events is out of fashion now, however, and the trend of the times insures that young people preparing for public life will get little or no experience in expressing themselves this way. Senator Everett Dirksen once said that every public servant should at least attempt to write poetry and plays (he himself being the author of at least one play and several poems), but the public reaction to this statement was far from kind.

Whether the typical student will engage in the type of esthetic communication mentioned above is problematical—but it is fairly certain that he will have occasion to participate in esthetic communication of a much baser sort—the speech or essay which is designed to "entertain." Admittedly it is a good distance from Lincoln's second inaugural to the after-dinner speeches given at the Athens, Ohio, Annual Elks Dinner— but the difference is one of degree rather than one of kind. A speaker of this kind has the same fundamental aims and ambitions as Lincoln— unless he fails badly in the task and descends to the level of simple comedy. It would be difficult for most of us to write a play as well as Arthur Miller does, or a poem as well as Carl Sandburg did. Few persons have much modesty when it comes to writing speeches which are going to commemorate a solemn occasion like a graduation or a dedication. As a consequence, the commencement platform is treated to a dreary procession of inarticulate public servants whose presence bespeaks a concern for political fence-mending rather than proven ability as an esthetic communicator. It would be hard for us to imagine a publisher inviting a well-known engineer to contribute a few poems because of his engineering ability—but the same process occurs over and over again in banquet halls (witness the halting delivery of the Big Ten football player at the annual sports banquet) throughout the country. The only general conclusion that can be drawn from such activity is that communication is poorly understood, and that perhaps when young people are better versed in what sort of things communication does and does not do, great improvement will be evident.

In spite of the general abuse of esthetic communication, we cannot simply say to ourselves that we will abandon it and deal with the other areas of communication instead. Admittedly esthetic expression is quite difficult, but the difficulty would seem to be a strange criterion for excluding a communicative form from our study. Most beginning courses in communication, however, choose not to treat this communicative form, primarily because study and preparation of this kind are arduous and most beginning courses simply do not have enough time for students to do this substitute "type" of preparation.

Let us now recapitulate all of the types of communication that we have been discussing, and see if we can present them all together, both to summarize the communicative purposes and to compare one with another:

COMMUNICATIVE PURPOSE	FUNCTION
SIMPLE COMMUNICATIONS	
Externalization	Express internal state or condition
Relaying	Act as mediator to unavailable outside stimulus or event
Mand	Specifies behavior which will be rewarding to source
ESTHETIC COMMUNICATIONS	Esthetic response, "appreciation"

(A third basic type of communication, which aims at the affecting of attitudes in the recipient, is called SUASORY communication and will be treated in Chapter 5.)

When we look at all of these together, we begin to realize that what may have seemed like a fairly simple process on the surface is actually a very complex set of interactions! And while these different purposes may seem strange at first, students will recognize most of the functions as being fairly familiar ones. Externalization, relaying, and manding are familiar processes and play a large part in our everyday lives.

Oral Communication—The Study of Speech

When we first look at the process of oral communication, we might think that the only distinguishing characteristic it has from general communication is the specialized choice of a channel—whether to voice the message or to write it. What bases can we use to decide on a particular channel, such as speech? What distinguishes oral communication from written—printed and otherwise? When should oral communication be the direct "interpersonal" kind, and when should it be relayed through electronic means?

One way to choose a channel is cost—in terms of time and money. Let us imagine for a moment that we are advising an executive who has a certain amount of information that he must relay to his subordinates. What shall he do—call a meeting and present the information orally, or dictate the message to his secretary and send it out to each of the receivers? The answer to questions like this lies in the cost of the subordinate's time and the secretary's time. Let us assume for a moment that each subordinate reads at the rate of 300 words per minute and receives $2.00 per hour in wages. If we have a message of a given length, say 3000 words, we can then figure out some rough cost estimates. Individuals retain written and spoken messages with about the same efficiency, but spoken messages are limited to the speaking rate of the source, usually about 100 words per minute compared to faster reading rates of at least 250 words and sometimes, in excellent readers, 500 or 600 words per minute. In our assumed reading rate of 300 words per minute, we have quite an advantage. In creating the written message, however, we have other costs—the secretary who takes the dictation, types up the stencil, and then mimeographs the finished product for distribution. Let us see how this all figures out for different numbers of subordinates.

If the communicator has 30 receivers at $2.00 per hour, the time they take for reading the 3000-word message will be ten minutes (assuming 300 words per minute for their reading rate). These ten minutes will cost $10.00. The secretary costs money too—she will take dictation one hour for the 3000 words, an hour and a half in typing, an hour in duplicating and typing (and don't forget the coffee break!). The typewriter, stencils, mimeograph machine, and paper all cost money, both in direct costs and in depreciation—one dollar in this example. So if the secretary costs $2.00 per hour, her wages will be $7.00 for the 3000 words, and the supplies and equipment cost will be at least another $1.00, raising the fixed cost of this kind of communication to $8.00. This gives us a total time and money cost of $18.00 for 3000 words. How much does it cost to communicate the same message to 30 receivers using the oral channel? 3000 words will take at least 30 minutes, at a speaking rate of 100 words per minute. At $2.00 per hour for each employee, this will cost the organization $30.00, a good bit more than the same message communicated by the written channel.

Does this mean that writing is cheaper than speaking? Not at all; for smaller audiences, the spoken channel is cheaper. When we do the same calculations for an audience of five members, we find that the written cost is $9.66 and the cost for the spoken channel is $5.00. For ten receivers, speaking costs $10.00 and writing costs $11.33. The graph in Figure 7 shows how these costs interact. There is a "break-even" point at approximately 13 receivers, where it doesn't matter which channel is used. At any point in the analysis, different factors might produce an entirely different graph—a raise in the secretary's wages, a higher reading rate by the receivers, and so on.

Sounds simple, doesn't it? And for rather simple messages, this kind of analysis provides a sound basis for choosing one channel over another. But when we begin to do more complex things with our communications, we must dig a little deeper into the differences between the spoken and written channel.

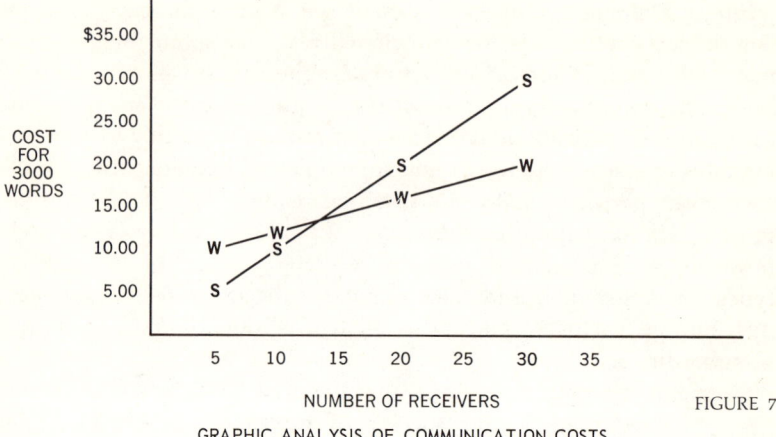

FIGURE 7
GRAPHIC ANALYSIS OF COMMUNICATION COSTS

The first and most obvious difference is feedback. This important process was mentioned in the beginning of this chapter, and you will remember that it is the process by which the source becomes the receiver, and vice versa, as the communication progresses. A communicator sends his message and is aware of what happened to that message when he sees the reaction of his receiver—and being aware of that reaction, he modifies his next message. When we talk together, one of us answers back, reacting to what was said earlier, and the first talker modifies his next statement on the basis of the reaction. A formal public speaker—if he's any good—modifies his message as he goes along to suit the reactions of his audience. This is a vital function with communication and alas! is not present in most written communications.

To see how this is so, consider what you would do if you wished to extract $50.00 from your father because you have an important date. Would you write him a letter or telephone? If you write a letter, you will receive either a "yes" or a "no." If you telephone, you can adjust your request to suit his circumstances—for example, you can come down to $40.00 and then $30.00, and so forth. You might explain how important the date is, and mention that your date's father owns a steel mill (if true!). If all that fails, you can try to secure a loan, and not an outright gift! In other words, you can do many things which depend on the receiver's reaction, that you could not have done by letter. You may have put all that information into the letter in the first place, but you cannot tell ahead of time what will be needed, and by overcommunicating you sometimes run the risk of insulting your receiver.

This is the main reason why large companies still use the salesman to handle the point distribution of their products—a brochure or a list of specifications for a generator simply do not communicate as well as a qualified salesman-engineer on the spot. The key difference is feedback and the intelligent use of it by the communicator. And while the written channel can have feedback, it is usually slow, inefficient, and ineffectual. By the time feedback occurs, the occasion for it is usually forgotten.

There is another consideration involved in the choice of the spoken channel (interpersonal communication) over the written channel. There is, in reality, more than one channel available when speech is used. Speech not only consists of the symbol systems used, but also utilizes other codes, such as voice, body movement, and whatever other visual codes are relevant. Consider the differences that arise between the reception of a cold, formal telegram that announces that your brother has been in a serious accident, and the same message delivered by a close friend. The telegram has limited information, and you immediately wish to know more. There is no way that the message can be tempered to reduce the shock to the receiver. Your friend, on the other hand, can tell you in a manner that reduces your shock, gives you further information about the accident, and conveys sympathy, support, and friendship in his presence and his voice.

There is really no limit to what inflection can do to a message. The proper inflection can convey so much more information than the written channel could ever hope to achieve that it is ridiculous to compare them. All of the infinite range of personal involvements—the emotions, feelings, and beliefs mentioned in our communication model —are much more easily and efficiently expressed by voice and bodily action than they ever could be in just words.

So there is more to our choice than simple efficiency—we have to consider our communicative task and make a channel choice based on that. It seems a valid rule to assert that most of the complex communicative tasks call for oral communication, while simple ones can rely on written ones for their implementation. Relaying and externalization might be easily accomplished by the written channel, along with simple mands. But when we make the relays, externalizations, and mands more complex, we almost certainly need to rely on the spoken channel. In communications that depend on attitudes for their success or failure, it should be immediately obvious that a communicator needs to have some initial assessment of the receiver's attitudes before change can take place. This depends almost solely on feedback, and is available almost exclusively in oral communication. And since attitudinal communications of necessity are more difficult than simple ones, more effort is needed in the communicative attempt. A good example of this is illustrated by a study of Miller and Hewgill.[24] They demonstrated

---

[24] Gerald R. Miller and Murray A. Hewgill, "The Effect of Variations in Non-Fluency on Audience Ratings of Source Credibility," *Quarterly Journal of Speech,* (Vol. L, 1964), p. 36.

that good delivery produced higher "credibility" for the communicator and subsequently greater acceptance of his message. It seems apparent that face-to-face communication with attendant feedback would add a good bit of efficiency to the type of communication that seeks to build attitudes.

Now that we've examined some of the differences between oral and written communication, we can make our choices in any given communicative situation. We can calculate the efficiency of each type if only simple communication is needed. If more complex communicative activity seems to be called for, then we need to make use of the additional channels of body and voice that oral communication gives us, together with the capacity for feedback that only face-to-face type situations have. Each communicative task needs to be evaluated on its own merits, and the communicator who gets in the habit of relying on one channel exclusively is likely to miss a good many of his communicative opportunities.

Differences in Communicative Skill Often in higher education, we assume that there is a general "communicative" ability that students are to learn, and having once learned this, they can then engage in listening, reading, writing, and speaking with equal facility. Unfortunately, this is not the case. A good bit of research has been completed concerning the relationships among the communicative skills, and most of it seems to indicate that the separate skills have little, if any, relationship to one another.[25] In other words, a good writer is *not* likely to be a good speaker and *vice versa*.

There seems to be an assumption in American education, however, that good speakers can be created by teaching students to become good writers, and that good oral communication will result from taking courses in English. Occasionally one sees "oral English" mentioned as a part of the English class curriculum, and the students are enjoined to put their writing into oral form. However, the kind of skills that go into making a good oral communicator are far different from the skills that make a good written communicator. Sensitivity to feedback, ability to use the voice well, and good adjustment in audience situations are quite important apart from the composition process of communication. In addition, preparation for oral communication is quite different than preparation for writing.

When we examine the amount of communicative activity that takes place in the different channels, we are struck by the overwhelming preponderance of speaking and listening as compared to writing and reading. Over 75 percent of our communication is oral, while only

---

[25] Samuel L. Becker, "Relationships among the Communication Skills," *Central States Speech Journal*, (Vol. XIV, 1963), p. 258.

25 percent is written.[26] It seems strange, therefore, that so much of education is given over to the craft of writing and so little is devoted to oral communication. What this means is that a student in a beginning course in oral communication should make extremely good use of his time—getting as much as he can for the short time he has to invest.

The Illusion of Success One of the things that makes oral communication so difficult to learn is that we are constantly engaged in the process with an illusion of success that is natural to the persistent optimism of humanity. We communicate a great deal daily, and cannot help but feel that much of this communication is sufficient, since we don't get fired, physically assaulted, or otherwise punished. The absence of negative feedback is usually due to the good manners of our receivers rather than the ability that we bring to the communicative process.

The late Frank Rarig of the University of Minnesota was fond of quoting Soren Kierkegaard's address to the young theological students, in which Kierkegaard commiserated at great length with the difficulties facing the young pastor who was to become a missionary—surely teaching Christianity to non-Christians would be a sorely trying job. But, Kierkegaard went on to say that their task is nothing compared to the task facing young pastors who would stay home and attempt to teach Christianity to the Christians! It is extremely difficult to learn anything if you are convinced one already knows it!

Just so, said Rarig, is the task of teaching beginning students communication. We are all communicators; our daily lives are filled with communicative activity. And when we add the illusion of success to this activity, it is sometimes very difficult to convince ourselves that we need to work, study, and improve ourselves in this respect. But such is the case, and study is, alas! necessary.

The Process of Oral Communication The models of communication that were presented earlier were fairly general, in that they described the process of communication in the simplest terms. In oral communication there is a good deal more involved than the general processes and we need to be more specific in the description that is used. You will recall that the figures showed the basic "message" or communicative behavior as the result of impressions or ideas being channeled through language and structure, through feelings, emotions, and beliefs, reaching a particular destination. In oral communication, each of these elements contributes to the form and content of the message in significant ways. For example, the communicator is stimulated by an environmental event and has a perception of that event as it has af-

---

[26] These are approximate percentages of transmission only. See pages 204–205 (in Listening chapter).

fected him. How this perception works actually becomes a part of the message. For example, if a given individual responds to the presence of juvenile delinquency in our society, we know several things about him immediately. To be aware of juvenile delinquency implies social awareness, general social concern, and probably a sense of public responsibility. In addition, the kind of external event that sparked the concern over juvenile delinquency also implies a given degree of expertise or implied knowledge. All of these elements are a part of the "message" that the receiver is given.

Similarly the language and structure of the message makes a decided difference in the reception of the message. If a speaker uses the term "irresponsible young hoodlums" for juvenile delinquents, then the word choice becomes highly communicative to the receiver. The general structuring of the content also becomes an element of message. Even so simple a thing as which element is considered first has importance.

It should be obvious that the feelings, emotions, and beliefs of the sender are part of the message that the receiver acquires as a result of the communicative interaction. The indignation, fear, or approval implied in a discussion of juvenile delinquency furnished information about the source of the communication, but also the material being communicated. And so, while we might have looked at the final behavior—the act of speaking, as the "message" in the communication —the fact is that the individual, his language, and his value system are all part of the final message that is received in an oral communication. Indeed, the actual delivery may be only a small part of the message!

The communication systems we studied earlier all had two interacting elements: a transmission system which *sends* a message and a receiving system which is the *target* of the message. The environment of the sender, including in it the potential receiver, generates the communication. Events external to both the potential sender and receiver may stimulate the initiation of a message. For example, two people are listening to a television broadcast from a war-torn country; the horror of the pictures interacts with both persons and finally, one individual may be internally stimulated to express his reactions to the events which are occurring. These specific reactions, in turn, may generate another message, exploring the subject of war in a more general way; finally, the speaker, because of the original stimulus, may find himself in a philosophical evaluation of war in our times.

The stimulus from the environment will not always be as dramatic or as strong as in the illustration. Physical discomfort may produce the question, "Do you mind if I open the window?" Similarly, silence in the setting may prompt one of the persons present to turn on the radio and ask of the other people present, "What station has music at this hour?"

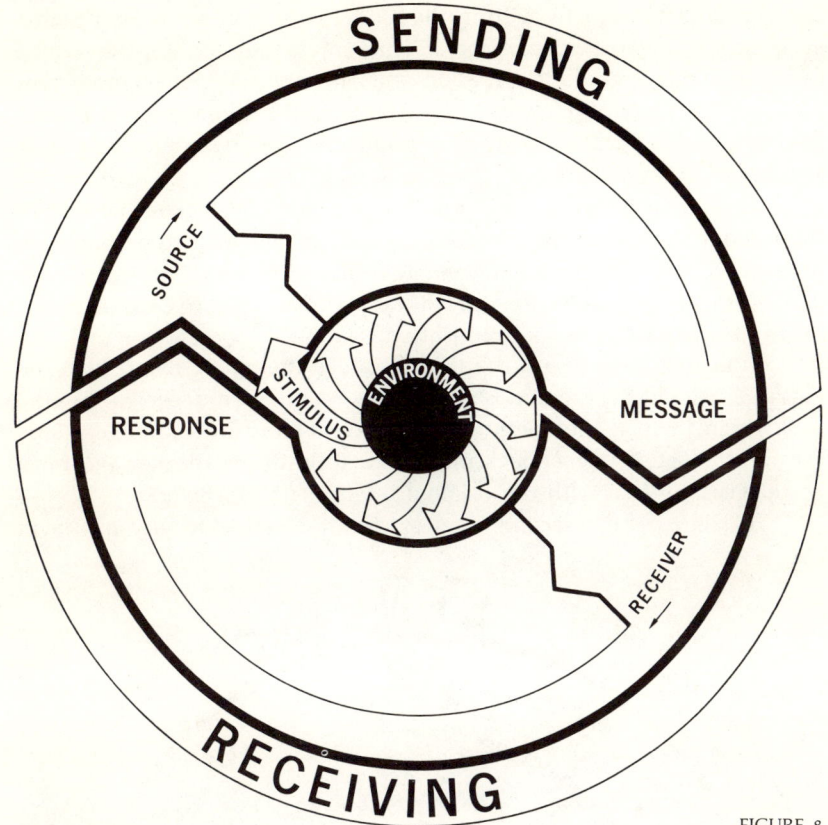

FIGURE 8

In any situation where two or more people are present or in contact, one person at some point initiates the sending aspect of communication and becomes the source of the message. Figure 8 illustrates this stage in the phenomenon of communication. Note that at this point, the source is himself a "message." Even before he begins to speak, the receiver perceives the message-source; he sees and interprets bodily activity and facial expression; he associates prior impressions he has had of the speaker, conditioning his own responses to the communicator.

At the same time, the potential receiver (the listener) begins to perceive his function and to behave in a way appropriate to this role. His behavior, like the speaker's, will be affected by the environment, his past experiences with the subject to be explored, his biases and interests, his attitudes toward the speaker, and his willingness to participate in this particular communication situation. And, he too, becomes a message-source, but for the speaker. In other words, he begins to provide feedback of a positive, neutral, or negative nature.

42 COMMUNICATION THEORY

It should be apparent from the model which we are building, that even before oral communication begins, interactions take place which can enhance the speaking situation and encourage the speaker to proceed with confidence. However, the nature of the interaction could also discourage the speaker with the result that he becomes defensive, aggressive, or even lethargic.

This interaction between the speaker and the listener continues throughout the extent of the communication, and sometimes after it. Its nature may change from time to time with peaks of agreement, disagreement, or neutrality. Or, it may remain positive or negative for the duration of the communication.

Both the speaker and the listener must attempt to insure that the message which the source sends is the same one received by the listener; in turn, if the communication event is to be completely successful, the listener's feedback must be helpful to the speaker and must be received by him with the original intent of the receiver.

In Figure 9, the second level of communicative activity has been

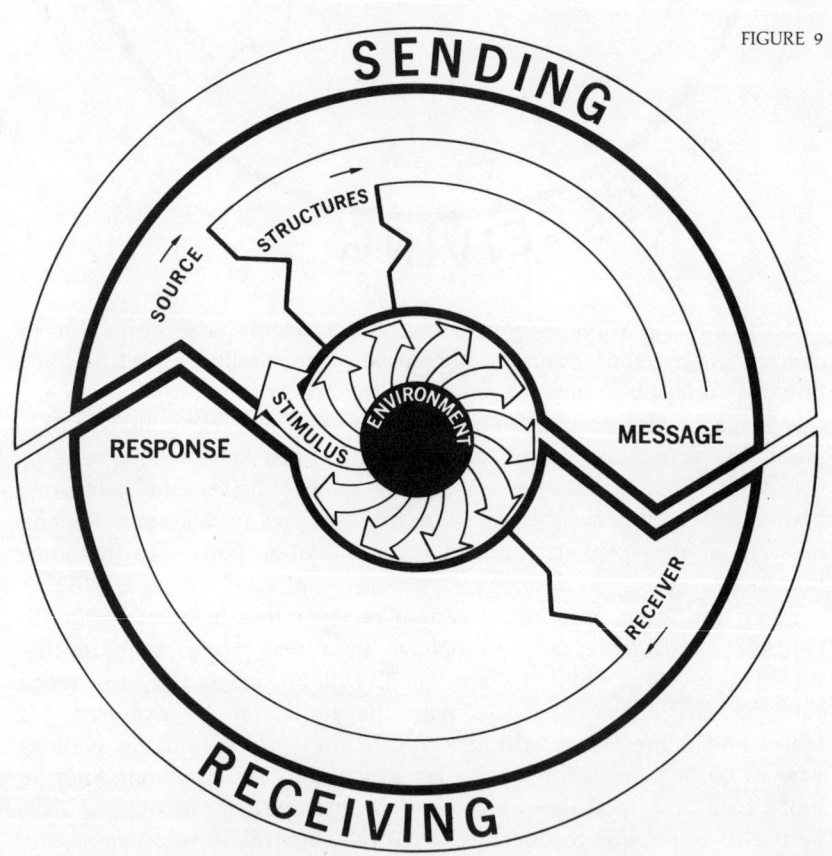

FIGURE 9

added to the "sending" portion of the model. The source, the speaker and idea-generator, now begins to structure his interaction, organizing the components internally and generally. Then he begins to think in terms of coding his ideas in a meaningful way, using language.

The receiver faces a similar activity; he must decode the message, recognizing not only the words used by the speaker, but the over-all structure of the message. However, this activity does not take place until the speaker's transmission has been accomplished.

At another level of communicative activity, the source interacts with his own values, opinions, and ideas; in other words, he evaluates his continuing message. This evaluation is an important part of communication, in that it is almost impossible for sources to ignore their own values in any circumstances. For instance, we often try to relay information free from value, but unconsciously attribute values to the relays. In externalizing, however, we are interested primarily in the values. In Figure 10, evaluation is added to the model as another step in the development of a message.

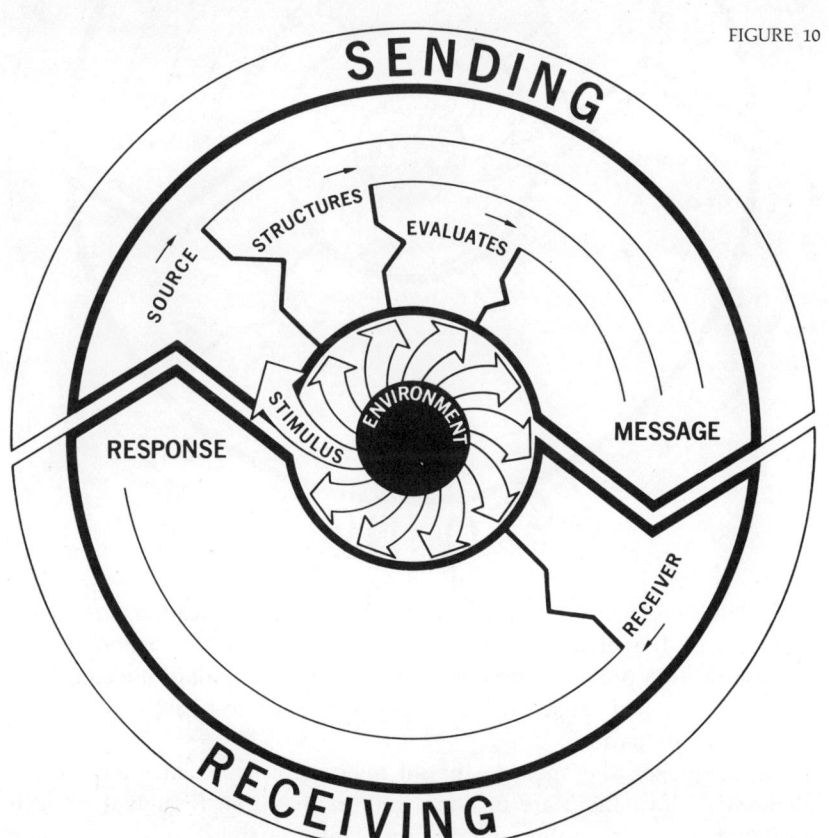

FIGURE 10

44 COMMUNICATION THEORY

It has been pointed out that the listener's activities are limited up to this point. He has been reacting to silent cues, for the most part. Obviously, the speaker must make use of the vocal mechanism if language is to serve its important function in relaying ideas. The source, the structure, and the evaluations of the sender are manifested in the physical activity that we call "delivery," which is the transmission system used to convert the silent cues to audible ones. Figure 11 illustrates the addition of this element to our communication system.

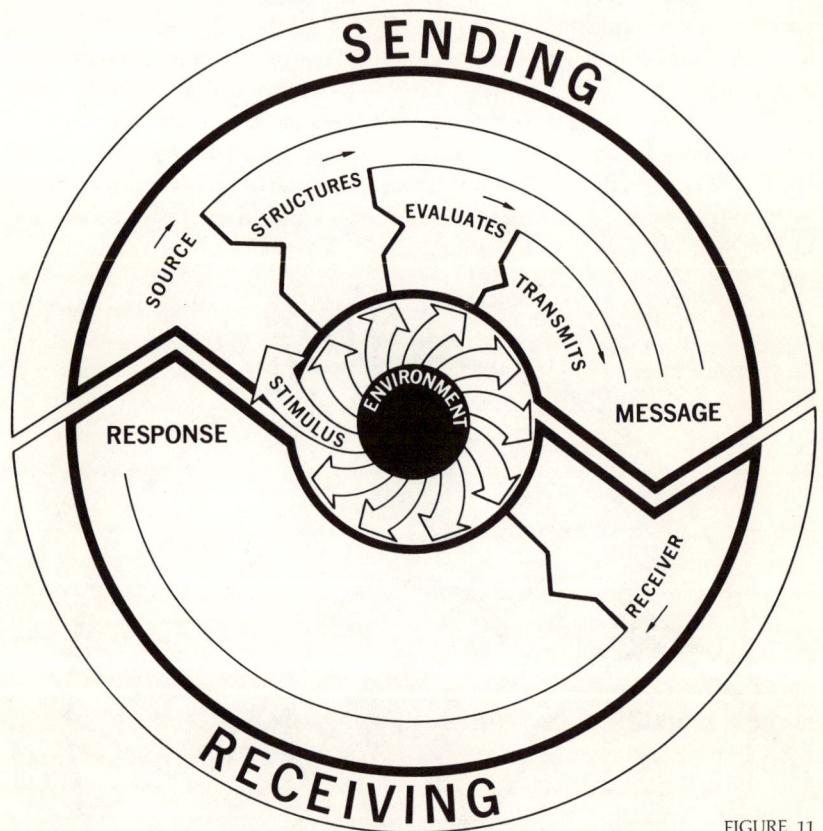

FIGURE 11

The "message," the total effect of the communication, now contains all of the elements that make up the sending portion of the communication process. The message is composed of all of the elements, and in a very real sense, this is a case of the whole being greater than the sum of its parts.

Obviously, the speaker should insure proper balance among the elements. All of them are of equal importance even though they each may not have the same dominance. Unfortunately, at times, some elements are disproportionately dominant and are likely, under certain circumstances, to distort the message. For example, a speaker may have a beautiful, resonant voice, impeccable articulation and pronunciation, and a most attractive physical appearance. His delivery and appearance may almost obliterate the other elements in the message. This is most unfortunate because it may result in undeserved acceptance of the total message.

The receiver is involved in a process similar to that of the source; however, the speaker's message, instead of the environment, is the listener's primary stimulus. In addition to being present in the situation, the listener must hear, comprehend and reconstruct the ideas being transmitted by the sender. Next, the listener evaluates the message; he balances ideas with facts he knows, experiences which he has had, and beliefs which he holds. He tests the speaker's ideas for truth, importance, and for information. And, finally, he reacts to the message as he receives and interprets it. His reaction, which is usually silent, is in the form of a special physical alertness, facial expressions, or relatively slight movements of some part of the body. These reactions may change often as new information is relayed and as the receiver's reactions to the material change. These reactions, called "feedback" or "responses" close the oral communication circuit by providing repetitive stimuli for the speaker.

Figure 12 on p. 46 shows the complete communication model, including all elements required for both sending and receiving messages. Note that the form of the model is determined by two arrows representing "sending" and "receiving." In a broad sense, the MESSAGE is the "warhead" of the sending arrow and the RESPONSE is the impact point of the receiving arrow.

The stimulus-response cycle is created and maintained throughout the extent of the communication. The model may seem to imply that one source keeps sending messages to one receiver. However, a speaker often finds himself in the position of conveying a message to more than one listener. Then he has the problem of attending to multiple responses.

From time to time, the roles of speaker and listener are exchanged as in a conversation or a group discussion. Each person in the group alternates roles and, therefore, responsibilities. A listener no longer must depend solely on silent communication, for as soon as one speaker has finished, the roles may be exchanged, and the original receiver may express himself audibly. Now, he assumes the responsibilities of transmission.

In turn, the speaker becomes the listener. This exchange of position is difficult for some people to accept. The speaker may be reluctant to give up his role and his chance to give vent to his feelings or beliefs. In turn, the listener, eager to assume the role of speaker,

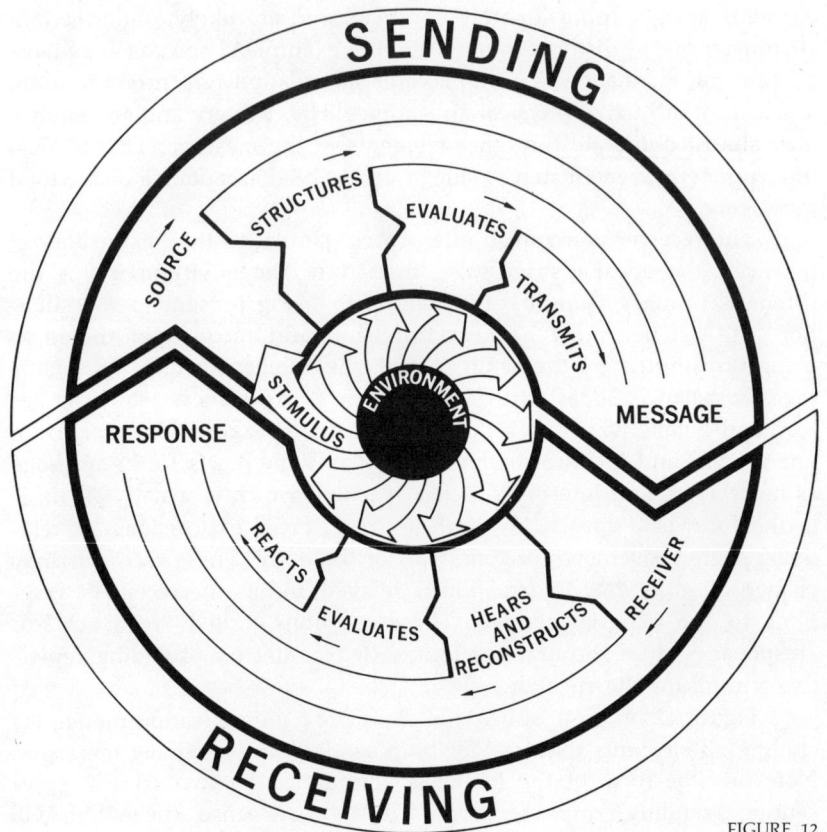

FIGURE 12

may be too preoccupied with his efforts to exchange roles, and may function ineffectively as a receiver.

The receiver's communication with the speaker is an important and immediate source of information. However, it is not the speaker's only source. The speaker hears *himself* and he should be able to make evaluations concerning his speech which may make it possible for him to clarify or otherwise improve his message.

This second type of feedback may influence and assist the source in many different ways, depending upon his awareness of it. Some examples may clarify this concept.

As he speaks, a person may hear himself pronounce a word incorrectly. He must make a decision at this moment whether it is important that he correct his error. In some cases, he will conclude that the change is not vital and go on talking. At another time, he may decide that for the purpose of clarity he should repeat the word accurately.

Or, as a speaker listens to himself explaining a process, he may realize that his first attempt has not produced a clear picture. He then reinforces his first effort by extending the discussion. He presents the idea in a different way, hoping to improve his explanation. Thus, he has depended upon his own feedback for one evaluation of effectiveness.

All people do not listen to themselves equally well; neither do they hear themselves equally well under all circumstances. As in the case of the listener, the speaker may hear himself without recognition or evaluation. This may be due to his intolerance of his own speech; his exclusive preoccupation with audience response; or many other divergent causes.

Neither do all speakers use their own reactions to their speech to the best advantage. Sometimes, for example, upon hearing an error in his speaking, the speaker becomes confused and embarrassed and consequently his message may be adversely affected. At the same time, the effectiveness of this feedback is diminished if the speaker listens to himself for the sheer pleasure of hearing himself.

A speaker is fortunate to have two constant checks on himself and should make every effort to use both his own and his listener's feedback as a means of continually improving his message.

The point was made earlier that elements present in the environment provide the stimulus for a potential communicator. These elements which are present in our surroundings can have a positive, motivational effect; however, they can also operate in a way that is detrimental to communication. Environmental conditions may and do operate at all stages of communication; therefore, they may interfere with any part of the communicative cycle, causing breakdowns to occur. The participants in a communication situation should be aware of both the negative and positive characteristics of the environment; they should take advantage of those environmental elements which seem to support them and they should learn to cope with those which are potentially negative and, therefore, detrimental.

This chapter has attempted to place the whole process of communication in a perspective that will be helpful to the students. Careful attention to terminology and definitions is needed in this first portion of your study, so that the processes which are discussed in greater detail in the following chapters will be understood.

2 THE SOURCE—THE BEGINNING OF COMMUNICATION

To improve as communicators, it seems reasonable to begin at the beginning—the source, or the generator of the message. How does one become a source for communication? What kinds of things do good sources do? What activities will help us improve ourselves as sources? These and other questions are the central concern of study of the individual as a communicative source. In the chapter that follows, we will analyze the process of generation of message variables that leads to creative communicative activity.

BECOMING A SOURCE

One of the first problems a beginning communicator has to face is the problem of subject matter. "What do I say?" is the first response of an individual who is told that he will be called on to "say a few words" at the forthcoming Elk's dinner. And for many of us, this question is of central importance in the communicative process. Happily, most of the time we do not have to search far. The situation may create the material for communication without the communicator becoming deeply involved in it. For example, if a speaker is called upon by the Daughters of the American Revolution to present the citizenship awards at their annual banquet, the choice of subject matter is abruptly limited by the audience and the task that has been set. This particular situation admits to few variants in source material, and the problem is not invention but the searching for significance within the subject matter delimited.

Invention

Traditionally the creation of significant things to say by the source has been treated as "rhetorical invention." In classical antiquity, a speaker was taught that five processes were involved in the study of communication: invention, organization, language, memory, and delivery. "Invention" was the most important to many rhetoricians, since the discovery of "ideas" was central to the whole process—all others seemed to emanate from it. The word "discovery" plays a large part in traditional treatises on communication—indeed, Aristotle uses "Discovery of the available means of persuasion" as his definition of the whole art of persuasive communication.

When a student faces a communicative situation with this kind of orientation, he usually feels that he must turn within himself, and become "creative" in a way that he really doesn't understand. Many students, not understanding how to be "creative" in this way, turn to fraternity files for subject matter and ignore the problem of their development as a source in communication. Nor is this confined to students. Many ministers, understandably concerned about finding a fresh subject for a sermon each week, turn to some of the well known little books of prepared sermons all ready for delivery. Many businessmen, when called on to speak publicly, simply have their secretaries "put something together." Small town newspaper editors rely heavily on wire service editorials to insert in their papers, so that they won't have to write their own editorials every day. And, as every student knows, prominent public figures retain on their staffs at least two or three individuals whose task it is to prepare speeches.

It should be immediately obvious to most readers that "public speaking" as practiced in this fashion has little to do with communication as we defined it in the first chapter. If we make the assumption that good communication is our goal, then we may be dealing with something quite different from "invention" in the traditional sense of the word. Yet much of our communication is going to take place in semi-formal settings that we call "speeches," and we need to prepare for these in ways that are obviously different from the simple relaying or extensionalizing that we discussed in the first chapter.

How can we treat this problem without referring to the classical notion of invention? Modern scholars would say that we cannot, since invention in rhetoric no longer has the classical connotations once attributed to it. But our problem still remains: how best to improve oneself as a source in the communicative interaction, and how to approach the process meaningfully in preparation for more formal communications. In other words, we need some systematic approach, so that communicators will not be forced to throw up their hands helplessly and say "What can I say?" when the occasion demands that they speak.

Situations and Sources

Fortunately, most of the time the communicative situation provides ready answers to these questions. Two main factors interact to produce our characteristics in the interaction: the audience and the task. Let us examine each of these in turn.

The Audience It is obvious that the audience limits and guides the content of any communication. In our earlier example, we mentioned the Daughters of the American Revolution as an audience with unique characteristics. We also could have mentioned the National Association of Manufacturers or the Communist Party Congress as groups with unique characteristics. What is it that makes one group different from another? Some characteristics come immediately to mind:

(1) *Age* The chronological age of any group is an important characteristic in the approach that a communicator will take. The cry of the student power movement has been "trust no one over thirty!" Indeed, there is some justification for this slogan, since our values and beliefs change drastically with age. To a group of nineteen-year olds, marijuana may be of compelling interest, worthy of a good deal of the communicator's attention. But for an audience of fifty-year-olds, the subject loses some of its compelling force.

(2) *Sex* The composition of the audience is drastically changed if it is homogeneous in respect to sex. An all-male audience has unique characteristics, both in subject matter interests and in the social expectancies that are present. For example, the draft looms large in the interests of males of a certain age group, but has only peripheral interest for females. Fashion and fashion changes will generally be of greater interest to females than to males. Some of these differences are more customary than real. World affairs is of great interest to most women, but if we ask a typical male about women's possible interest in this subject, he is likely to respond that women are more interested in flowers. Communicators have to determine whether the differences they attribute to sex are real or imaginary ones.

(3) *Occupation* This is one of the most obvious differences that occurs in audiences. The communicator who is getting ready to speak to the district convention of the Illinois Nurses' Association is furnished with a good many clues to the interests of his audience. Not only are the interests different, but the audience has a core of common experiences upon which the communicator can draw.

(4) *Other Factors* Many writers include common opinions, values, and interests as separate factors in audience analysis, as well as occa-

sional variables such as time and place of the speech, purpose of the meeting, and so on. We could continue to list these characteristics as they become known to us, and produce quite a list. Almost anything that makes an audience a homogeneous group is of import to the communicator, and is a factor that he should include.[1]

All of these audience variables are examined by the source to discover only one basic thing: the nature of the receivers that are going to enter into the communicative interaction with him. When this is determined, the source is ready to take his next step in the generation of material for the communication. Unfortunately, many times the audience characteristics that we have set out here are simply not known or are not available to the communicator. When this occurs, he can only guess as to what *might* be of interest to the audience and make adjustments in his behavior if his guesses prove to be wrong. Occasionally things work out so that the communicator has no control at all, and on these rare occasions, the whole communicative interaction can be a total loss. Such was the case with the popular after-dinner speaker who was invited to say a few words at a service club meeting. Arriving in town just in time for the dinner, he had no chance to chat with the members informally, and at the table he was absorbed in renewing an old friendship with the man sitting on his left. Thus, he hardly noticed that the atmosphere was rather subdued. Only after he arose did he sense tension and uncertainty. He began his speech, which was not completely serious in purpose. His discomfort increased as he became aware of the reluctance of the group to laugh with him. His speech became less and less orderly as he tried to break through to his listeners. He began to fumble for words; he hesitated more and more. In general, his usually fine delivery crumbled under the silent and cold reception by his audience.

It was not until after his speech that a member thought to tell him that, shortly before dinner, word had been received that the very popular mayor of the town, a member of the club, had been killed in an automobile accident.

Tasks If the communicator has some idea of what kind of receivers he will have in the communicative situation, he can now turn to the particular task of the communication. As we noted in Chapter 1, communication can be broken down into the main processes of relaying, externalizing, and manding, if we exclude the esthetic goals for the time being. (We will also exclude the attitudinal goals in this portion of our analysis.) But relaying, manding, and externalization as purposes are not enough—the communicator has to choose *what* to relay, mand, or

---

[1] For an excellent summary of many of these considerations see Theodore Clevenger, *Audience Analysis* (Indianapolis, 1965).

externalize. This choice of task is usually made on the basis of social significance and the state of the audience.

The principal requirement in the choice of subject matter is that the communicator should not waste his own time or the time of his audience. We can assume that waste is undesirable and we can see several kinds of communication that are immediately ruled out of our choice. For example, if we mean to relay, by definition we can only relay that about which the audience has no knowledge. If, on addressing the County Medical Association's monthly meeting, a speaker decides to relay to the assembled doctors his knowledge about how to give an intravenous feeding, the speaker is obviously wasting their time and his. This seems like such a simple requirement in choosing subject matter. But over and over again, we are witness to speakers who call for programs that are already adopted, present information that is common to us all, and advocate attitudes that the audience already assumes. In beginning classes in communication, we often see assignments presented on how to shine shoes, how to bake cakes, or Paul Revere's ride. A communicator who so obviously wastes his audience's time cannot have thought even momentarily about himself as a source in the interaction. The key to good choice in tasks lies in two processes: thinking and creating as a communicator. These will be examined in the next section.

THINKING

The most vital element in any office—whether it is part of a hospital, a small business, a doctor's or lawyer's office, an industry, or a research laboratory—is its filing system. Here is stored the past, present, and occasionally some of the future.

A competent filing clerk or secretary has carefully retained all the records which concern the operation directly or indirectly. At a moment's notice, she can locate specific information of any type because some place in these steel boxes, carefully classified and indexed, is the entire history of the organization.

Similarly, the college library is a storehouse of knowledge. Arranged in an orderly fashion on the tiers of shelves, the student finds reflections of the heart, soul, and mind of education. Man's knowledge of the universe is stored in the books which fill the stacks, together with his reactions, hopes for the future, and his criticisms of his environment.

Each of us has his own private library. We accumulate books from the time we are too young to read but old enough to look at pictures, to the time when our eyes are no longer sharp enough to see the print. These personal libraries reflect our backgrounds, our interests, our education—everything that has touched us during a lifetime. Our bookcases are filled with such volumes as *Little Women, Shakespeare's Works,* Horseman's *Encyclopedia,* Emily Post's *Etiquette, Abnormal Psychology,* a world atlas, *How to Improve Your Bridge Game,* and the Holy Bible.

But all of us have another important storehouse of knowledge. Its effectiveness is not limited in the same way that our libraries are. Its size and quality are not curtailed by lack of space or an overdrawn bank account. This storehouse of knowledge is the mind.

The human mind operates in miraculous ways. It accepts and stores sensations and impressions, recalls images, develops attitudes, resolves problems, and passes judgments. It also can sort and classify what it has recorded. Instead of going to the card catalog of the library or the table of contents of a book to locate particular information, one taps the index of his mind and recalls the necessary material.

Carefully stored in our minds is everything that has ever affected us. Furthermore, we have been able to categorize the material on a basis of relationships, so that it is possible for us to recall many widely separated experiences all of which pertain to the same thing. We then may make generalizations or draw conclusions from an analysis of impressions or facts we remember. In other words, there are folders in our mental filing system, dedicated to specific areas, which contain the accumulated experiences of a lifetime.

It is true, of course, that individual items are not always properly filed. They may have been perceived incorrectly or have not made an impression. But even those experiences which cannot be recalled or utilized in thinking have influenced and helped to form what is within memory.

The mental processes which must operate in order to prepare a message are thinking and creating.

The effectiveness of these functions of the mind in communication is dependent upon several factors:

1. The extent of the experiences and knowledge have been stored in the mind.
2. The sharpness and clarity of the original impressions.
3. The immediate evaluation that is made of the sensation.
4. The ability of the mind to establish degrees of relationship between isolated facts or impressions.
5. The orderliness of the filing system of the mind.
6. The ability of the mind to recall specific and appropriate material.
7. The facility with which all of the materials can be rearranged in order to achieve a desired effect.

8. The quality of evaluation which the mind exerts over the selection and arrangement of materials and ideas.

"Think before you speak" is an old maxim to which we often give lip service. Many of us have not stopped to consider the real meaning of this statement. But it deserves our attention, especially if it is extended to "Think before you speak and while you are speaking," because only with adequate mental manipulation can you effectively share with others what you have observed, studied, felt, believed, hoped, read, seen, or heard. Whether you are planning a formal ten-minute address or a retort to a friend with whom you are conversing, your speaking preparation begins with purposeful thinking.

Throughout your life you have been constantly exposed to stimuli of various types, which have reached you through sensory avenues, sometimes called the "Seven Doors to the Mind." This phrase is very descriptive because it suggests that you must open these doors in order to receive the many signals that seek entrance. Or said another way, you must be alert for and receptive to the desirable stimuli which confront you. Furthermore, you must make a conscious effort to relate the sensation to other impressions you have received, in order that it may be stored properly. This must be done if you want to retain it.

If any of the doors are closed, your mental file may have some very thin folders; there will be gaps in your facts, impressions, and feelings. The blind person, for example, misses the beauty of the colors of spring, the sad, bedraggled appearance of a hound dog, the serenity of a calm sea, and thousands of other pictures.

Sometimes sensory stimuli do not reach the person even though his senses are intact. This may be desirable at times. For example, it is fortunate that you can shut out or reject the noise outside your room while you are studying. You are utilizing your ability of selective perception and closing out that which is distracting to you.

At times, however, the rejection or lack of perception of stimuli can result in a great loss. The person who can see, but does not, misses opportunities for filling in gaps in his experience. This inability may be due to lack of motivation. He does not care whether or not he sees a specific picture, or else he has not had the appropriate background of experience to appreciate what he sees.

Thinking Depends upon Adequate Exposure to Stimuli

Fortunately, almost everyone is capable of receiving sensory stimuli, and the majority of us keep the channels at least partially open and unclogged. Signals literally pour into the brain through the doors of our perceptions. If you recall the first step in the communication model presented in Chapter 1, you will remember that the stimuli from the outside world are the beginning of the communicative process. Indeed, nothing communicative could occur if these channels were blocked. Let us examine some of the channels that we typically utilize in receiving data.

1. Through Our Ears From birth we are constantly exposed to auditory cues. We have all heard the whistle of a train, the bark of a dog, the whine of a motor, the Lord's Prayer said in unison in church, the voice of the teacher explaining the meaning of a word, the frightened whimper of a child, the majestic swell of organ music, the whirring of traffic on a super highway.

2. Through Our Eyes We were able to focus our eyes and see a fairly clear picture when we reached the age of eight or nine weeks. From then on, visual impressions have been constantly relayed to our brains. These pictures have varied from the first blurred impression of our mothers to an unbelievable kaleidoscope of images. They have included visual stimuli received from the printed page, from movie and television screens, from the paintings of great artists, and mostly from the world about us in action. The only time that these stimuli are completely blocked is when our eyes are closed. Think of the millions of pictures which our minds have received.

3. Through Our Sense of Touch Need any of us be reminded of the first time we poked our fingers into the fascinating, bright, blue-red-orange flame of a burning match? The searing pain which followed was a surprise and then a shock and perhaps was our first awareness of pain. We all remember how it feels to stroke a soft, fluffy Persian kitten; the wonderful sensation of the wet, cold sand of the beach as our feet touch it while walking.

4. Through Our Sense of Taste Every day, at least three times a day and probably more, we taste a variety of foods and liquids. Add to this the taste of cough syrup and drops; the glue of an envelope flap or stamp, the taste of a freshly lighted cigarette or of a lipstick.

5. Through Our Sense of Smell The odor of warm bread fresh from the oven intermingled with the smoky essence of frying bacon is an olfactory sensation that most of us have experienced. The world is full of distinctive odors: the slightly acrid but rich aroma of pipe smoke; the delicate odor of vanilla flavoring; ammonia fumes; the antiseptic smell of a hospital; the fragrances of new-mown hay; the fresh, clean smell of laundry soap; the unique odor of wet pavement in the summer.

6. Through Our Thermic Sense All of us have experienced the cold of a blustery, winter day and the oppressive, muggy heat following a rain storm on a hot summer day. There are other impressions of heat and cold: the refreshing cold of a plunge into a swimming pool; the warmth of an open fire alongside a skating rink; the searing heat of melted sugar; the scalding heat of hot coffee; the shock of ice pressed against the body.

7. *Through Our Motor Sense* Many of the sensations which are stored in our minds have had their source in movements involved in jitterbugging, going up and down stairs, typing, swallowing, swinging an ax, combing our hair, blinking our eyes, skating, playing tennis, ironing, driving a car, and so on. Almost every moment of our lives some part of our body is involved in some type of movement and the resulting sensations become a part of our memory.

This presentation of the various types of sensory perception has been oversimplified since each type has been discussed individually. However, it is a unique situation when only one sense is affected; most of the time, at least two and often more are stimulated simultaneously. You see the wild, uncontrolled surf breaking over the beach, you hear the roar of the waves as they race toward the shoreline, you feel the wind as it blows against your face and through your hair.

To further complicate the reception of these sensory impressions, the mind may have to accept multiple stimulations from one sense. You see not only the surf breaking on the shore, but also the small child running toward the water followed by an anxious mother. Or you hear the sea and the mother's cry, "Johnny, come back here."

In spite of this, the mind is able to receive these multiple impressions and is capable of sorting and identifying them. Or it can reject some of them. Moreover, the mind accepts, recalls, and relates images of stimuli which arrive in a haphazard, disorganized sequence, the manner in which sensory stimulations usually arrive.

In some cases our senses are stimulated indirectly or vicariously. The experience may be recreated for you in written form, on the movie or television screen; or you may receive it audibly from another's speech in face-to-face communication; or indirectly over a telephone, from a radio set, and so on.

For example, you may not have had the experience of watching an incendiary bomb dive toward your home, exploding within two blocks of the spot where you are standing. However, you can evoke the feelings of the real situation by reading a description of such an event in the newspaper. Likewise, you experience some of the terror and shock by listening to an actual witness describe his own experience. A movie may recreate the incident with such frightening vividness that temporarily, at least, your fear approximates the reality.

In these instances, you are able to appreciate the terror of the situation because you have a background of experience which has stimulated some of the same reactions. Perhaps you have seen a building burst into a mass of flames, the result of an explosion. Or you have viewed two cars racing toward one another on the highway and an inevitable crash. As you watched, you experienced some of the same suspense you would feel if a screaming bomb were aimed in your direction.

Regardless of how sensations reach you, the resulting impressions which are directed to your mind are encyclopedic at least in quantity. Their quality is dependent upon your ability to observe—to hear, to see, to feel, to smell, to taste, to experience heat, cold, and movement. In the case of the indirect stimulation, derived through reading and listening, the quality is dependent upon your ability to accept words as substitutes for actuality. In other words, instead of seeing a house burn, you see the words which describe the burning structure. Your interpretation of the words will be proportionate to the extent of your experience with fires.

By this time you must recognize that if your senses are intact, your mind is filled with a vast knowledge of the world about you. It should begin to be clear that the material stored is unique and extremely personal. While it is true that your actual experiences may have been similar to those of other people, the sensations you have stored may be quite different from theirs.

In the first place, the comparative sharpness of sensations caused by identical stimulations vary, due to differences in attention and observation. They will vary further because of differences in past experience. If your association with a particular situation has been limited, your sensations may reflect less impact. The extent of your interest in and appreciation of a particular type of stimulation will also have an effect on the resulting sensation. For example, if you are a skilled musician, you are likely to obtain more from hearing a symphony than the person who knows little about music.

Moreover, your sensations will be unlike those of other people because the stimulation is evaluated in terms of your highly individualized background. You have stored in your mind a combination of experiences which cannot be duplicated by any other person. An example may clarify this concept: A violent thunderstorm may be an exciting and exhilarating experience for one person. He has never had reason to fear it, and therefore, when it comes, he welcomes it for its beauty and excitement. Another person may see danger in the storm. These two people, as a result of different backgrounds of experience, react to the signs of the gathering storm in opposite ways. The resulting sensations, motivated by the same event, are quite different. The first sees beauty; the second sees only danger.

Since your mental storage file has a large supply of these highly individualized impressions, you must have something to say that is interesting and different. And certainly, some of your reactions to stimuli have been strong and thought-provoking. These are bound to come to the surface of your thinking mind as you are given the opportunity to speak and as you are motivated to share your thoughts with others. You *do* have an adequate background for communication—whether it is written or oral. At least, you have the necessary raw material.

Too often, however, a person does not recognize the potentialities of his mind. He makes little effort to recall and evaluate what is stored; in this case, his mental filing system might be labeled "dead storage." He excuses his lack of ideas by plaintively whining that he just hasn't anything important to say. The more often he excuses himself in this manner, the more often that he resists recall and evaluation, the more difficult it will be for him to think creatively, to develop attitudes, or to make judgments.

Thinking Involves Establishing Proper Relationships

The raw material of thinking is the stored sensations which must be classified and categorized. At the risk of carrying an analogy too far, let us assume that as impressions are received by the brain they are sorted on a basis of past experience, they are put into folders of the mind reserved for a particular subject. These sensory experiences are available then, any time that the mind recalls them. Try an experiment: Start with the word "party" and jot down quickly everything that comes to your mind. Limit your writing to two minutes. You will be amazed at the list of associations which you can devise in this short time interval. And your list will represent only a small part of your stored material dealing with this subject.

If you were successful in this experiment, we might assume that your party file is well organized and crammed with material. Your second step in thinking depends on your ability to remember and recall. Or to put it another way, the next thing you must do is to pull out all the files dealing with a particular area, in order that you may "brainstorm" the idea which you want to explore. You bring to a conscious level much more than you will need; but all of the material is necessary in order to ensure proper evaluation.

In the thinking process, words are substituted for actuality. You now deal with words instead of sensations, and you use them in much the same way that you do in oral speech. The objective, at this level, is to test the relationships of the recalled sensations in order to be able to arrive at a logical and sound conclusion, a vivid and accurate account, or an astute and meaningful deduction.

THE SOURCE—THE BEGINNING OF COMMUNICATION

Let us return to the example of the thunderstorm in order to clarify this concept. This time, the thunderstorm occurs in Kansas. A farmer pauses in his work and glances up at the gathering clouds, and he begins to talk to himself silently (he begins to think). If we could overhear this subvocal talk, this is what we would hear: "Oh, no! Not again. Those clouds look mighty suspicious to me. They're too much like the ones that ushered in that tornado last year; or are they? Maybe; they aren't quite so low. Well, I'll keep an eye on them. I wonder if we are in for it again. I wonder where the kids are. I wish they were in the house with their mother. I wonder if Mary remembered to put fresh water and food in the hurricane cellar. Last time we were stuck in there so long we ran out of water. Yes, and the flashlight battery gave out all too soon. Must remember to take a supply of candles this time, if we have to go down in the cellar. I must remember to fix that cellar door, too. I should have done it before. I'm glad the cattle are in the barn. Better check that door, too. The clouds seem to be getting heavier. Maybe we'll just have a good rain; crops are really taking a beating this year. They certainly could stand some rain. But if we have a blow like last year, they'll be leveled. Those clouds look mighty suspicious to me. Guess I'd better get moving if I'm going to get everything done before it's too late. I won't have too much time now."

As a result of this thinking, the man dashes to the house and calls out to his wife:

1. To find out where the children are.
2. To find out whether or not the cellar is stocked.
3. To remind her to take candles into the cellar.
4. To ask her to collect the children and make a dash for the storm shelter.

In the meantime, he thinks of several other things, in light of past experiences and needs, which are important:

1. He picks up some blankets, a raincoat, a small battery radio, to take to the shelter.
2. He turns off the pilots on the gas stove and water heater.
3. He puts the car in the barn and fastens the door securely.

When he arrives at the shelter, he calls to the children to come out and he explains to them what he thinks is happening. He attempts to direct their interest and attention toward this giant trick of nature and thus helps to eliminate some of their fears of the unknown.

This brief example should help you to understand thinking. The farmer was recalling his somewhat unrelated experiences with a tornado and applying them to the present situation. Although his thoughts seem irrational and disordered, he was simply exploring and evaluating the situation in order to reach some decisions. On the basis of his thought process, he arrived at very decisive and definite action and speech. The resulting communication was clear cut, purposeful, and well-organized.

This man saw the present in light of the past. He established the proper relationships. He arrived at logical conclusions—and when the full force of the tornado hit minutes later, the value of his clear thinking was evident.

His past experience with storms, especially with the frequent tornadoes in Kansas, made it possible for him to recognize the danger signals in the sky. He recalled events which had occurred during the last storm. He immediately remembered the fear of his children, for example, and knew that they probably were afraid this time. He thought of the preparations that should be made, recognizing the mistakes that had been made the year before. He recalled that they hadn't had enough fresh water and that the flashlight had given out too soon.

He kept comparing the weather signals with those which usually indicate trouble. Finally, on his analysis of the situation, on a basis of his comparison of the present with the past, on his predictions for the future, he was motivated to action and to speech. His actions and his speech were both highly rational and purposeful.

Just as with the farmer contemplating the storm, your ability for analytical thinking will provide you with solutions. But it will do much more, as it did for the farmer. It directed his action and it provided the source and the structure for his speech. And your thinking will provide the motivation, the source, and the structure of your oral communication.

When the need or opportunity for communication arises, because of the manner in which material is stored in your mind you always have an immediate source. If you will explore your mental files by thinking, you will discover something to say—something that cannot help but be worth sharing. The mental manipulations of the stored material will undoubtedly result in strong motivation for talking.

Thinking also reveals the weakness in an argument or in exposition. As you consider a problem and recall all of the information which you have in your mental filing system, after careful evaluation you may find that there are gaps. You will recognize the need for filling in these gaps and will seek help from storehouses of knowledge other than your mind.

A student complains that he has an idea but he just can't find a way to say it. Actually, the difficulty here is one concerned with words.

THE SOURCE—THE BEGINNING OF COMMUNICATION 61

The student does not have the language facility necessary to put his idea into words. The chances are, in this case, that he also has not been able to think his way through the subject, either; his silent language does not permit him to do so.

Thinking Assists You in the Process of Isolating General Topics

If you are in conversation with one or more people, the general topic may be chosen by anyone in the group. Whatever *you* introduce into the discussion will be motivated by a strong interest which has grown out of past experience. Note how often, in such a situation, you attempt to regulate the conversation so that it concentrates on subject matter that you are particularly interested in. This may be somewhat selfish, but it is also understandable. We tend to talk about the things we understand and appreciate. Personal though it is, there is no better example than the author of a text who forces conversations with his colleagues around to the problems concerned with the text. During the development of the manuscript, his energies, his dominating thoughts, his questions, and so on, are so centered in it that there is strong motivation to talk about it.

This is no excuse for a bore. But if self-stimulated general subjects represent the richest knowledge and experience of an individual, they are bound to be the most satisfactory. The speaker will have something to share. The subject becomes unsuitable only if the speaker has nothing new or challenging to offer.

When choosing a general topic for a communication, you thumb through the files of your mind. Without a doubt the topics that are full of experiences are the ones you will ultimately use. And probably you will be using topics that are a reflection of your major interests in school, of your leisure-time activities, and of your home. This is as it should be.

It would be presumptuous to attempt to list all of the general subjects or categories under which material is filed in the human mind. But to illustrate the meaning of a *general subject* and to stimulate you to think of more, here are a few:

Education	Government	Electronics
Religion	Communication	Human relations
Sports	Transportation	War
International relations	Nature	Peace
Isolationism	Philosophy	Justice
Entertainment	Salesmanship	Beliefs
Integration	Psychology	Hope

Juvenile delinquency	Literature	Tolerance
History	Geography	Leisure
Capitalism	Professions	Weather
Penology	Customs	Criticism
Capital punishment	Careers	Medicine
Marriage	Television	The family

CREATING

Once your general subject has been isolated, the really creative work begins. At this point, it is necessary for the speaker to crystallize and define the particular idea which he wishes to develop. Here, *creative thinking* is employed to define a purpose and to limit the extent of the discussion. The source, having decided on a general area for his communication, examines his mental files dealing with this general area. He recalls specific instances clustered around an image. He evaluates these, inspecting their relationships. He generalizes on the basis of his evaluations of his many impressions. Because all of his stored facts and impressions have been tempered by his reactions to them and his feeling about them, they are highly individualized and his generalization is likewise unique.

You have received millions of stimuli. You have evaluated many of these and reacted to them. Such a reaction becomes the motivating factor which stimulates you to want to share an idea with someone. The strength of the motivation will be a direct result of the sharpness of the original impressions received from observation and the mental consideration and evaluation of them.

For example, you read in a daily paper the shocking story of a riot in a large city. This may start a chain reaction in your thinking. You begin with an indirect picture of this particular violence. Then you begin to ask yourself, "Why?" You later see a television newsreel showing the arraignment of the people involved. You are amazed at their youth and their attitudes of belligerence. You recall an incident of minor consequence in your own school which reflected some of the same characteristic of unrest that these boys display. You try to picture yourself in such a situation and reject the image because of your devotion to your parents and the ideals which they have instilled in you.

Thinking about this subject may be intermittent, but each time you return to it your recollections and reactions begin to crystallize in opinion. There may be gaps in your knowledge concerning the topic and you seek the answers from other people or from books or magazines. You may begin to draw some conclusions which prompt you to share your attitudes and beliefs with other people. And so you say to your father, "It seems to me that many of our cities' problems are rooted in the lack of good schools." You have created an idea, incomplete at this point because it has not yet been fully explored, supported, and explained.

If your auditor asks you why you believe as you do, you proceed to outline your point of view, drawing from your stock of experiences, from your reading or listening. You adapt your material to the comprehension ability of your auditors. The resulting message is as creative as the picture produced by a painter, the song composed by a musician, or the chair designed by a cabinetmaker.

Of course, a single event such as a riot may evoke different responses from different people because of the uniqueness of each person's store of images. The twelve-year-old who reads the account in the paper reacts differently from the man of forty who reads it. An adolescent in the city and in the area where the incident took place reacts differently from another who lives in a serene rural area, far removed from the scene of the disturbances. And the young people who live in the district where the riot took place think about the event in different ways, depending upon their relationship to the gang. Thus each person has a potential for the creation of a highly individualized message.

To clarify this concept further, let us assume that four speakers have chosen the general subject of *education*. One is a lawyer who has been asked to give a commencement address. One is a high school principal who has consented to address a local service club. The third speaker is a college senior who is planning to give a special report in one of her classes. And finally, the last speaker is a comedian, a former schoolteacher, who is giving a monologue on a televised variety program. In each case, the speaker is influenced by his or her own background and experience and certain predictable factors in the speaking situation to select a suitable idea around which to build his speech:

1. The lawyer decides to talk about the need for continuing education throughout a lifetime.
2. The high school principal chooses as his subject, "The New Speed-up Program in Our High School."
3. The senior decides to defend American education against the charge that it is inferior to Russian education.
4. The comedian decides to share some of his amusing experiences with children.

Note that each speaker has drawn his subject from the large area of education. It is interesting to note, however, how different their specific subjects are. Each has been motivated to talk about his particular topic because he felt it suitable for him: it interested him; he has the background for it; he has had firsthand experience with it; and he is capable of doing a reasonably good job. Each speaker has also decided that his chosen topic should be interesting to, and appropriate for, his particular auditors, that there are values which would result for the listeners. Finally, in each case the choice of the specific subject was evaluated in terms of appropriateness for the occasion.

In other words, each speaker chose his particular facet of education in light of certain conclusions about the appropriateness of his subject. Many people have an instinct for selecting the most appropriate idea to share with others under all circumstances.

Also, some communicators have the ability to make almost any idea acceptable to almost any audience. With a rich background for the subject and a driving interest in it, they can transmit enthusiasm as well as ideas. The auditors will listen. It must be mentioned here that other factors may be operating to the speaker's advantage: unusual facility with the use of language, interesting and captivating use of vocal and physical reinforcement, among others. But the point is that he has taken a subject that another person may not have been able to handle effectively in the same situation.

For those of you who have difficulty finding the right specific speech topics for various speaking situations, the following guides may be of help:

1. *Choose a Subject that Interests you*   This is probably the most important advice that can be given to you. An interest in a subject provides you with strong motivation to share your ideas with other people. In turn, it generally creates in the speaker an infectious enthusiasm which is almost inevitably transferred to his listeners. With an audience made receptive by your own eagerness, you remove one obstacle to communication.

An interest in a subject almost guarantees that the subject is drawn from background and experience. In other words, you can't very well be interested in something you don't understand. Knowledge of the subject makes it possible for you to analyze it. You have at least the essential information necessary to establish relationships and draw tentative conclusions. You have personal experience with the topic which you can share with your auditors spontaneously and naturally. Although you may not have all the information necessary to explain a subject to your satisfaction, you do have other resources from which you can draw additional information.

Occasionally, your knowledge of a subject is limited, but you know enough about it to have developed a curiosity about it. If you are willing to do adequate research so that you become well acquainted with the area you propose to discuss, there is no reason for you to reject such a topic. But you must make a thorough study of the subject and not substitute rambling, unsubstantiated imagination for facts.

2. *Choose a Subject that Will Suit Your Audience* We have said that some speakers can present any subject so that it is acceptable to an audience. But if you are not able to do this, then you must select a subject that interests you *and* one that appeals to your listeners. It doesn't matter how important or interesting or familiar a topic is to the speaker, if he isn't able to transfer his enthusiasm to his auditors, the topic is not a good choice. The speaker has an obligation to choose a subject which will appeal to the people receiving the message. Moreover, he must be sure that the subject is worth while and that the time spent listening to the discussion of it will not be wasted.

Occasionally, a subject may be chosen because it is necessary to transmit certain information important to the listener. The topic may be unpleasant, such as a discussion of "Survival in Atomic Warfare." Because the listeners' lives may depend upon their comprehension of the material, the speaker *must* talk about it. Or the topic may simply be uninteresting. A parent often forces the exploration of a subject on his children because of the problem-solving value of the discussion. These choices are both justified because of the need which has motivated their discussion.

The speaker should find out as much as possible about his listeners in order that he may make a wise choice of subject. He will need to know something about their backgrounds, their educational accomplishments, their interests, the age range, and the sex ratio of the group.

He should also consider the possible attitudes that are a result of some of these characteristics, since they should influence the speaker at every moment of his speech preparation and delivery. (See Chapter 8 in which we present a more extensive discussion of this aspect of speaking.)

3. *Choose a Subject which Is Appropriate for the Occasion* The choice of subject must be further limited or influenced by the purpose of the meeting, the time of the year, the events which have preceded it or will follow it, and the time allotted to the speaker.

For example, it is rather pointless to try to deal with a very serious subject such as "Juvenile Delinquency" at a junior-senior banquet in a high school; just as out of place is a humorous subject used for a high school graduation address. The purposes of these two assemblies are incompatible with the topics.

Generally, it would be a waste of time to urge your listeners to have a chest X-ray when the state X-ray cruiser has recently visited their community and moved on. Likewise, some phase of the subject, "Christmas," would probably be unacceptable in July, though timely in December.

The same exceptions which have been explained in connection with the first two principles apply here. The person whose interest in a subject amounts to dedication and who has the unique ability of instinctively making the necessary adaptations, can talk about a subject that generally might not be suited to the occasion. You will have to decide whether you can take such a subject and handle it in such a way that it is not only acceptable but even exciting.

Let us go back to the general subject of *education* from which the four speakers drew their specific topics.

Other persons might have chosen different aspects of the field of education. Possibly there are thousands of well-defined ideas which could be drawn from this general area. Each speaker will choose the specific portion of the larger subject in terms of its suitability to him as a speaker, in terms of his audience and of the occasion. Among the many possibilities, here are a few:

1. Teachers' salaries must be raised to keep up with the steady increase in cost of living.
2. All teachers should be required to take refresher courses at least every five years.
3. Enter the teaching profession for a satisfying career.
4. Are your children learning to read well enough?
5. Can television take the place of the classroom teacher?
6. How can we motivate our children to learn?
7. Every student should be required to take four years of science in high school.
8. Let's curtail extracurricular activities in our colleges and universities.
9. The listening habits of college freshmen must be improved.
10. Vocational guidance programs are an important part of any high school curriculum.

OTHER SOURCE CHARACTERISTICS

We have now examined some of the processes that make up the creation of a source in the communicative process. Potential audiences and tasks stimulate the individual's creative and thinking functions, and produce the subject matter and materials for communication. There are other factors that contribute to sources that we have not discussed, however. In Chapter 1, the point was made that source characteristics become part of the message in the communicative interaction. "What you are speaks so loudly, I cannot hear what you say," was the famous quotation. Indeed, what we are does play an important part in the communicative interaction. Our next section will concern the two main source characteristics: adjustment and credibility.

Adjustment

"I don't want to get adjusted to this world," goes the first line of the frontier hymn. It was a fine song, but a poor sentiment. Most of us are vitally concerned with becoming adjusted to this world and the situations that this world forces upon us. We are also concerned with becoming adjusted to the communicative situation and meeting it in a confident fashion.

In many communicative situations, unfortunately, we are poorly adjusted. In an important interview we may feel nervous and ill at ease. In a formal speaking situation, the presence of an audience may cause a feeling of anxiety and cause our palms to perspire. Even in a classroom-speaking exercise, many students feel anxious and uncomfortable. Many persons list "confidence" as their principal goal in learning how to communicate orally, which illustrates how concerned most of us are with this anxiety.

In 1957, the School of Dramatic Art and Speech at Ohio University conducted extensive research regarding basic courses in speech.[2] One of the findings of that research is pertinent to this point. It was discovered that out of the 700 students enrolled in the Fundamentals of Speech course, 93 percent indicated that the most important result of taking a basic speech course should be a better personal adjustment to the speaking situation, and solutions to problems of "stage fright."

Ninety-seven percent of these students stated that they experienced fright to a significant degree.

Causes of Poor Adjustment

When we have a sincere desire to communicate and have done an excellent job in the thinking and creating steps of preparation for communication, and are still upset by the actual delivery of the communication, we commonly call this anxiety "stage fright," though it is not actually fright nor does it occur on the stage. Whatever we call it, we must acknowledge that it would be useful to concentrate on its mitigation, since poor adjustment very often contributes to poor communication. To achieve this purpose, we need to examine the possible

---

[2] School of Dramatic Art and Speech, Ohio University, *Year of Exploratory Research*, (unpublished manuscript), 1957, p. 84.

causes—the factors that contribute to poor adjustment. What we envision as a cause will depend largely on how we view the nature of our basic adjustment to other people, and, as you might have guessed, there are several different explanations that are commonly offered.

1. **The Psychoanalytic View** According to Freud, the "life force" in individuals has a counterpart, or opposite—"the death wish." In poorly adjusted individuals, this death wish is manifested in suicidal tendencies, but Freud believed that it was present in all of us to some degree. We more often see it exhibited in the compulsion to fail or to engage in self-destructive activities, such as alcoholism or gambling. In normal individuals, this force may manifest itself in nonadjustive behaviors, such as anxiety when an important communicative situation presents itself.

Freud's explanation is an imaginative and interesting one, and may contain a kernel of real truth. One of the principal difficulties with this point of view is that the theory seems to state that nothing constructive can be done about this anxiety short of psychoanalysis. This is not entirely consistent with the facts as we know them, and, while, lucrative for the psychoanalysts, is not very helpful for ordinary individuals who are interested in improving their communicative ability.

2. **The Field Theorists** One interesting point of view about human behavior has stated that we behave as we do because of fields of forces that act on us. This approach was largely the work of Kurt Lewin who borrowed heavily from vector algebra for basic pictures of social interactions in which we find ourselves. Simply stated, the theory held that when we were quite hungry, we could be viewed as being pushed in a given direction. In this case, individuals can be described as points, and the "pushes" on them can be described as vectors of the forces. No problems arise until two or more forces interact, giving rise to new directions. This is the case in the communicative interaction. The communicator is influenced by a force that pushes toward communication, and hence "approaches" the communicative situation. This force is the result of desires for social interaction, interest in the subject, and so on. At the same time, he is influenced by another force. This is the result of the realization that the situation contains danger of failure or of ridicule. This force can be called an "avoidance" force. Both of these operating together produce an "approach-avoidance" conflict, which is resolved by a new direction. Figure 13 represents how the approach-avoidance conflict is often resolved. As you can see, the conflict produces escape behavior, or tendencies to leave the field. This tendency is manifested as a basic anxiety reaction that we all experience in communicative situations.

Interpreting the situation this way offers a simple solution to the problem. All we need to do is to increase the force of approach and

THE SOURCE—THE BEGINNING OF COMMUNICATION

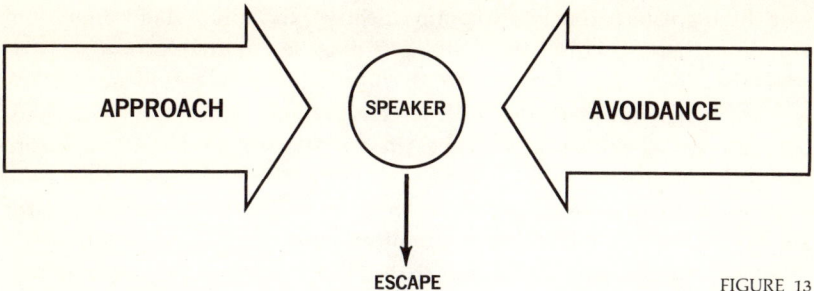

FIGURE 13

decrease the forces of avoidance, hence lessening the conflict. Unfortunately, we might also reduce the conflict by doing the opposite—resulting in no communication at all. Many persons do just this—they avoid communicative situations; in group discussions they are the last to speak out; they become known as the strong and silent type. Unfortunately being silent doesn't always connote being strong, but often only means that the avoidance has won over the approach.

We sometimes make a virtue out of this ("she's shy and retiring—very ladylike" or "he never chatters unnecessarily, only speaks when he has something to say"). Most people who have taken this path will admit that they would prefer to be able to join communicative situations more freely than they do.

We also have another problem in using field theory—how do we go about increasing or decreasing these forces? This is no simple question, with simple answers.

3. **Behavioral Theories** The "behaviorists" as a group are generally identified with that group of psychologists that assumes most of our behavior is a function of response-reward contingencies—that is, have resulted because of responses having occurred and a reward being given for that response. This is how we train animals to perform—when they respond appropriately to the command, we present them with food or water or some other desirable outcome. Many of us balk at interpreting our behavior in this way, since we are reluctant to admit that such simple things influence us. But we must admit that we are more influenced by this process than we care to admit. A great deal of our behavior was learned at a very early age when we were more "teachable," that is, much more rewardable in a behavioral sense. We can still be manipulted by rewards—money, grades, prestige, power, all are social rewards toward which men strive.

In the case of communication we would then reason that we have learned to speak because it was rewarding, awkward to avoid, or because it was punishing. Our learning history should explain the present state of rewards we get out of communication. There is some evidence to indicate that this is true. One researcher found that students who had greater anxiety in communicative situations had come from families where children were not given as much freedom of expression—that is, where the rule "children should be seen and not heard" was enforced. Another researcher concluded that anxiety decreases with the number of speech experiences in a classroom and must therefore be related to learning.

In this case, we can see that this interpretation of communicator anxiety has a good deal more to offer us in the classroom than do other approaches, since anything that is taught can usually be untaught or changed. We also know that certain kinds of rewards can be instrumental in the learning process. Most students find it helpful to realize that each experience in the classroom will be helpful in reducing their anxieties.

Adjustment as a communicator, then, is related to our general makeup, whether we interpret in Freudian expression, field theory, or behavioristic terms. Since most of us cannot afford psychoanalysis, we might choose to utilize the other approaches to adjustment—simply by gaining experience in communication and by attempting to make our "approach" valences stronger than the "avoidance" ones. This can be done by engaging in successful communication situations, and is one of the real values that a beginning course in communication can have for students.

THE SOURCE AND CONTROL

Now that we have described several aspects of the problem connected with the personal adjustment to the communicative act, it might be well to discuss the potential solutions to the problems. Is it possible to utilize your capacity and to guide your motivation into appropriate and constructive channels? The answer is a decided "yes," and this use of capacity and harnessing of motivation taken together are called "control."

Another question which requires answering is: How does one achieve control, particularly as it relates to the communication process? If one reduces the essential methods of achieving such control to the fewest number of possible alternatives, it begins to look as though there are, in general, two quite divergent points of view: the speaker-centered approach and the topic-centered approach.

A strange thing about these two methods is that they cannot be compromised or watered down to resemble each other. Both approaches have been used with success, but success has been much more likely to occur when one method has been used to the exclusion of the other. They are mutually detrimental to each other if used in combination.

In view of the fact that one method does not seem to be significantly or consistently superior to the other, we shall describe both approaches. You may decide for yourself which method you can use to the best advantage. If you feel you need help with this decision, consult your instructor.

The speaker-centered approach works on the assumption that the best possible way to cope with a given fear is to examine it and understand it. If you have an emotional problem, this approach directs you not to repress it, or avoid it, or even camouflage it. Instead, introspect (search within yourself); verbalize about what you find (bring it out into the open); obtain a feeling of release for having done so; and finally, become objective about it so that it no longer interferes with your effectiveness.

In other words, this method holds to the belief that if the communicator can begin to analyze and release his problem, he can gain insight. Furthermore, if he can gain insight, it is quite probable that he can change his behavior in the direction of improvement.

More specifically, there are three steps involved in the speaker-centered approach, and they are presented in outline for the purpose of easy review. Remember, though, that these suggestions are presented not with the intention to be specifically prescriptive but rather to be generally descriptive.

Step One. Analysis

A. Prepare an extensive autobiography of your communication experiences. Be sure to include an account of your participation in, or your avoidance of, formal, informal, and classroom situations. Be sure you picture the circumstances of these experiences accurately, and be certain you have described your role in these situations precisely.

B. Provide yourself and possibly your instructor with a check list of the outward signs of your approach-avoidance conflict and the inner conditions accompanying your fears.

Such a list might include shaky knees, trembling hands and fingers, an incessant spasm of a given muscle (frequently a small one, like an eyelid or the corner of the upper lip), increased perspiration—especially on the forehead and palms, a sudden onset of dryness of the mouth (the mucous membranes seem to cease their systemic secretions), a hollow feeling in the stomach (frequently occurring along with a sensation of "movement" or "butterflies" in the stomach), and a general feeling of being unable to move (a kind of paralysis or immobility which is characterized as much by heaviness as by the usual stiffness).

C. Describe as many conditions as your experiences will permit under which the signs appear to be magnified. Your description should include the various audience characteristics that disturb you, specific people you know who are difficult to talk to, and the kinds of situations in which you can predict trouble for yourself.

D. After your first speech in class, analyze your performance stressing the delivery aspects over the content. You will find it helpful, perhaps, to ask two of your classmates to assist you in the analysis. To give their task a little zest, and also to ensure a balance in the analysis, have one of the students look for the strong points of your performance (he takes the role of the complimenter); and the other student criticizes the weak spots (he has the role of the "razzer").

Step Two. Release

A. Keep a log or record of your communication experiences, using the autobiography as the beginning or foreword.
B. Make a speech for the purpose of externalizing, in which you describe your fear of speaking, its signs, its possible causes, and its treatment up to the time of your speech. Be sure you describe vividly and with imagery the emotional nature of your experiences. You might ask a few of your listeners to share and compare their own feelings about speaking situations, and perhaps generate an "all-in-the-same-boat" session.
C. Prepare a list of your avoidance devices or your "ways out" of speaking situations. Here you are trying to assess with cold, ruthless objectivity the liabilities of your approach-avoidance conflict. This list might mention such escape routes as feigned illness, absence, tardiness, forgetfulness, pleas for sympathy, asking questions which keep others talking, silence, oversleeping (so that you miss the situation), or falling asleep (when you are actually in the situation).
D. Prepare a description of yourself in which you stress your assets. This is literally your time to howl; you are to put your ego on parade. Mention everything about yourself that is worthwhile, desirable, valued by others as well as by you; and do not hesitate to brag. You may wish to add some humorous exaggerations regarding your greatness, and present this material as a light-touch speech to entertain.

Step Three. Objectivity

A. At three predetermined times in the semester present yourself with a progress report. Compare your autobiographic material with the progress you have made up to that particular time. List any changes you can observe. As a check on your accuracy, ask your instructor for such a progress report.
B. Prepare your last speech (or one of the earlier speeches, if your progress warrants it) for the final and conclusive proof of your achievement of control. "Let out all the stops." Be sure the content of your speech is strong; use language which enhances the idea of your message. When you present this speech, remember that this is the "big push" and you can prove to yourself and your audience that you have "broken through." If you feel apprehensive (and you should expect to because most people do), convert this nervous energy into the dynamics of your delivery; into the intensity of your voice, into the bodily action which enhances your message, and into the directness of your contact with the audience.

The topic-centered approach suggests a very different avenue of adjustment. It is supported by those authorities who believe that if one attempts to conquer fear by calling attention to it, he runs the risk of magnifying and intensifying that fear. If an individual is hypertense and wishes to avoid the speaking situation, it may not help to tell him that his hands tremble and he has poor eye contact. He needs to lose—not gain—consciousness of self. . . . He needs to pay more attention to what he says, and less attention to how he says it. If he can find a subject about which he has strong thoughts and intense feelings, he may be able to lose himself in the content of his topic. If his interest and motivation are potent enough, he will give in to the impulse to speak on that subject.

In the topic-centered approach, then, your behavior is changed indirectly; then the insight is attained. You surrender to the impulse to talk about your topic. You talk; and after talking, you can review what has happened. You can say to yourself, "Well look at me; I just talked up; I did not avoid, and I made my point."

The outline of the three steps in the topic-centered approach is presented below. Remember, these steps are not meant to be all-inclusive; they only indicate the aim of the approach and the general procedures used in attaining it.

Step One. Understanding the Goal

If you select the topic-centered approach, you will have to start by recognizing the rationale involved. You must bring to bear all of your intelligence and a considerable portion of your time, if this method is to help you to help yourself achieve control. You have to realize that your goal is to be able to release the ideas, thoughts, and feelings you have; and you must concentrate on these ideas, thoughts, and feelings. You must care enough about the topics you select to want to break through. Your goal, in short, is to be able and willing to communicate.

Step Two. The Means to the Goal

A. A crucial point in the success of this approach is the selection of meaningful, motivating topics. You may find that answering the following questions will help you select an optimum topic.
1. What is the most controversial subject you can think of?
2. What is the situation or activity in your life and time that you most want to change?
3. What is the situation or activity in your life and time which you most want to maintain or preserve?
4. What is the idea, event, object, or situation which you dislike the most?
5. What is the idea, event, object, situation, or personality that you like, love, or admire the most?
6. What is the most profound thought you have ever had?

7. Complete this sentence: "I firmly believe _____."

B. Getting wrapped up in your message is important in this approach, but it alone will not suffice. The ideas you decide to communicate must be so designed in your message that they will win the response you seek. The messages must be perfected and polished. Your outline will be a key to your success. The organization of your speech must be without error. Do not be easily satisfied with the composition of your message; be critical; concentrate on it.

C. Your ideas need support in terms of authoritative statements, testimonials, and quotations. You will have to review newspapers, magazines, and periodicals.

D. You may find it helpful to team up with someone in your class. You can listen to and analyze the speeches you are to make in class, stressing the content of the message rather than the delivery. If your teacher does not object, you can arrange to take opposite views on the same topic, and in this way add to the motivation value of an assignment.

E. One of the keys to this approach is the generation of the impulse to communicate. In order to facilitate your achievement of this end, you might ask your instructor to permit you to volunteer to take your turn speaking when that impulse occurs, instead of waiting for your name to be called from the class roll.

Step Three. Achieving the Goal

A. After the first half of the semester is over, you ought to provide yourself with progress reports. Once or twice a month you ought to review the topics you have prepared, assay the results of your communications in terms of their effect on your listeners and their effect on you. You might request the instructor to give you his impressions of your progress.

B. As your last speaking assignments come up, you can begin to polish your delivery. Now that you know that you can communicate when you want to, you will want to be sure that you are transmitting your communications as effectively as possible. Try to achieve variety of vocal attack (rate, pitch, loudness) and amplify your transmission with meaningful gestures, movement, and animation.

One further suggestion at this point: if you find that either of these two approaches is too difficult to work on by yourself, do not try to "go it alone" throughout the whole semester. Frequently you are the only one who knows that you need help. Usually help is available to you, if you seek it.

Do not procrastinate for long before you talk to your instructor. Make an appointment to see him; describe your problem to him (chances are he is familiar with the problem even if he is not well acquainted with you). If he can assist you, he will so inform you. If he cannot, he will be able to refer you to professional, qualified, and responsible people who can take up where your instructor leaves off.

THE SOURCE RESPONSIBILITY

If you were able to achieve everything that this chapter has suggested to you up to this point, it would be quite a miracle! However, it would not be enough. Indeed, even assuming that you thoroughly understood your method of approaching the speaking situation, and you could make use of all of the speaker's skills, and you were willing as well as able to communicate, you still have one more factor with which to contend.

If you know how to speak, if you know what to say, and if you want to say it, then say it! But be sure also that you know why you are saying it. It is not enough for the speaker to approach the speaking situation. He must enter that setting with responsibility. He must know that he is there to serve someone or something other than himself alone.

Let us examine this further. This is not an incidental issue. It is so pertinent that if you were to comprehend and respond affirmatively to only one part of this chapter, this is the part to attend. Professional teachers of speech can no longer abdicate this issue to those who would usurp it: the propagandistic politicians, the half-truth hucksters, the dangerously deceptive demagogues, and the pocketbook pirates of hidden persuaders. Adolph Hitler managed to approach his audience. He avoided very few opportunities to communicate. His messages led to hundreds of thousands of deaths.

The estimate that we spend 15 percent more than we intend at the supermarket and drugstore is said to be conservative. The advertisers, writers, and hawkers who bombard our ears with incessant commands and suave suggestions to get, get, get; and buy, buy, buy; and own, own, own, undoubtedly know what we know about communicating a message to win a response. But our future needs are ignored.

The trouble is that if man is to survive the many dangers of his world, he must be able to depend upon the messages he receives from his fellow men. This is more than a moral obligation; this is more than a plea to conscience. This is a demand for survival.

3 STRUCTURING THE MESSAGE

INTRODUCTION

The amount of formal preparation which precedes an oral communication varies greatly and depends upon the nature of the circumstances. A government official, invited to present a major convocation address on a college campus, will prepare extensively for such a task. He recognizes that his audience has certain expectations and that he has certain responsibilities as a representative of the government.

Similarly, the college professor has an obligation to communicate his knowledge effectively; his preparation is much more extensive because he must organize a large body of material into a course, then course units, and finally into individual lectures. His research is necessarily extensive in spite of the fact that he begins the planning of the course as a subject "expert." One of his most challenging problems centers on the need for reorganizing a large body of material into units (lectures) that must be presented in a logical sequence in a given amount of time or number of lectures.

We expect thorough preparation from a speaker in a formal situation. The man-hour loss can be very high if a speaker does not make good use of the time allotted him for a specific purpose, and auditors have every right to be resentful when a speaker takes advantage of his name or position and wastes the time of a group of listeners.

Of course, preparation takes different forms. A competent nuclear physicist has a lifetime of preparation in his area; he begins to prepare a formal presentation with a wealth of factual material at his fingertips. If he is asked to present a particular subject at a Sigma Xi (a graduate science honorary) meeting, because of his own competency in his field, there is no need for extensive exploration of the topic assigned to him. However, he does have problems of adaptation, selection, and organization.

Preparation for a formal presentation with one speaker and many auditors can involve several facets. It may involve extensive research of the topic, definition of a central idea, evaluation of and careful selection from the material assembled, and arrangement of the material in a manner which will be helpful to the listeners.

In some communication situations, preparation is limited to a thorough investigation of the topic without any attempt to structure a specific message. For example, the faculty of a department of speech decides that it would be advantageous to add a new type of major to its program. After many departmental meetings during which the purposes and nature of the degree have been explored, a program of study proposed, and degree requirements specified, the chairman must present his request to the curriculum committee of the university for final approval.

Even though the chairman has been present at all meetings of his department and is thoroughly conversant with the program, he probably will spend time in preparation for the meeting with the university committee members. This preparation will include a thorough review of the requirements, the intent of the degree, and the rationale for the addition. But he will probably go further in his preparation. He will review offerings in other departments to make sure that his program does not infringe upon or overlap with other programs. He may collect evidence to indicate that the new major, while innovative, is nonetheless being offered at a few other colleges. He may even assemble material relating to job opportunities for a person trained in a different way. He is not interested in structuring a "speech," for each of the committee members has received a copy of a written proposal. But he is preparing to answer the diversified questions which may be put to him by faculty members from other disciplines. He wants to reply to challenges in a way that will do nothing to detract from his and the program's credibility.

No one would dispute the need for preparation in formal and semi-formal settings. But is there preparation for the everyday oral communication in which we are involved? There is, but its nature is different. In a sense, your whole life is a preparation for talking. Your entire life experience provides you with the content; your talking draws on the knowledge, concepts, ideas, and feelings which you have acquired from your environment including contacts with people, books, formal education, entertainment, travel, and so forth. Admittedly, we are not equally well prepared to discuss any and all subjects, to make judgments in all instances, or to evaluate with equal competence all ideas with which we come in contact. But our exposures are so extensive that all of us are adequately prepared, from the standpoint of content, to meet everyday communication demands.

Obviously we do not preplan the structure of a message in a conversation, class discussion, or informal, unstructured "bull session." However, there is or should be structure or organization in these situations. The over-all structure is a function of all of the participants and its effectiveness is dependent upon the organizational ability of each individual. A topic is introduced by one person and is developed by all of the people present. Hopefully, there will be purpose, sequence, selectivity, and economy in the structure. Each speaker organizes his own contribution in a manner which will advance the discussion or amplify the idea. He also provides bridges from one idea to another, if he decides to shift from one focal point to another.

Preparation is an essential ingredient of good oral communication. An adequate knowledge of the subject is necessary in order for the speaker to plan the structure of his message. A carefully organized message will improve the speaker's chances of reaching an understanding with his receivers.

The processes of thinking and creating were explored in the previous chapter. These mental processes provide the raw and refined material necessary for sending written and oral messages. But a communicator can have a diversified collection of facts, ideas, concepts, feelings, and emotions relating to a particular general topic and still not be successful in achieving his purpose; the raw material must be organized into a coherent message.

A set of blueprints for a large building contains all of the information necessary for its construction. Not only are there plans for each individual room, hall, or closet, but the plans show these units *in relationship to each other.* Can you imagine the confusion if the detailed drawings for each room were on separate pages with no indication of relative positions in the building? Or can you imagine a contractor arriving at a building site to find piles of lumber, pipe, bricks, mortar, sand, concrete blocks, structural steel, and so on, but no blueprints. He has the raw materials necessary for construction but no idea how to "organize" them in the fabrication of the building. The blueprint would provide him with the structural plan. The architect, knowing the purpose of the building, should have devised a building plan that would meet the functional needs of those people and activities which will be housed in the structure.

An architect expects the building process to be an orderly one; he recognizes that the only way he can insure efficient construction is by providing a structured communication to the contractor in the form of blueprints and specifications. Without this complex but precise message, the builder is helpless, through no lack of skill on his part.

Listeners and readers also expect a communication to be orderly. People who read a daily newspaper learn the organizational pattern of the paper and expect to find related subjects in specific sections. Some readers, knowing the format of the paper, turn directly to the editorial page, intent on reading philosophical reflections on the issues of the day by competent columnists; others finish the front page, where important national news is featured, before turning to other sections; the youngsters in the family quickly turn to the page of comics; the sixteen-year old with a new driver's license flips to the classified advertising to see if, by any chance, a used car that meets his dad's specifications is listed. The editors of the paper have used a classification system to assist the readers in locating certain types of information.

But this orderliness would be of no importance, if the individual items in the paper were disorganized. Readers have a right to expect that each journalist participating in the preparation of the paper will do his best to present a structured report which is easy for the reader to follow. In the case of the newspaper, then, we have a master plan with many small, organized units.

The structure of a newspaper is not unlike the organization of a speech. The speaker, having chosen a topic, assembles materials relating to the topic. To begin with, he may simply list what appears to be ideas or facts which he feels he must present in order to achieve the purposeful presentation of the subject.

For example, a journalism major in a speech class may decide to talk about the organization of a typical newspaper. From his academic background and preliminary reading, he begins to list all of the features of the paper:

Subject: Organizational pattern of a newspaper
Topics:
    Editorials by managing editor
    National news reports
    International news reports
    Comics
    Human interest features
    Society notes
    Fillers
    Syndicated columns
    Advice columns
    Local news
    Sports
    Area news
    Special features
    Recipes

Tips on decorating
Household hints

The speaker may add to this list as he progresses with his planning; the important thing is that he has made his first effort to divide the subject into meaningful units. However, in this early stage of organization, the speaker has made no effort to group like items; this would be his next step. Let us look at his first effort at putting these items into a more meaningful arrangement:

Key idea: The organization of a newspaper follows a predetermined plan which facilitates easy handling and reading.
    News reports
        International
        National
        Local
        Area
    Editorials
        Local by newspaper staff
        Syndicated columns
        Letters to the editor
    Comics
    Society
    Advice columns
        For teenagers
        General
        Household hints
    Special features
        Crossword puzzle
        Horoscope
        Recipes
        Tips on decorating
    Human interest features
    Fillers

There may be several reshufflings of these topics before the speaker is satisfied that he has arrived at the most meaningful arrangement. The importance of this type of analysis cannot be overlooked. Each time that these topics are evaluated, some new ones may be added while others are dropped; each time, the speaker comes closer to a structural pattern in the form of an outline which will work for him and his prospective listeners.

An outline is a means to an end and not an end in itself. Too many novice speakers feel that once an outline is down on paper their work is finished. An outline for a speech serves much the same purpose that an armature does for a piece of sculpture. The twisted wire of the latter provides the general form for the finished product. The connective tissue of the clay and the details added by the sculptor's skill combine to form a work of art—the artist's medium of communication. The armature alone would have a completely different impact on a viewer.

Organization of an idea is facilitated by the speaker's attempts to construct and test a word diagram (outline) of his message. Such a plan makes it possible for the prospective talker to test relationships of major points, subordination of supporting materials, relationship of content to major intent, effectiveness of order, attention potential of introduction, continuity, and other considerations of less importance.

OUTLINING

There are many types of organizational patterns for a spoken message, all of which are variations of models that were developed by Greek philosophers as long as twenty-five hundred years ago. The authors of this text have found the following pattern well-adapted to the needs of most speakers:

    I. Introduction   (Functions as an attention-getting device.)
   II. Key idea   (States central idea of message.)
  III. Body   (Develops key idea in depth.)
  IV. Conclusion   (Reinforces key idea.)

This presentation of the over-all plan for a speech oversimplifies the concept of outlining and does not demonstrate the functional nature of the outline. As this chapter progresses, a working outline for a speech will be developed using the four-part plan introduced above.

The Introduction

The introduction to a speech exposes the general subject matter to the auditors. It also should be structured to capture the attention of the listeners and to focus that attention on the statement of the central or key idea. The attention of auditors is often lost in the first few minutes of a speech because the speaker shows little or no originality in content. The speaker who does not take full advantage of the potential of the introduction may not be able to regain the listeners' attention and direct it to the main part of his message. Prepare your audience for what is to come in a way that will heighten concentration and stimulate expectation.

There are many ways of beginning a speech. A speaker must decide at some point in his preparation, how he can best achieve the purpose of the introduction for his particular subject. An experienced speaker usually delays planning his introduction until he has formulated his key idea and developed the body and even the conclusion. With the major part of the task accomplished, he is in a better position to evaluate and develop an appropriate beginning for his message. Among the many types he may consider are the following:

1. **Illustration** Telling a story or an incident is a very effective way to begin a speech. Narration has great appeal if it is handled skillfully. The story must have a definite connection with the subject, however. If it does not, you are not providing an introduction to the topic; you are merely delaying the beginning of the speech.

The story must not only relate to the subject, but must also reflect the proper attitude toward it. It is disconcerting to listeners to have a very serious subject initiated with a humorous introduction, or vice versa. Following are two examples of introductions which have illustrations incorporated in them:

> A few years ago a Russian friend of mine went over to Paris and there visited Miliukoff, once one of the leaders of the Russian Duma during its brief and frustrated life. Miliukoff told him that he just had a visit from a Communist from Russia, a young man who had all his education from the Soviet State. This young man had asked him some questions.
>
> "Is it a fact, as I have been told," he asked, "that in the old Russia there were many political parties and they all disagreed?"
>
> "Yes," said Miliukoff, "there were many parties and they all disagreed."
> "And is it a fact," asked the young Communist, "that there were many newspapers and magazines that also had different theories about public affairs?"
>
> "Yes," said Miliukoff, "there were thousands of newspapers and periodicals, and most of them disagreed, too."
>
> "How odd!" exclaimed the young Communist, "when there is only one truth."
>
> That young Russian, it seems to me, gives us in a nutshell the best there is to say for the controlled press.—Raymond Gram Swing

> As I was driving my car down the highway the other day a woman in the car ahead suddenly turned left, and I narrowly averted an accident. She had endangered my life, and I said with contempt, "Oh, sure, a woman driver, a fool, a menace, what would you expect?" The old clichés—I automatically typed her, because it was easier, and it made me, a man, feel superior. It made no difference to my prejudiced mind that statistics show women cause far less traffic accidents, and that they drive on the average more cautiously and more safely than men. Facts prove the cliché fallacious.

Each time we think that way about a Negro, a Mexican, an Italian, an Irishman, a Jew, a Protestant, a Catholic, a capitalist, a laborer, a member of any group, we have helped to perpetuate the dangerous American myth that I wish to attack today.—Charles A. Endter

2. **Historical**   The speaker can make use of historical background material as a way of introducing his subject. Thus, he hopes not only to gain the attention of his listeners, but also provide them with a basis for understanding the subject as it is developed. In the following example, note how the speaker has accomplished this purpose.

Carved in the capstone above the door of the Hospital of Saint Michael at Rome are these words: "For the correction and instruction of profligate youth that they, who when idle were injurious, may, when taught, become useful to the state." This inscription, a landmark dividing two civilizations, was written when the world was just emerging from Medieval torture. Looking backward we see the Tombs of Inquisition losing themselves far into the shadows of barbarism. Forward, the inscription of Saint Michael pointed to the dawn of a fairer day in penal institutions. Written at the dawn of the eighteenth century, it has stood for some two hundred years as a prophetic vision of the time when a humane penal code should be established and wisely administered.—Benjamin L. Mather

3. **Striking Statement or Question**   One of the quickest and surest ways to capture the attention and interest of your auditors and to make them think is to begin your speech with a striking statement or question which will lead logically into a statement of your key idea. These two examples demonstrate this procedure for beginning a speech:

Home ownership on individual farms has been a great tradition in American history. Individual farm ownership was always recognized as the cornerstone of a free democratic society. Today the traditional national idea is being seriously challenged.

Less than half of our farm families own all the land they operate. Of the six million farm families in the United States, two million, eight hundred thousand, or 47 percent, are tenants, owning no land at all. Every ten years since 1880, when the first count of tenant farmers was made, the number of landless tenants has steadily increased.

The problem of tenancy is national in scope.—Henry A. Wallace

The first person to hear the human voice by telephone is still living. The first name to appear on the payroll of any organization giving telephone service is still on the payroll. A member of the first board of directors of the first telephone company still sits on the Board. It is still less than half of a century since the invention of the telephone, so that what I have to say must be considered only a part of the first chapter of the history of the telephone service.—Henry Bates Thayer

84   COMMUNICATION THEORY

4. **Quotation**   Another way of catching the fancy of the audience is to begin a speech with a quotation which has a definite relationship to the subject being discussed. Lines of poetry, quotations from the Bible or other works of literature, or statements by authorities are all suitable materials for introducing an idea to an audience. Here is a sample of an introduction which incorporates a quotation:

> The Navy used to have some lines of doggerel which began:
>
>> When in danger, when in doubt,
>> Run in circles, yell, and shout.
>
> That is about what we are doing in America today on the problem of crime. A thousand after-luncheon speakers, myself included, are trying to talk crime to death, and there is a great deal of yelling and shouting. We hold conferences and organize commissions and end by running in the same old circles. . . .—A. H. MacCormick

5. **Personal**   Sometimes the situation makes a personalized introduction almost a necessity. For example, the speaker who has been invited to speak at a large gathering such as a commencement exercise, having no direct contact with the listeners, takes this opportunity to express his thanks to all of them for their invitation. Or, if an honor is being bestowed by an organization represented by the auditors, the speaker may want to express appreciation publicly and he may do this effectively in his introduction. The following introduction is an example of this type:

> I was deeply moved when I was informed that the Directors of the Woodrow Wilson Foundation had decided to confer upon me the Foundation's medal and cite my efforts to bring about a lowering of international economic barriers as the reason for the award. I accept the honor with heartfelt gratitude. It evokes in me many memories of the long years during which the problem of improvement in the economic relations among the nations has been of absorbing interest to me.—Cordell Hull

The Key Idea

The key idea is a *one-sentence* statement of the central idea of a speech. It clearly and simply describes the limits of the topic and sometimes implies the purpose of the speech.

For example, a lawyer has been asked to talk to a service club about some practical aspect of the law. Recognizing that many men delay making a will and that such delinquency results in hardships for families in case of death, the lawyer-speaker settles on the following key idea:

STRUCTURING THE MESSAGE 85

Early preparation of a well-constructed will provides protection for your family.

Other lawyers might have chosen different aspects of the subject of "wills" resulting in key ideas such as these:

1. There really isn't any safe way to avoid probate of a will.
2. Under certain circumstances, it is wise to set up a trust fund for the protection of your family.
3. Prepare for making a will by listing all of your assets and by describing all of your responsibilities.
4. Have you ever thought of the consequences if you do not leave a will?

Each of these statements has met the requirements of a good key idea:

1. Each is a complete sentence.
2. Each one contains a single idea.
3. Each has been stated in a way which avoided awkward phrases or clauses such as "I am going to talk about . . . " "My key idea is . . . " "My thesis, today is . . . "

The use of a key idea is especially helpful to the beginning speaker. By stating his main idea early in the speech, directly after the introduction, he commits himself to a limited subject. All of the material selected for the speech may then be tested in light of the limits imposed by the key idea. Before making his final decision to include certain material, the speaker asks himself, "How does this relate to my key idea? Will it clarify my point of view? Will it advance the discussion of the central idea? Will it reflect my point of view? Will it reinforce in an interesting and vivid way?

The key idea also serves as a guide for listeners. Knowing the central idea of the speech will help them to focus attention on the important points and their relationships. The speaker literally leads the listener through the communication maze. (Key idea drill may be found on pages 236–237.)

The Body of the Speech

The main part (and largest part) of your speech explores in depth the prescribed and limited dimensions of the subject which has been suggested in the key idea. Because it will contain an analysis of the key statement, it will be made up of an appropriate number of self-limiting statements about the key idea. For example, the key idea, "Prepare for making a will by listing all of your assets and by describing all of your responsibilities," the speaker suggests two activities which are essential when the time comes that you approach a lawyer for help in formulating a will. The main points in the body of the speech then would be:

> Carefully explore and list all of your assets and long term liabilities in order to determine the nature of your projected estate.
>
> List all of your responsibilities as preparation for designating your heirs and their inheritances.

Now, if you made your working outline in the following manner, you have *listed* important ideas but you haven't suggested relationships between these points:

> Prepare for making a will by listing all of your assets and by describing all of your responsibilities.
>
> Carefully explore and list all of your potential assets and long term liabilities in order to determine the nature of your projected estate.
>
> List all of your responsibilities as preparation for designating your heirs and their inheritances.

A more meaningful arrangement would result from applying certain outlining principles:

>   I. Introduction: (unstructured at this point in preparation)
> II. Key idea: Prepare for making a will by listing all of your assets and by describing all of your responsibilities.
> III. Body:
>   A. Carefully explore and list all of your potential assets and long term liabilities in order to determine the nature of your projected estate.
>   B. List all of your responsibilities as preparation for designating your heirs and their inheritances.
> IV. Conclusion: (unstructured at this point in preparation)

With this arrangement, the plan of your message begins to take form. It should be apparent that the body of the speech, which will develop your key idea, represents approximately equivalent parts or divisions of the specific thought of the communicator.

In the example above, the body of the speech required only two main points; other subjects may require more in order to achieve the purpose of the speech. While there are no principles which limit the number of main points, it is wise for the speaker to choose a reasonable number that can be adequately explained in the amount of time at his disposal.

The major points in the body of the speech may take the form of explanations, arguments, defenses, challenges, and/or pleas. Taken together they provide the listeners with all of the material that they need in order to understand, believe, move toward action, or answer a cry for help.

Arrangement of Main Points Another problem facing the speaker is the arrangement of his main points within the body of the speech. In some speeches, the order of the subdivisions makes little difference. For example, in the partial outline below, it makes little difference whether the pulley is discussed first, or the wheel and axle, or the lever.

    I. Introduction: (unstructured at this point in preparation)
    II. Key idea: Simple machines are used frequently to reduce physical effort.
    III. Body:
        A. Use of pulley
        B. Use of wheel and axle
        C. Use of lever
    IV. Conclusion: (unstructured at this point in preparation)

In contrast, if the key idea were stated differently, "The basic physical principles upon which many of our modern machines are based can be traced back hundreds of years," would require a different type of arrangement. It would seem more meaningful to arrange the main points in a chronological order—according to time. In other words, it would be necessary to determine the approximate year or century that each (the pulley, the wheel and axle, and the lever) was invented. The main points would then be arranged chronologically.

Although there are no hard and fast rules regarding order within the body of the speech, you should be aware of some of the different possibilities and choose the one which will further your purpose most effectively.

1. *Chronological or Time Order* If the main points in the body of the speech are concerned with a sequence in time, the speaker makes use of chronological order. He begins at a certain point in time and progresses toward the present. Thus the episodes are presented as they occurred or as they should occur. The following outline exemplifies this type of arrangement:

    I. Introduction: (unstructured at this point in preparation)
    II. Key idea: John Smith has successfully combined political and academic careers.
    III. Body:
        A. Youth and education
        B. Early academic career
        C. Political activities

       D. Return to active academic career
    IV. Conclusion: (unstructured at this point in preparation)

2. *Place Order* A speaker, recently back from a visit to Rome, decides to describe Vatican City for his listeners. In place of discussing various features as they occur to him, he began by describing the first view of the whole complex as he drove up the avenue or as he stood in the huge square. He indicated the relationships of the various buildings and the impact that the total "City" has on the viewer. Next, he focused on each building, describing the exterior, moving into the first floor area, up the stairs to succeeding floors. His plan, then, was to begin at a point in space, move from outside to inside, from the bottom to the top or any other consistent pattern. The following sample illustration makes use of place order in the body of the speech on another topic:

      I. Introduction: (unstructured at this point in preparation)
     II. Key idea: A recent trip through Mt. Vernon revealed the wonders of this landmark.
    III. Body
         A. The grounds
            1. Size and shape
            2. Landscaping
            3. Approach to the building
         B. The exterior
            1. Architectural features
            2. Ornamentation
         C. The interior
            1. Architectural features
            2. Decoration
            3. Furnishings
    IV. Conclusion: (unstructured at this point in preparation)

3. *Logical Order* The subdivisions in the body of the speech may also be arranged in logical order. With this type of structure, there is a dependency relationship between the main points. That is, one part depends on the other for its position and together they form a logical relationship. In the next chapter we discuss the elements of logical order in more detail, but here we will only look at their position. The three main elements are *evidence, warrants,* and *claims,* and they usually follow in that order. Evidence refers to the facts and materials in the communication, claims are the conclusions that are drawn from these facts, and warrants are the assumptions that are made in order to draw the conclusions. Let us look at a sample of this kind of order:

     I. Introduction: (unstructured at this point in preparation)
    II. Key idea: Grades should be abolished.

III. Body:
   A. Grades, in college, motivate the students by creating anxieties.
   B. Anxiety is an undesirable element of a learning situation.
   C. Because they are motivated largely by anxiety, grades are a hindrance to learning and, therefore, should be abolished.

Here the fact that grades are anxiety-producing is the evidence and is presented first. The claim is that grades should be abolished. The warrant is the assumption that anxiety producers are fundamentally wrong in an educational setting and ought to be abolished. Students will find these three elements of logical order discussed in greater detail in the next chapter.

4. *Order Derived from Cognitive Imbalance* As we will discover in the fifth chapter, attitudes are changed by creating a state of attitudinal or cognitive imbalance in the listeners. This is done usually by demonstrating that two elements in the listeners' field of awareness are not consistent with one another. For example, if the communicator is perceived as an expert who can be trusted, the fact that he advocates a position different from the position of the audience will be incongruous with the way the audience would like to perceive him. The desired result should be attitude change, but certainly isn't always. In any event, the speaker's task is to demonstrate how incongruity can be resolved by attitude change and his speech sets out to do this. The following outline uses this type of order:

I. Introduction: (unstructured at this point).
II. Key idea: The Communist Chinese Government should be given diplomatic recognition by our country.
III. Body:
   A. In twelve years of study of the Far East, I have come to be highly familiar with Asian problems.
   B. My study has convinced me that the most effective manner of dealing with the Chinese would be within the framework of diplomatic recognition. (Imbalance)
   C. Therefore it is my hope that you will agree with me that this recognition will be extended.

As we will see in the next chapter, the listeners can restore the balance of their cognitive structure by disbelieving point A, so it becomes a fairly important part of the communication. Further details will be reserved for our discussion in the next chapter.

Developing the Body of the Speech

Completion of this much of the outline for a speech obviously cannot be achieved without knowledge of the subject. The source of the information which was required to develop the message this far may have come directly from the speaker's own knowledge and experience; however, it may have resulted from interviews with experts, discussions with people, letter writing, listening, or reading. At this point in preparation, some speakers are already expert in the subject and can proceed with further development of the main points within the body of the speech. Others, less competent in terms of the subject chosen, may have barely begun the job of researching the subject. Let us examine some of the resources available to the speaker who needs to explore his subject further.

1. *Talking with other people* is an appropriate source of information for certain types of subjects. This activity may take the formal structure of an interview or the informal approach of discussions or conversations with friends, colleagues, or families. In these give-and-take situations, much can be done to clarify the thinking of the speaker, to locate expert testimony, to discover the attitudes of people toward a particular situation, or to provide personal experiences all of which may help to clarify and amplify the point of view which the speaker has taken.

2. *Reading* is one of the richest sources of specific information. Any individual can find an abundance of material if he takes the trouble to locate it. We are surrounded by all types of resources including many newspapers and magazines in almost every home, textbooks which we use in our educational process, standard reference books, documents, pamphlets, periodicals, and books which are crammed into any library. The information is available if you try to find it *and* if you know how to go about finding it. Your library provides many services which should facilitate your location of specific sources.

    a. *The Card Catalog.* Every library catalogs its holdings and makes it available to potential users of the materials. The file of holdings, called the *card catalog,* contains a listing of every book available to the reader. If you know only the title of the book, you should be able to locate it.

    In the alphabetical file, you will find a card with the title; from this card you can determine the author and other bibliographical material you may desire. In addition, you can find the book's code number which is necessary if you wish to withdraw the book.

    Fortunately, every book is also listed by author and subject. If you are interested in finding material about the process and problems of probating a will, you might look under "law" or "wills" or "probate" and find books devoted to this subject. For example, you surely would find the fairly recent book, *How to Avoid Probate.* Or, if you wish to find material on the costumes traditionally worn in the Japanese Kabuki play, you would locate the file drawer containing the word "costume" and by thumbing through the cards you will eventually find a card labeled "costumes, Japanese." Or, you might look under "theater, Kabuki" and find a book which includes a section on costumes.

b. *Indexes* provide a very special service for the reader. In most libraries, a room or suite of rooms is set aside for periodicals, newspapers, professional journals, and the like. Usually, the current copies of all of these publications to which the library subscribes are kept in this section. In addition, the periodicals of the past years are stored in bound volumes which can be located through the serial catalog in this section.

There are numerous indexes which will help you to locate specific information. These indexes are issued regularly and list by subject all of the articles, features, and published speeches that have appeared in most of the periodicals. The following indexes may be of particular help:

READERS' GUIDE TO PERIODICAL LITERATURE
EDUCATION INDEX
ART INDEX
BOOK REVIEW DIGEST
BIOGRAPHY INDEX
INTERNATIONAL INDEX TO PERIODICALS
APPLIED SCIENCE AND TECHNOLOGY INDEX
PUBLISHERS' WEEKLY
NEW YORK TIMES INDEX

c. *Standard Reference Works.* Depending on your subject matter, you will often find pertinent material in the standard reference works in your library. In a communication that dealt with the consumption of alcohol in the United States, you might wish to look up the amount of business done by distilleries in the *Statistical Abstract of the United States.* There are hundreds of good standard references available in every library such as *Who's Who, World Almanac, Congressional Digest,* and *Dictionary of National Biography.* The student who cries "I can't find anything in the library pertinent to my topic" has usually not consulted the standard references. Indeed, if you are not familiar with the last three references on the above list, you probably could use a refresher tour through your library to see what they are and what they can do for you.

If you are preparing a speech using a topic with which you are not personally well-acquainted, you should read as much as possible about the topic. Even if you are fairly conversant with the subject, you will feel more expert if you do some additional study of the area.

In all of the reading you do, it is important that you are careful to extract the intent and purpose of the writer. Avoid quoting single sentences if you have not read the whole article or section. Otherwise, you may distort the meaning of the author.

Be sure, also, that you read all sources critically. Follow the developmental pattern of each author, as a basis for testing his conclusions. Simply because a writer has succeeded in appearing in print does not guarantee his reliability nor the validity of what he has written.

Every speaker should explore a variety of sources in an effort to expand his background. It is very likely that he will not share all of the materials he encounters in his research with his auditors, but the thoroughness of his preparation will be reflected in the assurance that comes with expertness.

The Conclusion

The last portion of a speech gives the speaker another opportunity to reinforce his idea. It provides one last chance to emphasize the purpose and to recreate his central idea. The conclusion may be structured in different ways to achieve its objective, and the speaker must give adequate consideration to the available forms in order that he selects the most appropriate type for his message.

1. **Summary** The most used, but not necessarily the best conclusion, is the summary. It is particularly useful in speeches where it is essential that information be relayed accurately. For example, in a military operation there is no room for error. A squad leader issues orders to the men under him and explains a complex tactic. With one minute left before the maneuver, it is unlikely that the sergeant will give a "pep" talk; instead, he will use that valuable time to go over the plan in brief.

In a summary, the speaker should not end his speech by saying "I have made the following three points. . . . " Rather, he should try to structure the conclusion in a way that will refocus the attention of his auditors. He will present essentially the same ideas which he has stressed in the body of the speech but will reword and restructure this part of his message so that it possesses a unity, polish, and impact of its own.

Here are two examples of conclusions whose function is to summarize:

> As you can see from the graph, the curves show the relation between steam generation at the load center and water generation at a distance, with coal prices within the range indicated. The transmission cost does not exceed 20 percent of the total cost of water power . . . nevertheless, water power, even when more costly than steam power, has a place where coal is costly and may be impossible to obtain. The great extension of hydro-electric stations in certain European countries can only be justified by their lack of coal supplies.—George Orrok

> I now propose that we establish by law an assurance against any such ill-balanced Court in the future. I propose that hereafter, when a Judge reaches the age of seventy, a new and younger Judge shall be added to the Court automatically. In this way, I propose to enforce a sound policy by law instead of leaving the composition of our federal courts, including the highest, to be determined by chance or the personal choice of individuals—

> I am favor of action through legislation:

> First, because I believe that it can be passed at this session of the Congress.
>
> Second, because it will provide a reinvigorated, liberal-minded judiciary necessary to furnish quicker and cheaper justice from bottom to top.
>
> Third, because it will provide a series of federal courts willing to enforce the Constitution as written and unwilling to assert legislative powers by writing into it their own political and economic policies.
>
> During the past half-century the balance of power between the three great branches of the federal government has been tipped out of balance by the courts in direct contradiction of the high purposes of the framers of the Constitution. It is my purpose to restore that balance. You who know me will accept my solemn assurance that in a world in which democracy is under attack I seek to make American democracy succeed. You and I will do our part.—Franklin D. Roosevelt

2. **Personal** In this type of conclusion, the speaker alludes to a personal experience, attitude, belief, or relationship which may give increased credibility or reinforcement to the central thought of his speech. For example, a Negro makes a plea for support of an open-housing bill in a speech to the League of Women Voters. In his introduction, he reconstructs the general conditions which a Negro faces when he attempts to find an adequate home for his family. In the body of the speech he develops reasons why this situation is undemocratic. Now, in planning his conclusion, he is faced with several alternatives. He could summarize his main points, stressing the logic of his arguments. He might make a plea for cooperation. Or, he might cite some examples or illustrations. Many of his friends have had problems in finding homes and he might generalize their plight.

However, our speaker has had some degrading experiences himself; doors have been slammed in his face; weak excuses have been made when the landlord finally discovered that he had been talking to a Negro over the phone. And so, the speaker finally decides to personalize his conclusion by exposing his own experiences. He recognizes that he will be giving "expert" testimony which should be more persuasive.

Personal conclusions may also be expressions of appreciation for the opportunity to explore a particular problem, rededication to a particular crusade or way of life, or tributes to other people who are promoting the concept explored by the speaker.

The following excerpt from one of Cordell Hull's speeches, illustrates the tone of a personal conclusion:

> Since this is an intimate occasion, permit me to end these brief remarks on a personal note. I have never faltered, and I never will falter, in my belief that enduring peace and the welfare of the nations are indissolubly connected with friendliness, fairness, equality, and the maxi-

mum practicable degree of freedom in international economic relations. I have never doubted the ability of statesmanship to create conditions in which relations of this type will become firmly established. I earnestly hope that no development will ever arise which will impel me to relinquish this belief. I shall continue to seek, as I have sought in the past, in whatever manner and in whatever measure time and circumstances may vouchsafe me, to translate these profound convictions into the realities of public service.—Cordell Hull

3. **Illustrative** The speaker may find it effective to close with a story, poem, or incident which illustrates the idea of his speech. The following examples demonstrate the use of an incident and a quotation as parts of illustrative conclusions:

Many of you, I am sure, have seen as I have, the inside of a slum tenement. You will know what it means for the father of a slum family to try to bring up his children with the manners and morals of a civilized society. You know the slums, realize the hopeless plight of a mother trying perhaps to nurse a sick child in a room without light, without air, without running water, and without adequate heat. There is no need to elaborate that picture. Perhaps Jacob Riis—the pioneer in the housing movement in this country—summed it up best when he said a generation ago:

> "The most pitiful victim in city life is not the slum child who dies, but the slum child who lives. Every time a child dies the nation loses a prospective citizen, but in every slum child the nation has a probable consumptive and a possible criminal. You cannot let people live like pigs and expect them to be good citizens . . ."— Jacob Riis

More than twenty-four centuries ago a thousand Spartans, hard pressed by tens of thousands of Persians at the pass of Thermophylae, knelt and took the old Spartan pledge of consecration: "I pledge that I will never desert my comrade in the ranks. I pledge that I will fight until death for my fatherland. I pledge that I will transmit the freedom and democracy of my Greece unmarred and even greater than it was transmitted to me." America is hard pressed today. There are problems on every hand. Her defenders must take as the Spartans of old, their pledge of faith: "I pledge that I will continue to serve my fellowman. I pledge that I will do everything in my power to solve the problems of my nation to the best interests of all her people. I pledge that I will transmit the freedom and democracy of my America unmarred and even greater than it was transmitted to me."—Gladys Pennington

4. **Stimulative** If the speaker wishes to stimulate or arouse strong feelings for his subject, he may further accomplish this purpose in the conclusion of his speech. He may make one last appeal for the auditors' consideration. Here is an example:

Republicans and fellow Americans! This is your call. Stop the retreat. In the chaos of doubt, confusion, and fear, yours is the task to command. Stop the retreat, and turning the eyes of your fellow Americans to the sunlight of freedom, lead the attack to retake, recapture, and reman the citadels of liberty. Thus can America be preserved. Thus can the peace, plenty, and security be re-established and expanded. Thus can the opportunity, the inheritance, and the spiritual future of your children be guaranteed. And thus you will win the gratitude of posterity and the blessing of Almighty God.—Herbert Hoover

Before you decide on the type of conclusion you will use in a particular speech, carefully go over all the material which you are including in the body of the speech. Repeat the key idea to yourself. Then recall the various types of endings you might use, and select the one which can do the best job of leaving the idea of the speech with your auditors. Be sure to do a thorough job of preparing this part of your speech because this is going to be the last impression that you leave with your listeners. It must be effective if you hope for a positive effect. (A suitable drill will be found on pages 240-242.)

STEPS IN PREPARING A FORMAL COMMUNICATION— A SPEECH

The preceding discussion has been concerned with the elements of structuring a message. In this section, a review of the whole process may be helpful. However, because we are concerned not only with the *theory* of structuring communication, but also the *activity* of the individual *preparing* a message, the process will be outlined in a slightly different and more functionally-oriented order.

1. The first challenge the prospective speaker faces is the selection of a *suitable topic*.
2. Next, the speaker must filter out a more *specific subject* which is narrow enough to be thoroughly explored in the time allotted to him.
3. The speaker then prepares his *basic outline*—the framework.
4. The *key idea* must be developed in a way that will describe the central idea and imply the purpose.
5. The material for the body of the communication must be acquired and structured and ordered.
6. A suitable conclusion should be devised.
7. Finally, the speaker should prepare an attention-getting introduction.

It should be noted that the introduction is the last concern of the speaker. You should not conclude that you leave this preparation until last because of its unimportance; rather, you delay devising the introduction *because* of its value. If you don't get the attention of your listeners during the first two or three minutes of your presentation, you may not be able to achieve it at all. So it is essential that the opening remarks be as strong if not stronger than other portions of your message.

By waiting until your preparation is nearly complete and all of your information is "in," you will have the best chance of developing an introduction that functions well. You will be in a better position to choose the type and content of this part of the speech if you know precisely how you plan to present the rest of the message; hence, the recommendation that you plan your introduction last.

EXPANDING THE OUTLINE

Up to this point in the discussion, the outlines have been relatively simple. For the most part, they have consisted of four main parts with a few major divisions in the body. Now it seems appropriate to explore outlining in greater detail.

It has been pointed out that an outline is a basic form on which you build a message. To be of the greatest help, it should follow certain principles which are well established and logical.

Outlining is a way of sorting materials into like groups. It is similar to a classification system. An office file is based on the same type of system. First, dividers are placed in the file; each divider is labeled according to a predetermined system. If the file contains correspondence, each divider will carry a letter of the alphabet and clerks will be expected to put correspondence from particular clients in the appropriate slot. However, because there probably will be many clients whose names begin with "A," folders will be labeled with the last names of the correspondents and will provide a particular storage place for letters from each person whose name begins with "A," "B," "C," and so on.

Obviously, this is not the only classification system that could be used for office files. The office manager chooses the one which is best suited to the needs of the particular organization.

The speech outline, then, is a classification system that will be useful to the person who is developing an oral message. It is based on certain organizational principles which have been explored and is structured on the basis of certain principles which have been established by experts in the field.

It has been pointed out that an outline shows relationships between the parts of a message. A system of notations has been developed which enables you to see these relationships. The basic outline which has been suggested to you consists of the introduction, the key idea, the body, and the conclusion. These are the main parts of the speech and are labeled with Roman numerals:

> I. Introduction:
> II. Key idea:
> III. Body:
> IV. Conclusion:

The notation system uses Roman numerals because of their size, implied dominance, importance, and "prestige" to label the largest segments in the outline. If a main part is subdividable, the outline should suggest that the subdivisions are only parts of the whole and this is accomplished by indenting. It is also helpful to have a label. This end could be accomplished in different ways. For example:

> I. Introduction:
>   Part 1:
>   Part 2:
>   Part 3:

This approach seems awkward and ungainly. So, we make use of capital letters for labeling these main subdivisions:

> I. Introduction:
>   A.
>   B.
>   C.

Let's apply this principle to an actual outline. Each time that an entry in the outline is divided, the subordinate parts are indented and labeled. The labels change with each step in subordination, alternating numerals and letters:

> III. Body:
>   A. (First main subdivision)
>   1. (First support for first main subdivision)
>   2. (Second support for first main subdivision)
>   a. (First support of 2)
>   b. (Second support of 2)
>   (1) (First support of b)
>   (2) (Second support of b)

B. (Second main subdivision)
   1. (First support of second subdivision)
   2. (Second support of second subdivision)
   3. (Third support of second subdivision)
C. (Third main subdivision)
   1. (First support of third subdivision)
   2. (Second support of third subdivision)
      a. (First support of C, 2)
      b. (Second support of C, 2)

You can avoid some of the common errors in outlining if you will try to remember these rules:

1. Never divide any point if you do not have at least two parts (supports) as a result of the division. For example, the following form is incorrect:

III. Body:
   A. ....
      1. ....
   B. ....

2. Alternate different forms of numbers and letters for labeling succeeding parts of your outline.

3. Be sure that the main points in the body of your speech represent approximately equivalent parts of the idea suggested in the key idea. This rule applies to any of the subdivisions in all four parts of your speech.

An outline may be made up largely of words or phrases or sentences. Study the differences in the two samples which follow:

Sample of a Sentence Outline

I. Introduction:
   A. About 1450 A.D., a new industry was founded.
   B. Johannes Gutenberg, with his movable type, laid the foundation for modern printing.
   C. A new process with old beginnings is encroaching on "type's" dominance.
II. Key idea: Lithography is coming into its own.
III. Body:
   A. Lithography or "offset" is not so new as some believe.
      1. Its name comes from the Greek words *lithos* and *graphein*, meaning "stone writing."
      2. Grease and water were used on stone to transfer drawings to paper.
   B. Modern offset uses zinc plates and photographic images.
      1. Plates are first treated.
      2. The developing is similar to stone-based lithography.

3. Offset press uses ink and water, with the images being transferred to paper via a rubber-covered cylinder.
IV. Conclusion:
A. Lithography is cheaper.
B. It is faster.
C. It is more accurate; a camera is better than an engraver.

Sample of a Topic Outline

I. Introduction:
A. Steel—an important and vital material
B. United States—a great steel producer
II. Key Idea: There are three important methods of producing steel.[1]
III. Body:
A. Blast furnace method
1. Description of furnace
2. The high line
3. Tapping
a. Hot metal
b. Slag
B. Bessemer process
1. Description of Bessemer
2. The process
a. Blowing
b. Time required
3. Tapping
C. Open hearth
1. Description of open hearth
a. Structure
b. Capacity
2. Charging
3. Tapping
a. Time
b. Method
c. Filling of molds
IV. Conclusion:
A. Advantages of each method
B. Comparative cost of each process

APPLICATION OF OUTLINING PRINCIPLES TO A SPECIFIC COMMUNICATION TASK

Let us assume that one of the authors has been asked to plan a year's program for a study group to which he belongs. The members of the organization have long been concerned with problems which face

---

[1] A key idea in a speech must express a complete thought. It should be stated as a sentence; hence the apparent inconsistency in the topic outline.

society, and throughout a long existence they have focused their attention each year on a particular area of concern. During the current year they are exploring the problem of conservation. The chairman of the year-long program was asked to divide the subject into meaningful units which were appropriate to the three-hour meetings and was further instructed to prepare one of these programs.

Conservation was a new subject to the chairman. Before he could begin to plan the year-long program it was necessary for him to explore the full and expanded meaning of the word in the United States. He discovered that the word "conservation" was related to the protection of our supply of water, soil, wildlife, plantlife, forests, and other natural resources. He decided that the series of presentations should logically begin with a discussion of the meaning and implications of the term "conservation." The first speaker would not only define the term but explain the need for an organized program of new laws, of citizen awareness, and of individual responsibilities. The first presentation, like all others, would be followed by a question period and general discussion by all members of the group.

It was decided, then, that each succeeding meeting would deal with one of the major divisions of the entire area of conservation, with the chairman assigned the responsibility of discussing the area of water conservation.

Let us follow the chairman through the outlining of his speech. Prior to the actual work on the speech, he went to the library and began an extensive program of reading. As he progressed with his part of the study, he felt a real need for contact with experts. A call to the local U.S. Department of Agricultural Soil Conservation resulted in a loan of carefully selected government bulletins and pamphlets, and books on the subject of conservation, and a promise of further help if it were necessary. A second call to another government agency resulted in a discussion with a wildlife expert. A further contact with a professor of chemical engineering on the university faculty produced other written materials of help to the speaker.

At this point, in all honesty, the speaker was somewhat confused. He had an abundance of material and no organizational plan for his presentation. He had far too much material to present and recognized that he had to become *selective* according to a *predetermined plan.*

Recognizing the help that a statement of his central purpose could provide, he attempted to write a crystal clear sentence that would both define and limit his subject. This effort resulted in the following key idea:

> Although water is indestructible and exists in sufficient quantity in the United States, we face a serious problem of pollution which may make our supply of safe water inadequate for our future needs.

This statement became a kind of testing device for all material he considered. If the material helped to develop this central idea, he put it aside for inclusion. However, if the material did not appear to advance the key idea, it was discarded.

The next step in his preparation was a tentative, stripped down, basic outline of the body of the speech.

I. Introduction: (unstructured at this point)
II. Key idea: Although water is indestructible and exists in sufficient quantity in the United States, we face a serious problem of pollution which may make our supply of safe water inadequate for our future needs.
III. Body:
   A. Water is indestructible and there appears to be an adequate supply on earth.
   B. Water usage has increased dramatically in the past 100 years.
   C. Conservationists are warning us that the supply of *safe* water, already inadequate in some areas, may not remain adequate for future use of all people in all parts of the United States.
   D. One of the most critical problems challenging our supply of safe water is pollution, caused by a variety of agents.
   E. Ground water presents special pollution problems.
IV. Conclusion: (unstructured at this point in preparation)

The key idea and these main points really tell the story of the problem of water pollution and its implications. However, there is insufficient detail, explanation, proof, and so on, for it to be really meaningful. In other words, the speaker's point that "Water usage has increased dramatically in the past 100 years," is not sufficiently clear for the average person. What is meant by "increased dramatically?" The listener's estimate may be quite different from that of the speaker.

So, in structuring the outline, the speaker begins to put in supports in the form of explanations, analogies and comparisons, illustrations, statistics, testimony, and specific instances. Let us briefly examine these types of supports.

1. *Explanation* is a clear and concise exposition of terms, ideas, issues, choices, and so forth. While explanation is the essence of speech which relays, it also is critical to the development of any idea regardless of its purpose.
2. *Analogy or comparison* is a form of support in which the speaker relies on the known or familiar as an aid in understanding the unknown or obscure. He may compare two like things, such as two houses, two poems, or two forms of music, or he may show similarities between two unlike things. In this text an analogy was used showing the similarity of function between blueprints for a building and the outline for a speech.

3. An *illustration* is a clear and vivid story which reinforces explanations or arguments. It is usually told in narrative form and may be factual or hypothetical.
4. *Statistics* may be used as proof. They are especially helpful in proving that a particular situation exists to the extent that you have indicated.
5. *Testimony* takes the form of direct quotations or paraphrases which may further amplify and/or substantiate the speaker's point of view.
6. *Specific instance.* A speaker may feel the need to reinforce a point by relating several examples. The variety provided by a series of illustrations offers unusually strong support for an idea. In order to relate many examples, however, it becomes necessary for him to merely sketch them, eliminating many details. This form of support is called "specific instance." The following example of this type of support illustrates the point that most people are called upon to discuss both concrete and abstract subjects:

The teacher deals with simple explanations of how to perform a certain assignment or experiment; but she also must discuss more abstract materials in connection with subject matter of the course. The lawyer must explain the intent of a law in simple, concrete terms to a client; but he may have to deal with highly abstract topics such as "truth," "judgment," "motivations," and so on, as he attempts to analyze his client's case for a jury. This he must also accomplish in a way which gets through to those who are listening. The football coach outlines new plays and defensive strategies for his squad in order to provide every player with necessary information; here he deals with concrete material on how the group may operate as a team to execute plays. At times the coach may be called upon to explain his philosophy of sportsmanship, a less concrete topic.

The speaker preparing the talk on "Conservation" now begins to arrange his material in the form of *supports* in a more detailed outline. A thorough analysis of his complete outline (which appears on pages 105 to 112) would require far too much space here. But let's look at the manner in which he has supported and developed a portion of the body of his speech.

II. Key idea: Although water is undestructible and exists in sufficient quantity in the United States, we face a serious problem of pollution which may make our supply of safe water inadequate for our future needs.

III. Body:
   A. Water is indestructible and there appears to be an adequate supply on earth.
      1. There is a natural pumping system which reuses the enormous reservoirs of the sea. *(Analogy)*
         a. Sun boils off billions of tons of water every day.
         b. Cool air condenses water into clouds of ice crystals. *(Explanation)*
         c. Gravity draws crystals to earth in form of rain, snow, hail, or sleet.
      2. Ultimately, then, the water in some form returns to replenish the oceans. *(Explanation)*
         a. Snow that falls ultimately returns to the sea though it may remain in the mountains for years before melting.
         b. Rain which seeps into the ground may be trapped for thousands of years in underground rock basins but eventually it finds its way back to the sea.
   B. Water usage has increased dramatically in the past 100 years.
      1. Adults require only three quarts of water per day for normal physiological functioning. *(Statistic)*
      2. However, the amount of water used is much greater than this known need. *(Comparison)*
         a. From 1900 to 1950, the amount of water used for other than power increased fourfold even though the population only doubled. *(Statistic)*
            (1) In 1900, 600 gallons of water were used per capita each day.
            (2) In 1950, this usage spiraled to 1100 gallons. *(Statistics)*
         b. By 1960, the per capita water usage was up to 1500 gallons per day. *(Statistic)*
      3. Why has this tremendous increase in water usage occurred?
         a. There has been a substantial increase in water used for industry and irrigation. *(Explanation)*
            (1) Water is the number one raw material of industry and its use has increased significantly with the phenomenal growth of industry. *(Explanation)*
               (a) In 1950, industry used an average of 77 billion gallons of water each day. *(Statistic)*
               (b) In 1955, water usage had jumped to 110 billion gallons per day. *(Statistic)*
               (c) 140 billion gallons were used each day in 1960. *(Statistic)*

(2) Irrigation, which permitted farmers to make use of land that lay idle because of inadequate moisture, has also accounted for part of the huge increase in water usage. *(Explanation)*
   (a) Irrigation requires 4 times as much water as cities and towns and 60% as much as industries. *(Statistic)*
   (b) About 60% of irrigation water is evaporated or transpired by crops. *(Statistic)*
   (c) About 70% of the water used for irrigation comes from surface sources; about 30% from ground water. *(Statistic)*
   (d) Seasonal need for irrigation water often puts strain on local water supplies. *(Explanation)*

b. Usage in cities and towns has increased from 95 gallons per day per capita in 1900 to 151 gallons in 1960, largely because of changes in standards of living, increasing use of labor-saving devices, and so on. *(Statistic)*
  (1) Ordinary and necessary family uses of water have sharply increased the amount of water used in the home. *(Explanation)*
    (a) A shower requires from 30 to 60 gallons of water and with daily bathing, the typical pattern in the United States, the volume of water used for personal cleanliness has jumped astronomically. *(Statistic)*
    (b) Five to seven gallons of water are necessary to flush a toilet. *(Statistic)*
    (c) An automatic washing machine uses 17 gallons for each cycle. *(Statistic)*
  (2) Other luxuries which consume millions of gallons of water include home and industrial air conditioning, lawn watering, automatic dishwashers, car washing, street washing, swimming pools, and an almost endless list of water uses. *(Explanation)*

c. Water usage for rural homes and livestock is estimated to be 2 billion gallons a day with the bulk of the supply coming from wells and springs. *(Statistic)*
  (1) There is a significant difference in

STRUCTURING THE MESSAGE 105

        the amount of water used in rural homes. *(Explanation)*
        (a) In homes with running water (and three-quarters of the farms are so equipped), the estimated use is 50 gallons per day per person. *(Statistic)*
        (b) In homes without running water, only 10 gallons per person are used. *(Statistic)*
    (2) Livestock needs account for a substantial percentage of water usage. *(Explanation)*
        (a) Milk cows require 20 gallons per day per animal. *(Statistic)*
        (b) Horses and other cattle require 10 gallons per day. *(Statistic)*
        (c) Sheep and goats need only 2 gallons. *(Statistic)*
        (d) Poultry require .04 to .06 of a gallon per day. *(Statistic)*

After completing the outline for the body of the speech, the conclusion and then the introduction must be structured and outlined. The entire outline for the speech on the threat and problems of water pollution is thus complete and is presented here for your study:

TITLE OF SPEECH: "How much of a threat is water pollution?"
PURPOSE: To relay
TYPE OF INTRODUCTION: Historical and Personal
TYPE OF ORDER IN THE BODY OF THE SPEECH: Logical
TYPE OF CONCLUSION: Summary
SOURCES OF MATERIAL USED IN THIS SPEECH:
    PERIODICALS:
        1. "The Crisis in Water: Its Sources, Pollution and Depletion," *Saturday Review*, October 23, 1965. (Entire issue devoted to this topic.)
        2. "Progress Report: 10 Years of Federal Pollution Control Aid," *Engineering News-Record*, September 22, 1966, pp. 24–27.
        3. Revelle, Roger, "Water," *Scientific American*, Vol. 209, (September 1963), pp. 92–108.
    PAMPHLETS:
        1. "Conquest of the Land through 7,000 Years," Agriculture Information Bulletin, No. 99, U.S. Department of Agriculture, Soil Conservation Service.
        2. "Fish Kills by Pollution, 1966," 7th Annual Report, Federal Water Pollution Control Administration, CWA-y, 1967. U.S. Government Printing Office.
        3. "Know Your Watersheds," U.S. Department of Agriculture, Forest Service, Leaflet No. 282, U.S. Government Printing Office, February 1948; revised September 1957; approved for reprinting April 1963.

4. "Sediment is Your Problem" Soil Conservation Service, United States Department of Agriculture, AIB 174, U.S. Government Printing Office, March 1958.
5. "Soil and Water Conservation: the Work of the U.S. Soil Conservation Service in Ohio," U.S. Department of Agriculture, Soil Conservation Service, Columbus, Ohio, July 1961.
6. "Water is a Matter of Survival and Pollution a Matter of Health," National Water Institute, New York City.
7. "Water Facts," U.S. Department of Agriculture, Soil Conservation Service, PA-337, U.S. Government Printing Office: 1964-OF–724–213.
8. "Water Pollution Control Program," U.S. Department of Health, Education, and Welfare, Federal Water Pollution Control Administration, Washington.
9. "Water Resources Activities in the United States—Pollution Abatement." Printed for the use of the Select Committee on National Water Resources, Committee Print No. 9, Pursuant to S. Res. 48, Eighty-Sixth Congress, U.S. Government Printing Office, Washington: 1960.

I. Introduction:
   A. Few of us have ever been truly thirsty.
      1. Those who have suffered that extreme of water deprivation report that there is no torture like the all-consuming desire for water, as the tongue swells and blackens, the body dehydrates, and the mind soon wanders.
      2. Death comes in a few days from thirst, but we can live for weeks without food.
   B. The old saying "You never miss the water till the well runs dry" certainly applies to all of us.
      1. For years now, the well has run better and better, thanks to our increased technology and sophisticated city water systems. Yet this was not always the case.
      2. The pioneers and settlers in Daniel Boone's day had to be careful to settle by a stream or spring to insure a safe, clean supply of water.
      3. Bitter battles have been fought for the possession of some muddy water hole or tiny stream which represented life and death to a community.
      4. Even today we find states like Arizona and California engaged in bitter legislative warfare over the possession of the output of one of our major western rivers.
   C. Water is the most important single ingredient in our life system.
      1. We are literally made of water, our bodies containing more of this substance than any other chemical.
      2. There is no element more important to agriculture or the raising of food animals.
      3. Nor is there any more important element in the manufacturing of most of our goods and services.
II. Key idea: Although water is indestructible and exists in sufficient quantity in the United States, we face a serious problem of pollution which may make our supply of safe water inadequate for our future needs.

III. Body:
  A. Water is indestructible and there appears to be an adequate supply on earth.
    1. There is a natural pumping system which reuses the enormous reservoirs of the sea.
       a. Sun boils off billions of tons of water every day.
       b. Cool air condenses water into clouds of ice crystals.
       c. Gravity draws crystals to earth in form of rain, snow, hail, or sleet.
    2. Ultimately, then, the water in some form returns to replenish the oceans.
       a. Snow that falls ultimately returns to the sea though it may remain in the mountains for years before melting.
       b. Rain which seeps into the ground may be trapped for thousands of years in underground rock basins but eventually it finds its way back to the sea.
    3. Pumping system produces an average of 30 inches of precipitation a year in the United States.
       a. This means that 4500 billions of gallons are available each day.
       b. Total stream flow derived from surface run off and ground water amounts to 8.5 inches a year and about 1200 billion gallons a day.
       c. Potential sustained supply for direct human use is four times the daily requirements at the present time.
  B. Water usage has increased dramatically in the past 100 years.
    1. Adults require only three quarts of water per day for normal physiological functioning.
    2. However, the amount of water used is much greater than this known need.
       a. From 1900 to 1950, the amount of water used for other than power increased fourfold even though the population only doubled.
          (1) In 1900, 600 gallons of water were used per capita each day.
          (2) In 1950, this usage spiraled to 1100 gallons.
       b. By 1960, the per capita water usage was up to 1500 gallons per day.
       c. Water needs are expected to more than double by 1980 while population will increase by only 45%.
       d. By 1980, then, the water supply will be equal to only two times the projected daily requirements.
    3. Why has this tremendous increase in water usage occurred?
       a. There has been a substantial increase in water used for industry and irrigation.
          (1) Water is the number one raw material of industry and its use has increased significantly with the phenomenal growth of industry.
             (a) In 1950, industry used an average of 77 billion gallons of water each day.
             (b) In 1955, water usage had jumped to 110 billion gallons per day.
             (c) 140 billion gallons were used each day in 1960.

(2) Irrigation, which permitted farmers to make use of land that lay idle because of inadequate moisture, has also accounted for part of the huge increase in water usage.
    (a) Irrigation requires 4 times as much water as cities and towns and 60% as much as industry.
    (b) Also 60% of irrigation water is evaporated or transpired by crops.
    (c) About 70% of the water used for irrigation comes from surface sources; about 30% from ground water.
    (d) Seasonal need for irrigation water often puts strain on local water supplies.

b. Usage in cities and towns has increased from 95 gallons per day per capita in 1900 to 151 gallons in 1960, largely because of changes in standards of living, increasing use of labor saving devices, and so on.
  (1) Ordinary and necessary family uses of water have sharply increased the amount of water used in the home.
    (a) A shower requires from 30 to 60 gallons of water and with daily bathing, the typical pattern in the United States, the volume of water used for personal cleanliness has jumped astronomically.
    (b) Five to seven gallons of water are necessary to flush a toilet.
    (c) An automatic washing machine uses 17 gallons for each cycle.
  (2) Other luxuries which consume millions of gallons of water include home and industrial air conditioning, lawn watering, automatic dishwashers, car washing, street washing, swimming pools, and an almost endless list of other water uses.

c. Water usage for rural homes and livestock is estimated to be 2 billion gallons a day with the bulk of the supply coming from wells and springs.
  (1) There is a significant difference in the amount of water used in rural homes.
    (a) In homes with running water (and three-quarters of the farms are so equipped), the estimate used is 50 gallons per day per person.
    (b) In homes without running water, only 10 gallons per person are used.
  (2) Livestock needs account for a substantial percentage of water usage.
    (a) Milk cows require 20 gallons per day per animal.
    (b) Horses and other cattle require 10 gallons per day.
    (c) Hogs need 3 gallons a day.
    (d) Sheep and goats need only 2 gallons a day.
    (e) Poultry require .04 to .06 of a gallon each day.

C. Conservationists are warning us that the supply of safe water, already inadequate in some areas, may not remain adequate for future use of all people in all parts of the United States.
  1. One-half of the 125 million people who use public water supplies can't be sure of sufficient water to put out a fire on a hot summer day.

2. Water was rationed in well over 1000 communities in a recent year.
3. In towns of 25,000 population and over, alarming deficiencies are being noted.
    a. One of 5 water utilities is deficient in supply.
    b. Two out of 5 are deficient in transmission.
    c. One out of 3 is deficient in pumping capacity.
    d. Two out of 5 are deficient in treatment capacity.
    e. Ground and elevation storage show deficiencies of 29% and 43%, respectively.
    f. Distribution improvements are required in 57% of our water systems.
D. One of the most critical problems challenging our supply of safe water is pollution, caused by a variety of agents.
    1. Sewage and other oxygen demanding wastes coming mostly from domestic sewage and from such industries as food processing plants account for a substantial amount of water pollution.
    2. Infectious agents are carried into streams, lakes, and ground water sources by wastes from municipalities, sanatoria, and industries such as tanning and slaughtering plants which discharge materials containing human and animal wastes.
        a. These disease-causing organisms may cause typhoid fever, a variety of viral infections and intestinal disorders if the water is ingested.
        b. They also may cause the same diseases if an individual comes in contact with the water in a recreational area such as a swimming pool or lake.
    3. There has been increased use of fertilizers containing such nutrients as nitrogen and phosphorous which have found their way into water sources.
        a. These elements occur in streams under natural conditions but are introduced in larger quantities by discharges of municipal sewage, industrial wastes, and chemical fertilizers.
        b. These elements in excess are particularly serious because they are not removed by ordinary sewage treatment processes.
    4. Organic chemical exotics such as detergents, new insecticides, pesticides, and weed killers are adding another dimension to the problems of pollution.
    5. Other mineral and chemical substances such as salt, metals, metal compounds, acids, and manufactured chemicals are further complicating the pollution problem.
        a. Natural deposits of salt drain into river basins, and brine is discharged as a by-product when oil is pumped out of the ground.
        b. Industrial wastes and drainage from coal mines are the primary source of acid in our water.
        c. Industrial wastes also contain other mineral and chemical substances.
    6. Radio-active substances are creating unusual problems when these materials find their way into our water supplies.
        a. Conventional water treatment plants in use today are not

designed to provide protection against small concentrations of such hazardous materials.
- b. Because of difficulty of processing and expense involved, treatment plants probably will not be designed in the near future to meet this problem.
7. If water is heated and returned to the rivers and lakes, a different type of pollution problem develops.
   - a. Water used in cooling in steel mills and petroleum refineries returns to streams, rivers, or other storage areas at a higher temperature and thus transfer heat to these bodies of water.
   - b. Amount of oxygen held in solution diminishes as temperature increases with the net effect of additional pollution.
8. Sedimentation, another source of water contamination, results from soils and mineral particles being washed from the land by storms and flood waters into streams, irrigation ditches, reservoirs, and other water storage facilities.
   - a. Sedimentation is harmful to living organisms.
     - (1) Silt harms fish, destroying spawning grounds and eggs of game fish.
     - (2) Muddy waters shade light, interfering with growth of microscopic plants which provide food for insects and fish.
     - (3) Deep pools which provided refuge for fish during a dry season fill with sand and silt causing the death of many game fish.
     - (4) Silt clogs drainage systems.
   - b. Of greater significance, perhaps, is the effect sedimentation has on the storage potential for water.
     - (1) More than 3200 water supply reservoirs are losing water storage capacity each year due to sediment.
     - (2) Additional filtering and settling of sediment is required raising the cost of water to the consumer.
     - (3) One-third of electric power which is generated in the United States comes from hydro-electric plants and when reservoirs serving these plants become silted, they produce less electricity.
     - (4) Flood control reservoirs are also victims of sedimentation.
     - (5) Natural storage areas such as streams, lakes, rivers, and so on are silting thereby reducing capacity.
       - (a) The rate of erosion before conservation treatments had been applied, amounted to about 78 million tons of sediment each year.
       - (b) In 1963, the average loss to the nation's reservoirs was estimated at 850,000 acre-feet annually.
         - (1) Reservoirs lose most of their value when they are 50 to 60 percent silted.
         - (2) Their useful life, therefore, may be as little as 15 or 20 years where sedimentation rates are highest and storage capacity is small, as with farm ponds.
         - (3) The bed of the Rio Grande River is rising 1 foot every 12 years.

E. Ground water presents special pollution problems.
  1. We don't have enough knowledge of the problems of ground water pollution to deal with it effectively.
  2. There seem to be, however, extensive effects of ground water pollution.
     a. Underground waters are out of reach and move only a few feet a day, and may require years before pollution is detected in these places.
     b. May require years for recovery from pollution and the affected water may never regain its original quality.
  3. This type of pollution may lead to numerous public health problems.
  4. With anticipated growth in population, the demand for ground water should double by 1980.
     a. We must insure that this source produces safe water.
     b. We must protect this source from further contaminations.

IV. Conclusion:
  A. Basically the water pollution crisis is caused by three things.
    1. More people and more industries are dumping more and more complex wastes into our waterways.
    2. We have continued our earlier bad habits of dumping wastes into rivers and streams without thought or care.
       a. We need to spend more money to treat these wastes.
       b. Government agencies at various levels need more clearly defined enforcement powers to protect our water.
    3. Lack of scientific knowledge has delayed improvements in sewage treatment processes.
  B. A move in the right direction was the Federal Quality Act of 1965 which the Federal Water Pollution Control Administration established in 1965.
    1. The administration will operate laboratories and research projects throughout the country.
    2. Act provides for the establishment of Federal standards of water quality which will be set up in consultation with state and local agencies.
    3. Eighty million dollars has been provided to develop ways of correcting pollutional effects of combined storm and sanitary sewers.
  C. In a guest editorial in the October 23 (1965) issue of the *Saturday Review*, the Secretary of the Interior, Stewart L. Udall, says, "water is the conservation scandal of our generation," and suggests certain principles to eradicate our problems.
    1. We must learn to respect water and treat it as a resource to be sought, recovered, processed, utilized, reclaimed, and reutilized at the expense of the consuming public.
    2. We must learn how, and then act, to clean up our rivers, to combat pollution at its source, to reuse and manage our water on the philosophical premise that it is a resource to be used for the common benefit.
    3. We must accelerate research and develop activities that will enable us to augment existing supplies, particularly in arid areas.
    4. Our public planning must achieve new heights if the protec-

tion of our watershed and watercourses becomes an essential element of public policy.

Admittedly, this is a long and detailed outline for a rather lengthy speech. However, a good outline for a shorter speech will be just as detailed even though it is not as lengthy. Too often the beginning speaker is tempted to devise his outline just before he presents his speech; as a result, not only is it sketchy, but more critical, its function has been completely misunderstood.

Remember, the purpose of an outline is to assist the speaker in his effort to prepare a message which is orderly, logical, clear, and comprehensive in light of the time allotted to him for delivering the speech. The importance of good organization cannot be overemphasized. In at least one research project, it was found that "disorder can affect comprehension adversely and that the amount of loss of clarity becomes greater as the degree of disorganization occurs."[2] Remember, also, that the outline is a means to an end and not an end in itself. Once structured, you must focus on the problems associated with transmitting the complete message to your listeners. The real test is whether you can relay the information suggested in your outline in a way which will interest them, heighten attention, and above all achieve understanding.

[2] Donald K. Darnell, "The Relation Between Sentence Order and Comprehension," *Speech Monographs*, (Vol. XXX, 1963), p. 100.

4 LANGUAGE

THE NATURE AND FUNCTION OF LANGUAGE[1]

Our World of Words

What kind of a world do we live in? How would you answer this question? There are many possible answers, all of them at least partially true. One can say that in a very real and important sense we live in a world of words. To a surprisingly large extent, what we have, what we do, and what we are depends upon our use of words. The *desire* to "communicate" is universal in the animal world. The *ability* to communicate is likewise universal, but this ability varies from the most simple forms of chemical stimulation between one paramecium and another, to amazingly complex and efficient systems among some insects, birds, and animals. Only mankind, however, has developed the ability to communicate with words; that is, to use a language made up of spoken and written symbols that have arbitrary meanings—in short, to use a code.

In a large measure, it is man's power to use words that sets him apart from all other species and makes him a thinking, writing, talking being who is able to dominate other forms of life, to remake his environment, and to ponder the mysteries of his life in relation to the universe. This, of course, is by no means a new idea. A Roman teacher of speech by the name of Quintillian expressed it very well some nine-

---

[1] The authors are indebted to Dr. Claude E. Kantner who contributed Chapter I in the second revision of SPEECH FOR EVERYDAY USE. Much of the material contained in his "The Nature, Function, and Problems of Language," which appeared in the last edition is contained in the first part of this chapter.

teen hundred years ago when he wrote, "God, the all-powerful father of nature and creator of the world, hath exalted man above every other animal by no character so potent as the faculty of speech."[2]

Even though our ability to use words is unique, we tend to take them for granted as a natural part of our world, like the very air we breathe. From the time we draw in our first breath and emit it as a cry of protest until the last expiration, we are surrounded by words. Day in and day out we are bathed in words as enveloping and all pervasive as the bubbles in a bubble bath. Think for a moment of the amount of talking you hear and do each day. Think of the unrelenting barrage of words from radio and television loud-speakers and from letters, billboards, newspapers, magazines, and books.

Our Casual Attitude toward Language

It is small wonder that something so common as speech is often taken so lightly. Moreover, we normally begin to understand and to use language in early infancy without any realization that what we are doing is in any way difficult, unusual, or important. From one point of view, we learn to speak too easily too soon, and by the time we are old enough to understand the significance of speaking, our speech habits have already become fixed and largely automatic. The result is that we take our ability to use language for granted, as a part of our natural heritage and environment. Even the ability to read and write, which is acquired somewhat later by a more conscious effort, is also so lightly esteemed that many of us resist any effort to improve our mastery of these vital skills. In this country, we regard literacy as commonplace and hence somewhat unimportant; in other countries where millions are still unable to read or write it is regarded as the miracle it actually is.

Four Indispensable Tools: Speaking, Listening, Writing, Reading

Yet it is a mistake to take our native language too casually. Have you ever seen a child who, although otherwise seemingly normal, was unable to learn to speak? Or to hear speech? Or both? Do you know an adult who as the result of an accident or a disease has lost his power of speech? Or of understanding speech? Or of writing? There are such people and they live in helpless frustration and isolation, deprived of the most important means of acquiring knowledge and of sharing

[2] Institutes of Oratory ii, 16.

experiences with other people. Knowing one personally brings quick awareness of the vital importance of these quite ordinary skills.

Remember that most of what you learn in college depends upon your ability to write, read, speak, and listen. These are the basic and indispensable tools with which we acquire and express knowledge. All of them are without question skills that can be improved. No matter how poor or how good a student may be, improvement is always possible with proper guidance and effort. Nothing that you can do as a student is more rewarding than the time and effort you give to increasing the mastery of your native language.

A Difficult and Complex Process

Our use of language, whether in oral or written form, is not only important, but also one of the most complicated and difficult abilities that we are ever called upon to learn or perform. It is difficult both to produce and to use. In terms of the muscular coordination and the complexity of the activities of the nervous system, the act of speaking is still the mechanical miracle of all time. When we consider also that we rely chiefly on language to understand and represent the world we live in, including ourselves, the difficulty of the process becomes even more apparent. We have in language a tool of almost limitless capacity and flexibility with which we attempt to relate ourselves to a universe of infinite complexity. This means that no one can achieve perfect mastery of his language because language and living, the world of words and the world of things, are irrevocably intertwined.

The Importance of Speech to the Individual

Despite the very real difficulty of the process, nearly all of us do learn to use language, although, of course, not equally well and seldom to the best of our ability. Yet the ability to speak and write well is of crucial importance, not only in acquiring an education, but also in the daily business of living among people in our efforts to adjust to, and achieve some degree of influence over the social culture in which we live. Moreover, it is apparent that the ability to use language well is especially important to a person who is preparing himself for a career in a profession, in business, or in industry. Both personal happiness and vocational success are dependent upon the ability to communicate orally. Our relations with other members of our family and with our friends and neighbors are influenced by our speech. In many lines of work, job success in terms of promotion and achievement is closely linked to ability in speech. Finally, both our contributions to the general welfare of the society in which we live and the values we derive from our various social groupings are heavily influenced by written and spoken language.

Yet, unfortunately, many people, including far too many college students, are so stumbling and inarticulate in their speech that they become inhibited in their interpersonal relations, handicapped in their work, and ineffective in any verbal participation in social or public affairs. In a very real sense their "freedom *of* speech" is abridged even though our society still leaves them relatively free *to* speak, if they can and will. A student with a limited vocabulary, who is lacking in the ability to speak, read, or write his own language is ill-prepared either for college study or for life in the complex twentieth-century world in which he must live.

BARRIERS TO UNDERSTANDING

The Crucial Importance of Understanding

If it is true that contemporary man is reaching out to conquer space itself, it is also true that he is plagued by fears that all may not be well with the world he lives in. To put it bluntly, he hears that his world may collapse around him due to some major catastrophe brought about by the inability of people to understand each other and to live together amicably. It seems probable that much of the current "hippie" psychology is basically a loss of faith in man's ability to keep his own house in order.

Some evidence of this concern is to be found in the increasing attention to "relations" in our times, so that we are becoming more aware of the problems involved in intrapersonal relations, interpersonal relations, interracial relations, and so on. At one time, not so long ago, there was considerable optimistic hope that increased opportunities for communication would surely bring increased understanding and some semblance of world "brotherhood." Certainly, there is no denying that increased travel facilities and tremendous advances in electronic communication during the last few decades have multiplied a thousandfold the opportunities for both face-to-face speech and for long distance and mass communication. It is also clear that there has been no proportionate increase in human understanding, and it is becoming painfully evident that *something more than the opportunity to communicate is needed*. It is indeed one of the ironies of our time that many who long for some magic formula that will enable us to live in amity with Arabs, Asians, and Africans are quite unable to get along with their own wives, neighbors, or coworkers, and—all too frequently—even with themselves. *Increased opportunities for communication may result only in an increase in the number of breakdowns in communication.* Since we are rightly concerned with this problem, it is appropriate that we review some and predict other barriers to understanding that arise out of man's communication.

Barriers Imposed by the Use of Words

Throughout the various chapters in this book, communication barriers have been or will be pointed out to you. These barriers are related to the personality of the speaker, his voice and articulation-pronunciation, the structure of his message, and other factors which are essential to and important in oral communication.

Strange as it may seem, one of the most common sources of misunderstandings is the fact that we talk and write with "words." On the surface, and especially if you take your language for granted, you will tend to think that this is a ridiculous statement. On closer examination, however, we see that there are at least three ways in which our use of words leads us into misunderstandings.

1. **We Tend to Assume that Everyone Else "Speaks Our Language"** Even when we are talking to a "foreigner," we sometimes catch ourselves raising our voices in the apparent belief that if we speak English loudly enough he should be able to understand us. The trouble is, of course, that although we are both using what we call words, we are not using the same "code." This is easy enough to see in the case of the foreigner and we usually understand, at least in principle, that even among our friends words may mean different things to different people.

There seems, however, to be a powerful tendency that leads us to assume unconsciously that the words we use have the same meaning for the other person as for us—an assumption that is all the more powerful and dangerous because it is partly true. Indeed it has to be partly true if we are to communicate at all. The very fact that some of our meanings are similar, lulls us into a sense of false security, and we forget the possibility of dangerous differences. Note also the natural human tendency to assume that the other person's meanings are the same as ours, and not that ours are the same as his.

The point in question is this: How can you be sure that the strange noises you make in your throat and mouth that somehow manage to cause membranes, tiny bones, and some liquid to vibrate in my hearing mechanism and that eventually reach my brain as nerve impulses, mean to me what you think they mean to you? If you were a tenderfoot scout standing on the top of a hill and waving a pair of flags to a comparative stranger on the top of a distant hill, would you be sure that he understood your signals?

It is too easy to become overconfident of our ability to communicate with words, whereas in fact the use of language ought to be approached with humility and a deep respect for the problems it presents. Instead of assuming that everyone speaks the same language, it might be wiser to reflect that in some respects at least everyone speaks a "foreign" language and that from our somewhat isolated little hilltops we keep trying as best we can to get a message across the gap to another person on his hilltop.

2. **We Try to Talk About a Very Complex World with a Very Limited Vocabulary** Some people have the idea that there is less danger of misunderstanding when only a limited number of short and "simple" words are used. This is far from the whole truth. A small number of simple words may be serviceable in expressing a small number of simple ideas in a gross fashion, but, unfortunately, what goes on inside us and around us is not simple. It is tremendously complex. To attempt to talk about our complicated world with a vocabulary of no more than a few thousand words is like trying to describe a six-ring circus with a one-ring vocabulary or like trying to build a modern house with only an ax and a bucksaw. Although these statements seem obvious, there is a surprising amount of resistance to learning new words even during those four years when we are "getting educated." Yet it seems clear that if we want to express shades of meaning more subtle than "lousy" and "cool" and if we want to think and talk intelligently about the world we live in, we will have to acquire a vocabulary that is equal to the task.

3. **We May be Suffering from Verbal Inflation** The parallel between words as a medium for the exchange of ideas and money for the exchange of goods is striking. Apparently, if there is too much money in circulation in relation to the available goods, money becomes cheap and buys less and less. The currency is said to be debased, and at some point in the process we lose confidence in our medium of exchange. One cannot help wondering if our verbal currency is in the process of being debased and cheapened. It may be that our retinas and eardrums are being assaulted with words so continuously and overwhelmingly that we no longer pay much attention or have confidence in either the spoken or the written word.

More important than the mere number of words, however, is the fact that much of what we see and hear simply cannot be trusted. It is not sound currency; it is not backed by integrity; it is not true to facts; in all too many instances it is deliberately intended to distort, deceive, and misrepresent. Only recently, a well-known national magazine told us in effect that we are naïve if we continue to believe that all price tags with marked-down prices mean what they say. Not knowing which price tags to believe and which to distrust, we come to suspect all.

The cautious listener and reader is being forced, whether he likes it or not, to adopt an attitude of cynical disbelief toward more and more of the language used in advertising, press releases, propaganda materials, and much of both public and private speaking. This attitude may be necessary self-protection, but it does not indicate a healthy state of verbal currency. We may venture a statement that our civilization is just as dependent upon soundness and essential trustworthiness of its language currency for the exchange of ideas as it is upon sound money. Our use of language is based on trust just as truly as is the paper dollar or the check. If talk is becoming cheap, so cheap that it is getting to be worthless, our loss of faith in its trustworthiness could be serious.

We should also be aware that the purposes and practices of much of our present advertising and of many of the "persuasive techniques" used in speaking and writing in general are in direct and dangerous conflict with the purposes and practices of education. Ideally, education seeks to lead us toward the "truth," to supply us with "facts" and knowledge, to teach us to weigh evidence and use reason—in short, to act like rational human beings whose judgments are mature and deliberate. Quite to the contrary, much of modern advertising as well as of other forms of speaking and writing is deliberately intended to induce us to act quickly, automatically, and emotionally, without weighing the evidence or using our reason and to act on the basis of pseudo facts and information so distorted, oversimplified, and dramatized as to be essentially false. Some of the best and most expensive brains in the country are constantly figuring out ways to do this more effectively. The struggle between the purveyors of education and the sellers of soap at times seems woefully unequal.

Language—a Calculated Risk

While it is possible to do many things to reduce the possibilities of friction and misunderstanding in communication, it should be evident that speech is truly a calculated risk. Every time we talk (or write) we take the chance of being misunderstood, and it is often just when we take for granted that we understand and are being understood that we are most likely to get into trouble. It is safer to be fully aware of the risks in each communicative situation and put up a mental warning sign: DANGER, MEN TALKING.

LANGUAGE—TOOL OF COMMUNICATION

The word "language" has many meanings. In any discussion of communication, language, as Webster's *Seventh New Collegiate Dic-*

tionary defines it, refers to "the words, their pronunciation, and the methods of combining them used and understood by a considerable community."[3] A study of language in communication, then, must deal with word selection and ways of putting words together in a meaningful pattern.

It is important that language be considered in connection with speech. Without it, of course, oral communication is impossible. Without language, our only means of direct communication would be facial expressions and gestures. Language is the essence of thinking, and therefore of writing, reading, speaking, and listening. According to psychologist George A. Miller, "Thinking is never more precise than the language it uses. Even if it is, the additional precision is lost as soon as we try to communicate the thought to someone. The importance of a precise language is most clearly demonstrated by the value of mathematical language in science. It is only necessary to compare the Arabic with the Roman system of numbers in order to recognize the tremendous advantage a good notation has over a poor one."[4]

Our code or system of notation for oral and written communication is made up of words. We think, write, and speak in word sequences. Therefore, we must have an adequate storehouse of words for all purposes, the ability to recall them when they are needed, and the skill to put them together with the proper grammatical and thought relationships.

Our language potential is great. We have a basically good notation system. We have thousands of words with varying degrees of specificity, vividness, and color. Principles for word order and word relationships have been developed over the centuries, and certain rules have been prescribed concerning word order and form for our own English language.

The purpose of this section is to explore the various problems connected with the selection of appropriate words, the arrangement of words in the proper order to carry intended meaning, and the various grammatical forms dictated by general usage.

Words and Their Meanings

It has been pointed out that thinking can be no better than the language it uses. The first and smallest unit that can be discussed in relation to language is the *word*. Hence, this discussion of language should properly concern itself first with *words*.

---

[3] By permission. From Webster's *Seventh New Collegiate Dictionary* © 1969 by G. & C. Merriam Co., Publishers of the Merriam-Webster Dictionaries.

[4] George A. Miller, *Language and Communication*, (New York: 1951), p. 223.

In speaking, the choice of words is of the utmost importance. Proper selection will eliminate one source of possible breakdown in the communication cycle. Too often, careless or thoughtless use of words prevents a meeting of the minds of the speaker and listener. The words used by the speaker may stir up unfavorable reactions in the auditor which interfere with his comprehension; hence, the transmission-reception system breaks down.

Moreover, inaccurate or indefinite words may make it difficult for the listener to understand the message which is being transmitted to him. The speaker who does not have specific words in his working vocabulary may be unable to explain or describe in a way that will be understood by his auditors. Part of the problem with words lies in their meanings. Basically, all words with the exception of connectives and supporting ones such as "and" and "but," have two types of meanings: *historical* and *connotative*.

Historical or Denotative Meaning The historical meaning of a word is generally construed as the dictionary meaning that is accepted or agreed upon at a given time by all who know the word. For example, Webster's *Seventh New Collegiate Dictionary* defines "home" as follows: "A family's place of residence." This is the first definition given for the word. There are other meanings: "2. The social unit formed by a family living together. 3. A congenial environment. 4. A place of origin. 5. The objective in various games. . . ."[5]

These definitions show that the meaning of a word may broaden or otherwise change; for example, the association of the word "home" with baseball is fairly recent. The evolution of a word may result in a marked change in meaning. For example, in Duane Clayton Barnes' book, *Wordlore*, he points out some interesting changes in word meanings. According to Mr. Barnes, a "chap was once a peddler."[6] "The word 'marshall,' now used as a high military rank, had a lowly beginning as 'horse servant.'" "'Aftermath' . . . was originally a farm term and meant *literally* an 'after-mowing,' a second mowing."[7]

All words have a dictionary meaning which represents the current definition. This fact makes it possible to use words in creating an idea which can be transmitted through the vocal mechanism of the speaker. It is important that both the speaker and listener know which meaning is intended if the transmission is to be accurate. The word itself is not important; only the associated meaning is of concern.

For example, there is truth in the statement that a "rose by any other name would smell as sweet." The name which has been attached

---

[5] By permission. From Webster's *Seventh New Collegiate Dictionary* © 1969 by G. & C. Merriam Co.

[6] Duane Clayton Barnes, *Wordlore*, (New York, 1948), p. 34.

[7] Duane Clayton Barnes, *Wordlore*, p. 76.

to the flower which we identify as a rose is of little significance in itself; its importance lies in its code—in the association that we have made between the letters or sounds of r-o-s-e and a flower of a particular shape, texture, and so on. By common agreement, the printed word "rose," or its acoustic counterpart is used to label a specific type of vegetation; through the use of this label we are able to identify a particular flower.

Connotative Meaning This meaning of a word generally cannot be found in a dictionary. It is the personal meaning which one attaches to the word, the interpretation which is a result of the individual's past experiences and exposures to the word.

For example, in contrast to the historical meaning of the word "home," generally the connotative meaning includes or is a reaction to the individual's recollections of his home environment. It may suggest love, warmth, comfort, privacy, and many other positive reactions. However, if one's experiences with a home have been generally unhappy, the connotative meanings may be quite the opposite.

Remember that we store literally hundreds of thousands of sensory impressions in our brains. As we are exposed to new stimuli, we may form new word meanings or the established meanings may be reinforced.

Sometimes a communicator may use a word without recognizing that the connotation of the word is such that it will elicit an unexpected response from his listeners. The story is told, for example, of a professor giving an orientation lecture to an audience of approximately three thousand freshmen. As he progressed in his speech, he was amazed to see several girls in the front rows break into tears. The speaker realized, too late, that in illustrating a point he had used the word "mother" several times and evoked a response which seemed out of place in the excitement of becoming a part of a university family. The homesick girls' connotative meanings for the word "mother" progressed to "home," "love," "family," "tenderness," "sister," "father," "alone," and "homesick."

The connotative meaning of a word may dictate its use by a speaker; however, it also may interfere with the reception of a message by another. It may dominate the logical meaning of the word so completely that the original or intended meaning of the word is lost. This is one of the problems with which both the speaker and listener must be concerned.

Concrete vs. Abstract Words Ogden and Richards in their book, *The Meaning of Meaning*,[8] point out that every word has what they term a "referent," the object or attribute which the word symbolizes. The term "New York City" has its referent in a particular city. When you use the symbol "home," the referent is usually your own home.

---

[8] Charles K. Ogden and I. A. Richards, *The Meaning of Meaning*, (New York, 1923).

1. *Concrete Words* These are symbols, according to Webster again, "naming a thing, or a class of things, as opposed to naming a quality or attribute."

The word "cigarette" is the name of a thing, while "relaxation" represents an attribute. Only the former is an example of a concrete word. Other examples of this type of word are "mother," "soldier," "book," "movie," "radio," and "church." In each instance the referent is the thing, the class of things or persons being alluded to.

2. *Abstract Words* In contrast to concrete words, abstract words are the names for qualities and attributes. Such words as "relaxation," "humanity," "love," "sacrifice," and "worship," do not denote an actual object.

It should be apparent that concrete words are likely to carry more specific meanings than abstract words. Since the referent for the former is something that can be seen or heard or felt (in the physical sense), there is a smaller margin of meaning error than in the case of abstract words. Hence, there is likely to be less misunderstanding, less chance for a breakdown in communication between the speaker and the listener.

Abstract words have feelings, emotions, attitudes, ideas, and the like as their referents. Hence, since these characteristics are peculiar to an individual and are formed as a result of his own past experiences, the referents for such words as "truth," "democracy," "ethics," "honest," "coward," or "freedom" are likely to be different for different people.

Thus, the speaker may encounter difficulty in his use of abstract words. His meaning may not be the meaning of his listener. As a result, there may be a breakdown in communication.

In this discussion, you have been introduced to historical and connotative meanings of words and to two different types of words—concrete and abstract. Of the many problems associated with word usage, the following are of primary concern:

1. The connotative meaning of a word may overshadow and distort its historical meaning.
2. The referent of a word may be different for different people.
3. The referents of abstract words are highly individualized because they do not exist in actuality.

For words to function effectively as a part of the language of speech, they must convey the speaker's intended meaning. This is possible only if the speaker explains his meaning of any word which is *likely* to have different referents for different people. For example, if he is talking about "freedom of the press," he must explain what he means; otherwise, there is likely to be misunderstanding of the word "freedom."

The speaker will find that the less concrete and the more abstract the word is, the greater the precautions he must take to insure that his meaning will be that of his listeners.

Words are only signposts to understanding. In his book, *Language Habits in Human Affairs*, the late Irving J. Lee says:

> A sign or expression may concern or designate or describe something, or rather, he who uses the expression may intend to refer to something by it, e.g., to an object, or a property, or a state of affairs.
>
> Words are vocal sounds or letter combinations which symbolize or signify something. They . . . have no other function except to direct attention. The words now being read by the reader for instance are directing his attention to something; to the fact that words are attention directors. . . . Thus the word *gold* directs attention to a yellow, incorrodible, dense metal of atomic weight 197, and the word *vertebrate* to a class of animals having spinal columns.
>
> Words may be thought of as signs which name that for which they are signs: *table* is the name of an object, *red* of a quality, *run* of an activity, *ever* of a relation.
>
> Thus words may be considered as *pointers, indicators, forms of representation*, which are intended to correspond to anything whatsoever that may exist, that may be experienced, or that anyone might want to talk about. Or put another way, words may be used for the almost *endless naming* of the inexhaustible electronic events, objects, persons, situations, relations, etc., observed in the world outside-our-skins, along with sensations, feelings, beliefs, opinions, values, tensions, affective states, etc. experienced inside-our-skins.[9]

These signposts that words represent will be clear only if the words are thoughtfully chosen and properly defined so that they point the way directly and accurately. The speaker must do all he can to prevent his listener from getting lost in his own personal meanings.

Language and Attitude Change

In discussing connotative meaning, we saw that language conveys a good deal of our inner thoughts and attitudes. It is only logical that in communicating to change attitudes that we will make use of language that is appropriate to the goal that we have set for ourselves. The language event interacts with the speaker and the audience, and conveys to the audience the intensity with which the speaker advocates his message. As you will see from the description of balance in Chapter 5, the imbalance that results in attitude change is brought about by a high-prestige source advocating an additudinal position different

[9] Irving J. Lee, *Language Habits in Human Affairs*, (New York, 1941), p. 15.

from the one the audience holds. The strength of this advocacy is largely a matter of language.

How does this process occur? Bowers has studied the effect of words that had strong connotative meaning in an experiment on attitude change. He found that more intense expression conveys stronger attitudes than did the conventional expression.[10] But for a listener who had moderate views, the use of extreme language is apt to have a boomerang effect. This is entirely consistent with a balance hypothesis, and the student should work out the details for himself as an exercise. It would seem that audience analysis is the key to successful language in the structuring of attitudinal communications.

CHOICE AND ARRANGEMENT OF WORDS

"Words have no fixed meanings; they have the power of designating referents and of stimulating awareness of meaning in individuals. We use words as though they were dippers, the same dippers for everybody, but the stuff that is dipped up with the dipper depends upon the body of stuff from which it is dipped. And when we use words we are always dipping into ourselves."[11] In this statement by Charlton Laird, he implies that language is the product of the individual communicator. If we accept this point of view, we must also perceive that the speaker or writer has a difficult challenge; he must choose the most appropriate words from his personal vocabulary and organize or arrange them in the way which is most likely to convey his exact meaning, feeling, hope, or challenge. Hopefully, his vocabulary is large and includes words which will permit him to be specific, vivid, affective, and accurate. He must be able to select words which can convey information accurately, which can illustrate and describe vividly, and/or which can elicit specific receiver attitudes or behavior.

However, words cannot achieve these goals if they are written or spoken at random. We are accustomed to certain structuring in the English language. Generally, words are put together in an accepted sequence in a unit that is designated as a "sentence." Granted, at times the sentence is abbreviated to a clause or phrase, and the receiver is able to supply the missing words. A small child who is just beginning to learn established patterns of word order and sentence structure is not misunderstood when he says, "Me cold," or just "Drink." However, as a child grows intellectually, as his world becomes more complex, and

[10] John Waite Bowers, "Language Intensity, Social Introversion, and Attitude Change," *Speech Monographs*, XXX (1963), p. 345.
[11] Charlton Laird, *Thinking about Language*, (New York, 1964), p. 37.

as society demands more of him, he must move in the direction of language patterns which come closer to those of the educated majority.

Language abilities should parallel intellectual and physical development. The immature language habits of the child are certainly not appropriate to the adolescent; neither is the typical slang of the adolescent compatible with the young or mature adult.

It must be admitted that while there are general rules for choice of the appropriate form of word and for the arrangement of words in a sentence, language is constantly changing. Most of these changes are gradual so that there is enough stability in language patterns to give the communicator a sense of security.

Many educators feel that "correct" pronunciation increases the credibility of the speaker; likewise, many speech teachers feel that language usage which approximates the patterns of the educated also adds to the believability of the speaker.

The educated man, then, should have a knowledge of established grammatical principles. He must understand the most effective ways of interweaving phrases and clauses in sentences. He must recognize the advantages of variety in sentence length and complexity as an attention holding device, and should recognize acceptable construction of a sentence in light of its function in the message.

Sentences have been traditionally classified as *declarative, interrogative, imperative,* and *exclamatory.* The speaker will probably use all of these types, his choice being dictated by the nature of the message which he is trying to convey. Moreover, he should make an effort to achieve variety in sentence length. A change of pace is desirable. Many long and complex sentences in sequence may create lethargy or confusion and thereby, lose auditor attention. Too many short sentences in quick succession may also confuse the listener.

There are many grammatical problems which the communicator faces. One of the most common problems and one which often generates negative listener reaction is the inability of the speaker to recognize proper agreement between the subject and verb. Such deviations as "they was," and "the gentlemen was," are far too common. Speakers probably make these errors more often with words which require a singular verb, such as "each" and "any." As a result, we may hear "Each of the plants need watering" instead of "Each of the plants needs watering."

Frequent errors are also made in choosing the appropriate tense for a verb. It is not unusual to hear "he come," "he had ran," or "he had went."

We often laugh at the attempts of foreigners to use English. In a recent letter from a businessman in Hong Kong, the writer said:

> We heartily thank our customers to give us business for 1968. In return, we sincerely give them all our blessings and kind regards and wish them enjoying prosperities in 1969.
>
> It is our policy to supply first class material, the high fashion goods and elegant style with reasonable price. We always offer our best and prompt services to customers in aim to make them convenience in every respect. . . . We welcome your criticism and claim, we will pay you remedies whenever occurred.

We can't help but smile upon reading this message. We are amused by the awkwardness of the language, by the misuse of words and forms of words. The writer did not follow our grammatical rules but this didn't prevent us from understanding most of his message—perhaps all that he intended.

We are "pleasantly intolerant" of this merchant's language. Often, however, we justify our own misuse of language, saying, "But that's what most of my friends say." We are quick to point out the errors that our foreign friend has made; yet we do not perceive the errors we make ourselves.

Sometimes, the meaning of a sentence can actually be distorted because of the careless choice of words or word forms, or because of a strange word order. For example, the meaning of the following sentences has been distorted, primarily through an ill-chosen word order:

1. He rushed up on the porch and lying under the mat he found the key.
2. I turned off the television set when the announcer came on to eat.
3. The ballplayer threw his bat in the air as the umpire called "strike three" and walked disgustedly to the bench.

If an individual takes the trouble and makes the effort to speak, we must assume that he hopes his auditors will understand him. If this is a true assumption, we would expect the sender of the message to make every effort within his ability to insure that his ideas reach the receiver intact. His effort must include attention to discriminating word choice and acceptable grammatical structure.

A more remote and less personal responsibility is expressed by W. Nelson Francis in his *History of English:*

> As times have changed, language too has changed to meet the needs of each generation. It is just as wrong to speak "decay" of language as to see in it an inevitable progress. Language is what people make it. In every generation there are those who use it skillfully and those who use it clumsily; those who use it honestly and those who use it corruptly. The final lesson of its history is that not only poets and scholars,

but ordinary citizens as well have a hand in shaping the language of their time. This is our privilege and our responsibility.[12]

POSITIVE APPROACH TO BETTER LANGUAGE USAGE

There are certain positive steps which you can take in order to improve the language aspect of oral communication: (1) *Use words which convey precise or exact meanings;* (2) *Avoid overworked, general purpose words when there are better ones;* (3) *Use vivid and colorful language;* (4) *Adapt your language to the situation;* (5) *Always use language that is in good taste;* (6) *Avoid verbosity;* (7) *Make a real effort to build a vocabulary which will serve you efficiently in the great variety of speaking situations which you will face.*

Be Exact

First of all, choose words that convey precisely what you mean. If there is any possibility of misunderstanding, modify the words in a way that will help your listener to receive your intended meaning. Depend upon words and word sequences to transmit your idea *intact* to your listeners.

Say exactly what you mean. Try to avoid the repetition of the phrase, "What I really mean is. . . ." Say what you mean the first time. Likewise, avoid depending upon catch-all phrases such as, "like that," or "and everything," or "and all of that." Extend your discussion to include all the material in concrete terms.

Do not rely on *approximation* when exactness is required. Of course, there are instances when exactness can be carried too far. For example, in using statistics in the support of an idea, the speaker should round the figures out. It is not necessary to quote "$1,632,320.11" in its entirety. Round the figure off to $1,630,000."

This does not mean that you can always depend on approximation. For example, in the following, lack of information or unwillingness to reveal statistics which were requested caused the speaker to respond without exactness:

> A member of a board of directors of an important industry was dissatisfied with the annual report presented by one of the officers. Following it, he asked, "Just what is the amount of our indebtedness at this moment?" The answer came back, "It is somewhere between one and three million dollars."

[12] W. Nelson Francis, *The History of English*, (New York: W. W. Norton & Company, Inc., 1963), p. vi.

The second question he put was, "How did the sales volume compare with last year's?" The answer was an indefinite, "Oh, so-so." Next, the questioner asked, "How does the number of employees at the present time compare with last year's number?" The answer was equally vague: "Just a small drop, but approximately the same."

The man asking the questions wanted exact figures; however, he learned no more than he had from the original report. When the occasion for exactness arises, the speaker must comply with the demands of the situation. He must not hide his ignorance behind approximations. Too often lack of specificity is the result of lack of information or is a method of deception. If it is necessary that you be exact, secure the information from reliable sources and use exact language to transmit the information.

The serious student of written and oral language tries to form the habit of preciseness. He practices giving directions accurately, describing objects, scenes, and events so that they are clear, and reports things he has heard or seen as clearly as possible.

Avoid Overworked Words

There are too many speakers who make use of common words which no longer express an exact meaning. The word "beautiful," for example, has developed into an all-purpose symbol which lacks preciseness. You meet a friend on the campus and you remark, "It's a beautiful day." Coming away from the stadium you hear someone else say, "That was a beautiful game." That night you walk onto the dance floor and say to your partner, "My, but you're beautiful tonight." Then your date looks across the room and notes, "Helen has a beautiful dress on tonight." The word *beautiful* has developed into an overworked, all-purpose word which lacks specific meaning.

How much more precise the comments would have been if the speakers had said: "It's a crisp, clear day," and "I've never seen near-perfection in football before today; both teams were playing over their heads," and "Helen's dress is smartly tailored."

Many words are in this category of overworked words. Among them is the term "nice." This word is used in so many different ways that it has lost its exactness. Other examples include, "good," "bad," "gorgeous," "well," and "monstrous." These words have been worked to death. They have lost any vividness of meaning they originally had. When you say, "It's a beautiful day," exactly what do you mean by the word "beautiful"? Equally important, what do your listeners interpret it as meaning?

Other words convey more exact images. Such symbols as "delicate," "fragile," "bombastic," "arrogant," and "superficial," still retain more clear-cut delineations and therefore are more useful to the speaker.

Everyone interested in improving the language level of his communication should make an attempt to eliminate worn-out words from his speaking and writing vocabulary; he should try to be more exact in his word choice and more imaginative in word selection.

Be Vivid

There are times when utilitarian language suffices in speech. The engineer who issues orders to his men depends on the exactness and clarity of his language to explain the job. The lawyer, trying to clarify a legal point for a client, depends on specificity. The teacher must explain a geometry problem with concrete language. Everyone must first achieve clarity in language.

But there are occasions when more than exactness becomes necessary. In some classrooms, in social situations, and a host of other places, the speaker and his auditors require the beauty and color which can be achieved through language that will stimulate the senses of the listener. To catch and hold attention the speaker must be more descriptive, using words to recall color, taste, feeling, motion, and all the other sensory impressions filed away in their mental storehouses.

Everyone, then, should have a large supply of different levels of words. You should be able to produce at will, clear, concise, and exact words which are necessary to intellectual comprehension. In addition you must have a supply of vibrant, novel, and colorful symbols, which add vividness and freshness to your speech. These appeal more to the emotional understanding of your listener. Moreover, you should recall from your own experiences images which reinforce your explanation or description or argument.

Color may be added to speaking, then, through the words themselves. But this is not the only way. Well-told and imaginative analogies and comparisons and other attention-holding illustrations also add to the vividness of speech.

Let us examine some of the brilliant language used by Winston Churchill in his speech, "The Twentieth Century—Its Promise and Its Realization."[13] Early in this speech, Churchill says: "In the first half of the twentieth century, *fanned by the crimson wings of war*, the conquest of the air affected profoundly human affairs."

Note the vivid image created by the italicized words. Another

---

[13] Winston Churchill, "The Twentieth Century—Its Promise and Its Realization," *The Age of Danger*, Harold F. Harding, Editor, (New York, 1952).

speaker might have said, "In the first part of the twentieth century, the war was responsible for air developments which were later to affect people greatly." This lacks the imagery and style of the original statement. It is ordinary.

Churchill goes on to say later in the speech: "After four years of hideous mechanical slaughter, illuminated by infinite sacrifice, but not remarkably relieved by strategy or generalship, the victorious allies assembled at Versailles."

The reader feels the strength of this statement. The words "hideous mechanical slaughter" are loaded with imagery and condemnation. The following phrase, "illuminated by infinite sacrifice," is said with dignity, and the words suggest the quality of the sacrifice that men had made.

This particular speech is rich in vivid and colorful language. Examine the following excerpts and try to analyze what Churchill has achieved with words:

> There remains, however, a key of deliverance. It is the same key which was searched for by those who labored to set up the World Court at The Hague in the early years of the century.
>
> Human beings and human societies are not structures that are built or machines that are forged. They are plants that grow and must be tended as such.
>
> Life is a test and this world a place of trial.
>
> I say that the flame of Christian ethics is still our highest guide. To guard and cherish it is our first interest, both spiritually, and materially.
>
> Under the impact of Communism all the free nations are being welded together as they never have been before and never could be, but for the harsh external pressures to which they are subjected.

The poet, of course, makes use of impressive language. He appeals to the senses of his readers through the use of colorful and vivid words and many of the other devices mentioned above. Consider, for example, how Longfellow described the village blacksmith:

> Under a spreading chestnut tree
>   The village smithy stands;
> The smith, a mighty man is he
>   With large and sinewy hands;
> And the muscles of his brawny arms
>   Are strong as iron bands.

How much less forcefully and effectively some people might describe this scene: "The blacksmith shop is under a big tree and the blacksmith is a really big guy." This sentence lacks the vividness achieved through the words "mighty," "sinewy," "brawny," and "iron bands." With these words, the poet has added atmosphere, feeling, and color.

Examine, also, the following image carved by the master artist, Edgar Allan Poe. Notice the quality of its language.

> At midnight, in the month of June,
> I stand beneath the mystic moon.
> An opiate vapor, dewy, dim,
> Exhales from out her golden rim,
> And softly dripping, drop by drop,
> Upon the quiet mountain top,
> Steals drowsily and musically
> Into the universal valley.
>
> from "The Sleeper"

Churchill, Poe, and Longfellow all demonstrate a mastery of language that few students can expect to acquire. However, all of us can improve the quality of our language. Many college students develop considerable skill in the use of language. The following excerpts from student orations attest to this fact:

> In a few more years, I will not hear the purr or thrill at the flash of silver. I will only know that somewhere up in that endless blue, a supersonic plane is flying at 1700 miles per hour—940 miles faster than the speed of sound—three times faster than man has ever traveled—faster than a nerve impulse! I gasp as I try to comprehend these facts. Everything is being planned, designed, and produced—not exactly with the ideas of aiding humanity nor even with the ideas of providing extreme comfort, but with the idea that we must be speeded up—we must go faster![14]

> I want to describe to you a mental metamorphosis. It took place on a trip West in the summer of 1945—a trip that turned out to be a journey through thought as well as through distance. My first important stop on the trip West was at the Grand Canyon, one of nature's most magnificent spectacles. It's an awesome sight, really, this gigantic, gaping hole in the earth—some fourteen miles across and over a mile deep into the earth. Standing on the rim of that vast Canyon, a human being can feel very small and insignificant. I was one of a small group one morning gathered at a lookout to hear a lecture on the history and background of the Canyon. The speaker, we soon found, was quite impressed with the magnificence and grandeur of the Canyon, as compared to the smallness and unimportance of man. He spoke of the agelessness of the Canyon, of how it had taken thousands and thousands of years for the wind and the rain to change certain basic rock formations. He told of the fossils embedded in the rock—the last remains of animals that the Canyon had passively watched come and go. He pointed to us and told

---

[14] Elsie Cory, "Faster, Faster, We Must Run Faster," *Winning Orations*, (Evanston, Ill., 1947), p. 43.

us how unimportant we were in the over-all picture of nature and history—how meaningless our short lives. Time, he said, meant nothing to the Canyon. Time was a man-made device. He scoffed at how concerned little man was with his mere three score and ten years on earth. The Canyon, he said, would go on forever, while little man would come and pass away like any other line of animal.[15]

In a very real sense we are living in a storm which today is blowing not only on a desolate island in the Pacific, but which is smacking dangerously against our whole global structure. The United Nations have stretched a fly tent of security over the world, but the pity of it is that soon there won't be enough stakes to peg it down. The winds of war are sweeping in under our fly tent of world security and puffing it up. Every time they do, some of the stakes pull loose. Palestine with its seething Jewish problem, India's cry for freedom, China's factions, the daily border incidents of Greece, and Poland's mythical free elections all indicate that the stakes are giving away. If enough of them pull loose, the fly tent of world security will collapse. In the studied conviction of Harrison Browne, the next time the fly tent goes down it will be "curtains."[16]

There is another reason for using imagery-laden language. Descriptive language may clarify abstract words or ideas which the speaker wishes to discuss. Abstract words may have highly individualized meanings, the result of the past experiences of the individual. Thus the speaker and his listener may not attach the same interpretation to an abstract word, and the meaning intended by the speaker is not received by the auditor. The speaker's real intent is lost.

Examine the word "beauty," or "beautiful" again. In conveying the abstract idea to a listener that your mother is a beautiful woman, your real meaning may not be clear. In order to make sure that your auditors understand what you mean, you must do more than make a bare statement of fact. You must draw a word picture, using vivid, descriptive terms which will help your listeners to see your mother as you do: as a beautiful woman.

Describe your mother's face, her hair, her carriage, her voice, her hands, the touch of her hands—all that make her a beautiful person to you. After all, is not our concept of beauty made up of a variety of sensory impressions? So that your listeners can understand this and other abstract words, you should build a series of concrete word pictures or images.

In a sense, accurate and colorful language may be considered elevated language. If you take special care to select and use appropriate words which say exactly what you mean, your language level is bound

[15] Seymour Tuchow, "The People Make History," *Winning Orations*, (Evanston, Ill., 1947), p. 19.
[16] Harold Brack, "The Center Pole," *Winning Orations*, (Evanston, Ill., 1947), p. 5.

to be on a high plane. Contrary to the beliefs of many people, the term *elevated language* is not synonymous with obscurity and difficulty.

Instead, elevated language makes it possible for the speaker to say what he is thinking with maximum effectiveness. The language of the poet or the dramatist or the philosopher may or may not be elevated, depending upon the skill of the writer to adapt his language to his idea and to his receivers. Sometimes, because we do not understand what we read or hear, we assume that the material is too elevated. Perhaps the reason is rather that the material was not meant for us, or the artist has done his job ineffectually.

Occasionally, words are invented because the speaker has not been able to locate an established symbol which has the necessary impact. Sometimes he will use an established word in a new context. These new words or meanings eventually become a part of our language and may even be included in standard dictionaries. A word such as "wallop" may become acceptable as a synonym for "impact." It also fills a need for a colorful word. Other examples of coined words or meanings which have been accepted or partially accepted recently include: *zip* (He is full of zip today); *charge* (I get a real charge out of being in a play), *brunt, dud, chortle, bamboozle, grumble, chump, foist,* and so on.

Adapt Your Language to the Situation

Throughout this text, it has been emphasized that the speaker should keep his audience in mind. This has been discussed in relation to choice of subject, choice of material, and to organization. It also applies to the choice of language. For example, the language of Emerson would not be appropriate in a Boy Scout meeting; at the same time, it would be completely out of place to use *wallop, charge,* and *zip* in a student-faculty committee meeting.

The speaker must design the language of his speaking so that it is suitable for the ages of his listeners, for their backgrounds and education, and for the occasion. The language appropriate for a junior high school group would not necessarily be appropriate for college students or a group of professional men. The language of the courtroom or the service club differs from that of the house of worship. Moreover, the language of a convention of engineers or scientists might be entirely different from that used by a speaker for a Memorial Day celebration.

Always Use Language That Is in Good Taste

Almost inevitably your audience will resist you if your language is punctuated with slang or swearing. Swearing, particularly, has no place in anyone's language. Likewise, words such as "guts," "nigger," "hunky," should not be used as expressions of disgust or as a means of stirring up hate. These words are generally offensive and cannot be considered appropriate for any occasion.

Slang, while it is usually inoffensive, is out of place in many speaking situations. If you are an educated person, you should not rely on these words to transmit information. There are much more precise and colorful words which are available to you which are not only appropriate but in better taste. Slang phrases are usually transitory; the ones which were used by your parents have long been lost. They rarely become an accepted part of the vocabulary of a language.

Avoid Verbosity

A speaker should use all the words necessary in order to transmit an idea. He should use all the necessary imagery to make the idea vivid for his listeners.

However, there is a limit which the speaker must not exceed. Too many speakers indulge in overamplification. They are too profuse in illustrations and specific instances. In an attempt to arouse the listeners' emotions, they go on and on, building images until the original effect has been lost and the auditors become bored.

The skillful speaker must sense when he has given his auditors enough so that they have comprehended. He must choose his supporting materials discriminately, using only the best to create his idea. He may have to discard some of his examples, but in so doing, he will strengthen, not weaken, his message. His listeners will not be lost in a maze of material.

Build a Vocabulary

This is a continuous process which everyone must consciously cultivate. The vocabulary of the eight-year-old is usually adequate for his thought processes, but his storehouse of words is not adequate for the college freshman. Likewise, the vocabulary of the university student may not be extensive enough for the professional man.

You must try to keep adding to your usable speaking vocabulary. When you encounter words in your reading and listening which are not a part of your oral vocabulary, make the effort to transfer them to your speaking. As your usable vocabulary grows, it becomes easier to be exact and vivid. You will discover, also, that you rely less and less on abstract, indefinite, and tasteless language.

It is difficult to give any specific information to guarantee you a richer and more useful vocabulary. Actually your development will depend upon your interest in this area and your determination to improve.

Vocabulary drills, as useful as they may be in some situations, are not stimulating or exciting. Making work out of language development may eliminate the possibility of enjoyment and may eventually curb the desire to investigate words and their usage.

Satisfaction and enjoyment, and appreciation of the need for exactness should be the stimuli which move you to experiment with language. You will find that the addition of a single word to your working vocabulary provides you with a real feeling of accomplishment. You will find yourself incorporating that word into your conversation and writing with increasing frequency. And the oftener you use it, the more conscious you will be that it has a specific meaning that no other word in your vocabulary possesses.

Actually it is satisfaction and enjoyment and need which stimulate children to learn new words. Many children, upon acquiring a new word, use it over and over again, seeming to derive tremendous gratification out of its use.

We go out of our way to meet new and strong people. We seek them out, talk with them, and prod them for new ideas. We secure a great deal of pleasure and stimulation from such associations, together with new ideas and philosophies which enhance our basic understanding of the universe and things within the universe.

The same procedure may be followed with words. You may seek out new words and learn to know and understand them. Your familiarity with them helps to make them a part of you. Then, when their use becomes automatic, the resulting fluency and preciseness of language provides you with an abiding sense of satisfaction. Moreover, as your vocabulary increases and your choice of words becomes more exact, your listeners obtain greater esthetic enjoyment from your speaking.

Strive to be an artist in the selection of your words, to be accurate in the arrangement of those words into sentences, to be logical in the arrangement of these sentences into a complete whole, and work constantly toward the goal of vivid, colorful, and dignified speech.

TRANSITIONS

So far in this chapter, you have been introduced to the problems and challenges of using language in order to convey your ideas. The emphasis has been largely on the need for accuracy and vividness in language. But the speaker faces another problem which is language-centered. He must join together the independent units of his speech so that its continuity is unbroken. This, too, is a function of language. It is accomplished through the use of transitions which bridge the gap between ideas.

The length and nature of these transitions depend upon the nature of the material in each unit. In some instances the transition consists of one sentence, while in another a whole paragraph may be necessary. If the organization of a speech is clear, the relationship between each unit is inherent and needs only to be demonstrated by the speaker.

This problem of effective passage from one portion of oral discourse to another may appear to be comparatively minor at first, just as getting across a gully or river may appear simple. It may be possible to reach the other side of a river by simply throwing a few planks across. However, the building of a solid and attractive bridge is more difficult and requires planning and construction based upon sound physical and artistic principles.

So, too, the job of building effective transitions must be done carefully and with certain basic principles in mind. Remember, first of all, that a shift from one part of a speech to another should not be abrupt. Give your audience time to adjust its thinking to the new idea after filing away the old. You may wish to summarize briefly the point you have just made and then point to the new idea in your transitional statement. For example, Robert Forsythe does this in one of his speeches, "Justice in Jeopardy," saying, "At this point we have considered the problem of injustice as it exists in the army and have proposed a solution. Now you may well ask, why is this any concern of ours?"

Avoid making the shift obvious by implying or saying, "Since I have finished with this point, we are ready to move on to a new idea." Avoid overuse of such incomplete transitions as "next," "then," and "also."

Perhaps a few examples will clarify this concept of transitions. In an oration entitled, "The Center Pole," Harold Brack in the first part of his speech discusses the policy of international cooperation which the town of Middletown, Ohio, has adopted. As he moves on to a discussion of what other areas or organizations are doing to further this spirit, he says, "What has happened in Middletown is only the beginning of a great American effort to support the General Assembly and make it the voice of the people of the world." This sentence is the connecting link between two parts of his speech.

Robert L. Kincaid, in his speech "Lincoln and the Loyal South," uses a simple transition most effectively:

A few months later, General Grant made an inspection trip over the

Wilderness Road from Strawberry Plains in Tennessee, through Cumberland Gap, to Lexington, Kentucky. On this journey he was greeted by the people like a hero. Writing later in his *Memoirs,* he said: "I found a great many people at home along the route, both in Tennessee and Kentucky, and almost universally intensely loyal. They would collect in little places where they would stop evenings, to see me."

This attitude of the mountain people was confirmed by the experiences of the Confederate general, Kirby-Smith, when he made his invasion of Kentucky from Tennessee in the fall of 1862. General Kirby-Smith, moving. . . .

The inexperienced speaker will find such phrases or words as "in addition to," "besides," "not only," "then, too," and "but so far," useful in creating connective sentences.

There is no doubt that the use of suitable transitions is a difficult part of speech composition. However, through the use of effective transitions, the speaker may secure a polish and finish which could not be attained in any other way.

5 COMMUNICATING TO AFFECT ATTITUDES

Students who have diligently followed the development of this book thus far have seen how to take communication through to the construction of a fairly involved speech. For many of us, this is as far as we need to progress in the study of communication. But as you may remember from study of the model in Chapter 1, communicative behavior also is channeled through the emotions, values, and attitudes that the listener and speaker possess. The role of these attitudes and values in the communicative interaction is fairly important in many kinds of communicative tasks. Therefore, our next major task is to examine the kinds of communication that are more closely involved with attitudes than relays, externalizations, or mands.

There are few words in English more misused than the word "attitude"—we are thought to have an "attitude" about most everything. "Attitude" has come to mean almost any kind of evaluative reaction to internal or external stimuli. We are said to have attitudes about cucumbers, Sophia Loren, the hydrogen bomb, and Barry Goldwater. Social psychologists have variously defined attitudes as "habit strength," "predisposition to respond," and "manifestation of value systems." Most general usage assumes that attitudes are internal states or predispositions to respond in particular ways, such as a political position, or an evaluation of a certain kind of behavior. Most definitions assume that an attitude about lemon meringue pie is substantially the same as an attitude about W. C. Fields or the diplomatic recognition of China. This point is defensible heuristically, but is certainly not very useful. A more valuable definition of attitude has been proposed by Leonard W. Doob, who believes that attitudes should first of all be of some significance in our society.[1] He also feels that attitudes are implicit, or not visible (the response potential we discussed in Chapter 1) and capable of producing their own motivations, or drives.

To be sure, Doob's definition of attitude calls for value judgments. It is not always easy to decide if something is socially significant—but this is a value judgment that must be made if this approach to communication is to be productive at all. On a practical level, it is fairly easy to distinguish between evaluations of Sophia Loren and evaluations of the Mississippi school system, even though our evaluations of Miss Loren may have a kind of social significance of their own. Like all definitions of this kind, it is not defensible in its extremity, but is a highly useful one for the introductory study of communication.

If we can agree that attitudes are socially significant, implicit, motivating reactions, we can now examine the types of communication that are importantly related to attitudes in the receiver. As we have seen, the externalization expresses source attitudes, but has no stated intent concerning the receiver's attitudes. For attitudinal types of communications, we will use the word *suasory*, a term used by Donald Bryant for the basic classification of this kind of discourse.[2] Suasory communication, then, is communication which has as its object the attitudinal structure or restructuring of the receiver—a strengthening, weakening, or other kind of modification. Suasory communication is different from the simple communicative forms presented in Chapter 1 —in that it aims at some socially significant reaction in the society. Some similarity may be observed between the mand and suasory communication, in that the suasory communication, like the mand, specifies a response on the part of the receiver. The important difference between the two is that the response specified by the suasory communication is attitudinal, and quite different qualitatively from the ordinary responses on the mand. Suasory communication can be viewed as a special case of the mand. To assert that the two are the same since they both aim at some kind of behavior, however, would be like asserting that the Beatles and Beethoven are the same since they both are involved with music. However lovely we may feel John Lennon's melodies are, we must admit that the two kinds of music are enormously different in form, content, method of performance, and audience response. So it is with ordinary mands and suasory communication.

[1] Leonard W. Doob, "The Behavior of Attitudes," *Psychological Review*, (Vol. LIV 1947), p. 135.
[2] Donald C. Bryant, "Rhetoric: Its Function and Its Scope," *Quarterly Journal of Speech*, (Vol. XXXIX, 1953), p. 35.

They may not differ in complexity, but they do have a completely different approach to audience responses.

Another important distinction of the suasory form of communication is the various dimensions possible in the attitudes of the receiver. It is possible to affect the receiver's attitudes in many ways, since attitudes are not simple reactions, but fairly complex structures depending on some very different psychological processes. Rosenberg and Hovland have characterized the important differences in attitudes by a three-part classification system.[3] They have divided attitudes into three basic processes: affective, cognitive, and behavioral. Affective responses are the nonverbal, "emotional" responses that are usually manifested in the behavior of our sympathetic nervous system—heart rate, perspiration, pupil dilation, and others. We have characterized such attitudes by "emotional" terms, such as "anger," "fear," and the like— and these make up an important part of our attitudes. Cognitive responses are the perceptual and "imaging" functions of attitudes, and reflect the way we perceive our environment and/or other persons. A highly prejudiced person, for example, has an entirely different cognition of Negroes than do less prejudiced persons. Finally, attitudes are manifested through overt behavior of individuals. Voting, buying, and other forms of behavior are good examples of the overt kind of responses that are related to attitudes.

Rosenberg and Hovland's distinctions do not necessarily imply that these attitudinal components always take place separately—in fact, the three usually occur together. If I have a strong objection to the war in Vietnam, I am likely to get angry about it (affective), view the military establishment as hired killers (cognitive), and involve myself in various protestations against the war (behavioral). However, it should be immediately apparent that each of these does not depend on the other. It is quite possible to have change in cognitive attitude without affective or behavioral change. We are all familiar with individuals who "feel" that capital punishment ought to be abolished, or that China should be given diplomatic recognition, but who have never put these "feelings" into "action" or recognizable behaviors. Most college students are convinced that studying is important; that they should study a good bit, but have in actuality, a much different cognitive structure of studying and an even different behavioral approach. So while we may see all three of the attitudinal components at work simultaneously, they are not of necessity linked and may often occur quite separately. And it is common to see communications which are aimed at each of

---

[3] Milton Rosenberg and Carl I. Hovland, *Attitude, Organization and Change*, (New Haven, Conn., 1960), p. 3.

these components separately. A message that is aimed at affective arousal will take a very different course from a message that is only interested in cognitive change, and messages that aim at behavioral attitude change will be even more different. Much confusion has existed in past descriptions of suasory discourse because of the failure to distinguish between these three functions and the assumption that a change in one inevitably leads to a change in the other. Many writers feel that if we change the cognitive attitude about integration, behavior will follow—an assumption that has been proved wrong again and again, both by research and the experiences of civil rights workers.

Suasory communication, then, can be sensibly divided into communication that aims at cognitive, affective, and behavioral processes. Let us examine our communication model again and see how it relates to this kind of communications.

The source of the communication, the speaker, who has been affected by the events of his environment may put the events of his

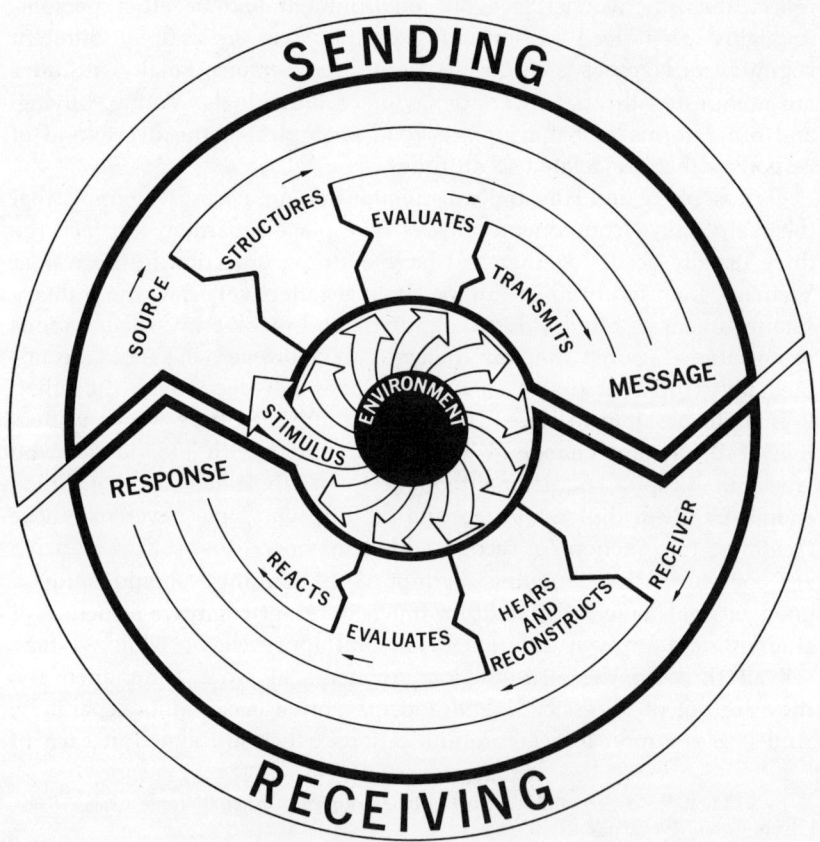

experience into an organized linguistic form, and this may pass through the value system of the source. This value system necessarily modifies the form of the message, since the individual's value system is now *part* of the message. These values pass into and through the delivery component and affect the receiver in a different manner than the simpler forms of communication. Whereas the relays, externalizations, and mands were communicative acts that interacted and passed through the attitudes and emotional responses of the listener, suasory communication aims at *alteration* or *modification* of these values and attitudes. The resultant receiver responses can be expressed in the communicative interaction in at least three ways—the affective, cognitive, and behavioral dimensions of Rosenberg and Hovland. Which of the three we decide to aim for will have great influence on the kinds of communicative action we are using; each of these is different enough to specify them as different communicative forms.

So now to our three simpler forms of communication, we must add three important attitudinal communication aims—suasory communication that is either affective, cognitive, or behavioral. Each of these three is typically found in most suasory communications—but it is also possible for each of the three to be the focus of a given communicative act. We have now expanded the purposes of communication a great deal. Let us look at the purposes as we now can compare them:

COMMUNICATIVE PURPOSE	FUNCTION
SIMPLE COMMUNICATIONS	
Externalization	Express internal state of condition
Relaying	Act as mediator to unavailable outside stimulus or event
Mand	Specifies behavior which will be rewarding to source
ESTHETIC COMMUNICATION	Esthetic response, "appreciation"
SUASORY COMMUNICATIONS	
Cognitive	Affect cognitions, states of "knowing," images, frames of reference
Affective	Bring about "emotional" arousal, psychological disruptions, discomfort
Behavioral	Overt and observable behavior, buying, voting, agreement, and so on.

Communication, as we have examined it in this book, can take on any one or combination of the purposes tabled above. There may be other forms of communication—some more simple and some more complex than the above kinds of communicative events—but these express most of the tasks that will face the great majority of us in our interactions with other people. And the main thing to remember about the distinctions drawn here is that each of them may require different approaches and methodology. Our next job is to examine the methodology inherent in preparing suasory discourse.

At this point, the student is possessed of enough basic information to do a creditable job of communicating in many situations. He knows what is needed to perform the first steps involved in presentation. But now he needs to think past the simple communicative tasks to the attitudinal framework—communications which are designed to change attitudes. These kinds of communication call for a greater emphasis on content in the form of evidence, and a more formal rigor in the kind of thought processes that are used—in the form of logic. The net result should be attitude change, which follows communication that is adequately constructed and coded.

EVIDENCE

When you hear the word "evidence," you may immediately think of Perry Mason and the jury—trying to discover the evidence in a given case. To be sure, evidence has a legalistic aura, and we tend to overvalue its use in terms of "proof." Actually, evidence can be viewed as anything that induces a state of belief in your audience, and while we generally feel that some kinds of evidence are better than others, the ultimate test of any kind of evidence is the effect it has. Gerald Miller has defined evidence as "those data that are intended to induce a sense of belief in the proposition."[4] So if you are trying to convince an individual who is a strong believer in astrology, you might just as well cite the position of the stars to convince him as the laboratory research of the American Cancer Society.

This pragmatic point of view is not as callous as it sounds; most receivers are sensible enough to recognize good evidence and detect the bad. A communicator who habitually cites false evidence or distorts the facts soon acquires a reputation for this sort of thing—and while he may be effective for one communication, he soon loses credibility as time passes. This is why the communicator, in the long run, must consider not only what is effective, but what will be effective over a long

[4] Gerald R. Miller, *Perspectives in Argumentation*, (Evanston, Ill., 1966), p. 24.

period of time. And for the long run, communicators must get into the habit of using evidence that will not come back to haunt them in future communicative situations.

What Makes Evidence Effective?

There is no good answer to the problem of what seems to make evidence effective. Probably the best answer lies in the creation of a special "set" of believability around the source, who is presenting a given point of view. Sometimes evidence is not as good as the citation of personal experience. In one study, for example, a communicator cited evidence in the form of testimony by an expert which supported his point of view. In another version, the same communicator cited his own personal experiences with the subject in question. Each of these communications was presented to different audiences, and when the results were compared, the researchers found that the personal experiences produced more attitude change than did the expert opinion.[5]

In another study, experimenters found that audiences could not distinguish "sincere" speakers—who spoke from their convictions—from insincere speakers—who spoke on a subject exactly opposite to their own positions.[6] This apparently indicates that a speaker could very well be just as deceitful as he wished and still be effective. In addition, there is some evidence that "good" evidence is no better than ordinary evidence. An experiment by Cathcart demonstrated that when a speaker used evidence, he was more effective than when he did not—but when he made his evidence "better" by attributing it to high-prestige sources, the amount of opinion change dropped.[7] We would have less confidence in this finding if it had not been replicated for different kinds of tests[8] and if there were no other research findings supporting this conclusion. However, studies by Dresser[9] and Anderson[10] both show no relationship between "good" evidence and amount of opinion or attitude change, supporting Cathcart's finding.

[5] Jerry N. Ostermeier, "Effects of Type and Frequency of Reference upon Perceived Source Credibility and Attitude Change," Speech Monographs, (Vol. XXXIV, 1967), p. 137.

[6] R. A. Hildreth, "An Experimental Study of Audience's Ability to Distinguish between Sincere and Insincere Speakers," Thesis Abstract, Speech Monographs, (Vol. XXI, 1954), p. 146.

[7] Robert S. Cathcart, "Four Methods of Presenting Evidence," Speech Monographs, (Vol. XXII, 1955), p. 227.

[8] Recent experimentation at Ohio University showed the same results somewhat with semantic differential and Likert-type attitude test.

[9] William R. Dresser, "Effects of 'Satisfactory' and 'Unsatisfactory' Evidence in a Speech of Advocacy," Speech Monographs, (Vol. XXX, 1963), p. 302.

[10] Delmar C. Anderson, "The Effects of Various Uses of Authoritative Testimony in Persuasive Speaking," Unpublished M. A. Thesis, Ohio State University, 1958.

This seems to be a dismal conclusion—that an audience will be affected equally by bad evidence as well as by good evidence. Unfortunately, there is no escaping it. Communicators must recognize that they can be effective in the short run using any kind of deceit, and make their choices based on what exists, and not what they would wish things to be. The choice facing a communicator is fundamentally an ethical one, and must be made on this basis. Probably the best answer is to be found in the comparison between short-term and long-term effects of communication. Hardly any of us will be engaged in communications that are "one-shot" only—situations where we will never again see the audience and want to communicate with them again. Communicators exist in a social framework, and must, of necessity, conform to the demands of that social framework over a long period of time. The question of the use of evidence must be made in terms of the communicator's long-term needs, as well as the short-term demands for effectiveness. And so, from this point of view, the choice becomes a difficult one.

Evidence and the Communication Model

As you will recall from examining the basic diagram of *relaying* on page 23 a communicator interacts with his external environment and presents the experience of his environment to a second individual in the interaction. In a sense, all evidence is relaying. Suppose, for example, you want to introduce the experience of a given antipollution program in another community in support of a kind of program you wish to support. You might present the "facts" of the successful program, both in terms of what action was taken, and whatever result was observed in the rivers and streams. What you are now doing is *relaying* the events of our common external environment that your receivers do not have available in their own experiences or perceptions. You may have observed these events directly or secondhand, through the experiences of others—in which case, you are acting as individual "C" acted in the Westley-MacLean model on page 23.

A common term for this kind of evidence is "facts." Communicators are enjoined to present the "facts" in a given instance and to base their communications only on the available facts. "Just the facts, ma'am," says the popular detective in a television series. Communicators are sometimes prone to go beyond the facts in a situation and embroider them with their own conclusions. The processes of conclusion-making will be discussed later in this chapter, and have little to do with the facts.

What exactly is a fact? The best answer is "an event in the external environment." And when the communicator uses a "fact" in his communication, he is no longer dealing with the event itself—he has passed it through his perceptual system and clothed it in language. What he now has is a "factual statement" which has the ability of being verified by the senses. This is how we determine a factual statement from conclusions. If we can verify the statement through one of our senses, the statement is factual. Notice that the *capability* of verification is the important part of this distinction—not the actual verification itself. To *verify* something means to determine its accuracy or inaccuracy, and factual statements are verified by a test of whether the event is present or not.

Let's look at some common statements and see if they are factual or not. "There is a bell in St. Patrick's cathedral" is a factual statement, because we can go to New York and inspect the cathedral to see whether the bell is hanging there or not. "The national capital is in Seattle, Washington" is another factual statement. While not true, we can verify the statement by either observing the capital in Washington, D.C., or verifying the absence of it in Seattle. Common usage for the term "fact" centers on the accuracy of the statement. We commonly say "That's a fact," when we mean "That's a true statement." Whether or not a statement is verified is not implied by the use of the term *fact*, only the *capability* of verification. Obviously we want to use verified factual statements only in our communications, but before we can tell what we are doing in the communicative interaction, we must know what kinds of statements we are making.

A moment's reflection brings out one other very important characteristic of factual statements—they are not all equally easy to verify. If you hear me say "The President of the United States has an ulcer" you will recognize the statement for what it is—a factual one, since it is possible to examine the interior of the President's stomach and see what is developing. In practice, however, we are going to encounter great difficulty in this verification, and we might even conclude that such verification (for us, at least) is impossible. Just because a statement is capable of verification does not indicate that it is, in practice, verifiable, and we must often operate on many factual statements that have not been verified in direct experience. Suppose your physician says "I think you have an ulcer—you'd better stop smoking and take care of your stomach." We might ask him to verify the statement by operating and directly examining your stomach. On the other hand, you might think it is more sensible to do what he says and see what happens, on the ground that the cessation of smoking is going to be easier on you than the operation. It all depends on how important smoking is to you —this is the crux of the verification problem. If it is terribly important to know what the results are, we may go ahead with the costs of the verification. If not, we may accept the inference about the physical event and consider it an operational fact.

In addition, many events or occurrences are far removed from us in space and time. Much debate has attended the question "Who shot first in the Arab-Israeli war of 1967?" Obviously we cannot roll the clock back and see, so we must depend on the firsthand reports of witnesses. Whether or not these witnesses are reliable and unbiased then becomes the important consideration in the evaluation of the factual statement. The whole fabric of history is full of accurate and inaccurate reporting. And when we move past recorded history into legend, we have great difficulty in establishing factual bases for our statements. Consider the statement "Jesus had a beard." Almost every representation of Jesus we see in paintings, statuary, and illustrations show him with a long, flowing beard—leading many people to consider that this is an accurate representation of his correct physical appearance. All we have to go on is that most Jews of that time wore beards because shaving was not permitted by the Law, and since Jesus was Jewish and religious, we assume that he did not shave. On the other hand, Jesus was quite impatient with many aspects of Hebraic law, and was not above violating many old precepts and substituting new ones for them. The recorded testimony of some first-century Christians is the only evidence we have of Jesus' whole life—Josephus, a contemporary historian, ignores him entirely—so the lack of mention of a beard in the Gospels certainly is not evidence that Jesus did not shave. Is this a trivial question? Of course it is, but it is on such trivial questions that much of our emotions, feelings, and beliefs are based. Since we *wish* them to be true, we begin to imagine that they are factual, and sometimes make tragic mistakes.

In the Korean war, General Douglas MacArthur had put together an important victory over the North Koreans—by holding out in the Pusan perimeter and then successfully landing marines at Inchon. The war had started when the North Koreans crossed the 38th parallel in Korea, and MacArthur had the choice of pushing the enemy to this parallel and then stopping, or, since the North Koreans were roundly defeated, pushing on into North Korea and capturing the North. He decided to go north to the Yalu River—the border of Korea and China —and based his decision on these "facts": (1) The Chinese and Russians were not interested in the existence of a Communist North Korean State, (2) The Chinese were not capable of military intervention, and (3) The Chinese were generally poor soldiers. All three "facts" had been reported to MacArthur in good faith by his intelligence officers. However, the actual state of affairs was quite different. Malenkov could not afford a communist defeat politically, nor could the new government of Communist China. The existence of hostile troops on the Yalu River was not acceptable to either country politically. Second, there were, at the time of the push across the parallel, over 600,000 well-armed, well-equipped Chinese troops poised on the Yalu River, ready to cross. Intelligence officers estimated their strength at approximately 25,000 to 30,000. Third, the "fact" about the quality of the Chinese soldier was largely the result of observing Chiang's troops in action against the Japanese and the Chinese Red army. Unfortunately, the Red army as organized by Mao Tse-tung turned out to be an entirely different sort of army, manned by a tough, resourceful kind of soldier, well-equipped by the Russians. The result of MacArthur's blunder was foreordained by the poor intelligence that he was given—and the "facts" that his subordinates gave him were determined less by verification and observation than the desire that they be so. The existence of a communist North Korean government was something that should be stamped out if possible, and apparently the judgment of the intelligence officers was influenced by their desires in the situation.

We must remember, while looking at examples of this kind, that this particular mistake was made by highly trained, expert, and well-informed individuals whose job was the reportage of facts. This emphasizes the extreme importance of placing the accuracy of factual verification in a communicative situation. If a communication is based on verifiable factual statements, it has quite a different basis than an inference based on a given probability that the statement is true. The quality of the communication, therefore, depends on how the communicator represents the evidence to the receiver; it is easy to report a "probable" factual statement as if it had been carefully verified and was acceptable in this way.

Types of Evidence

There are three types of evidence that play an important part in communication: *examples, testimony,* and *statistics.* Let us look at each one in turn, remembering that they are all reported as factual statements, supposedly representing an event in the external environment of the communicators.

Examples are fairly common in the communicative interaction, and are best defined as a single instance of the event that is in question. We are using an example when we say "It's expensive to drive in New York—the toll on the George Washington bridge is fifty cents." To really nail down the statement, we probably should report the toll for the Holland tunnel, the Triborough bridge, and so forth, but by picking out a single instance that is *representative* of the other instances, we communicate more efficiently.

Many communicators forget the requirement that an example be representative. "Boy, are Africans primitive;" we hear. "I know a man from Tanzania who had tribal tattoos all over his face." The reporter may have known the only Tanzanian in America who had tribal tattoos, and may be reporting a "fact" that does not support his conclusions. African tattoos are not very different from the gorgeous tattooed heart with "mother" on it that many American sailors display. It is easy to see that an example is not really very good "proof," and is best used only to clarify a given statement.

Testimony is a factual statement that alleges that a given individual made a statement that you are reporting. "The American military is too strong," you may say. "When President Eisenhower retired, he warned Americans against the increasing influence the military establishment has on our lives." The value of your evidence rests on three things: the *relevance* of the testimony to your point, the *expertness* of the source you are quoting, and the *credibility* the source has with your audience. It is tempting to use as testimony the source who has credibility only; your effectiveness will be enhanced. Advertisers seem to believe in this process wholeheartedly; the endless parade of sports figures eloquently extolling the virtues of a given shaving cream is apparently pretty effective in inducing the gullible to pay the extra money that the advertising adds to the cost of the shaving cream.

But at the same time, it would be pretty silly for a communicator to choose as his witness the most obscure, unknown expert that he could find; obviously some sort of balance would seem to be required here. Here, as in most other matters, good judgment is required to prevent both the abuse of the use of testimony and the ineffectiveness of a poor source. Students often say "What can I do? This is what I have to work with." They forget that as responsible communicators, they have an obligation to *find* acceptable material for their communication, and the process here is not at all easy—good evidence must be rooted out diligently.

The third kind of evidence is statistics—a much abused kind of evidence in communication. The world is full of persons who are suspicious of statistics and statisticians, mostly because statistical evidence has a way of failing to fit our expectations. Consider the continuing furor over the Surgeon General's report of the connection between cigarette smoking and lung cancer. The evidence as presented is a fairly convincing indictment of cigarette smoking, yet it has not had much effect on the practice of smoking in our country. The tobacco industry, on the other hand, has condemned the Surgeon General's report as only "statistical," as if that were a criticism of the contents. What does it mean when we say that evidence is "statistical," rather than something else?

To be statistical, evidence must satisfy only one requirement—the observations made must be rigorous enough to warrant mathematical description. In the case of the Surgeon General's report, the death rate of smokers and nonsmokers was carefully observed for many years. "Death rate" is a concept that means that, from comparable populations, so many individuals per thousand died every year. Age, sex, general health, and other characteristics are carefully controlled. When these two groups are compared, it is observed that many more smokers are dying than nonsmokers—not just from lung cancer, but from many other causes. Whether or not the smoking caused the deaths is still unproven; however, the *association* of smoking with a higher death rate is incontrovertible. This is what it means to have statistical evidence, and the question of causation follows from the statistics. In other words, the statistics do not prove that smoking causes lung cancer deaths; the statistics prove that more smokers have lung cancer than nonsmokers. The inference that follows—that smoking causes the higher death rate—is a logical one. When we look at this particular case, we are hard put to explain the statistics any other way, and there seems to be no other factor that presents a satisfactory cause of death. But in many other kinds of statistical evidence, there are alternative explanations.

Consider the commonly cited statistic concerning the income of college graduates as compared with the income level of those without college degrees. High school guidance counselors are fond of citing this kind of statistic to prove that a college degree is worth a given amount of money to the student. Not too long ago, former President Johnson cited the same statistic as proof of the value of education. Fundamentally, what the statistical evidence proves is that college graduates, on the average, will make more money in their lifetimes than nongraduates. But is there any other factor that could explain the relationship between a diploma and higher income? Is it possible that more individuals with ability tend to go to college, and that the ability is what produces the income and not the diploma? Or is it possible that individuals who have parents with money will go to college in greater numbers than individuals who come from poor families—and as a result that the individuals who come from well-to-do backgrounds have a better advantage in earning high incomes than the individuals who come from poorer backgrounds? Both explanations are not only possible, but highly plausible, and illustrate one of the characteristics of statistical evidence. Association does not in and of itself prove causation, and the attributing of cause is a logical process that is separate from the statistical evidence. In the case of the figures on smoking and lung cancer, no good alternative explanation is offered, unless we, like the tobacco industry, are willing to hypothesize some mysterious death cause which has not yet been identified, and which, strangely enough, more smokers seem to have than anyone else.

One more example may serve to make the point clearer. In a recent study of the academic behavior of undergraduate men, it was discovered that men with automobiles got poorer grades than did men without automobiles. Immediately a great hue and cry went up throughout college faculties all over the country: ban cars from the campus—they cause poor grades! Most faculty members are somewhat suspicious of the student car problem for other reasons—student cars are typically creating enormous parking problems almost everywhere in the country. A later study of the relationship between academic achievement and car ownership showed that students who were poor academic risks to begin with—low high school grades, insufficient motivational structures, and the like—were much more likely to be the students who thought that cars were important in campus life. And so, while it is clear that automobile ownership is associated with poor scholarship, it is by no means clear which causes which—and it is highly doubtful that banning cars will cause those poor in academic ability to improve their performance in the classroom.

In short, statistics are events observed in such a manner that we are justified in describing them numerically, and may be said to show a kind of association between events. Beyond this, statistics cannot be said to *prove* causation and must be interpreted with care. But in spite of this caution, a statistical citation is often the best form of evidence that a communicator can find—when compared with the alternatives, the example and testimony.

In some discussions of evidence, an evidence form called the *hypothetical example* is often recommended for communicators who are seeking support for their statements. Hypothetical examples are not really evidence, since they are fabricated by the communicator to explain or clarify a point. This process involves the imaginary instance. For example, a communicator will say something like, "What does the average student in a ghetto school face every day? Let us look at the typical ghetto schoolroom, where Juan, a Puerto Rican student, begins his day . . . " and goes on in that vein. There is no Juan, but the use of the hypothetical example personalizes the other information presented in the communication. This kind of usage is common and may be very helpful to the communicator who has a difficult point to make. But hypothetical examples should not be considered as evidence, since they do not relate to external events. They are not statements of fact but only rhetorical devices.

Let us summarize briefly the points we have made so far concerning evidence. Evidence is that part of the communicative interaction that is represented in the communication model as the "external event," and is then translated into factual statements by the communicator. Evidence is not proof, but only the beginning of proof. Evidence may be used in all types of communications, but is usually thought of in terms of the attitudinal communications. Evidence usually takes three forms:

the example, the statistic, and testimony. All three should be used, insofar as it is possible.

LOGIC

Evidence does not always prove the points that the communicator wishes to make, and to go beyond the simple citation of evidence, the communicator must make use of logical constructions. Logic is a word that can take on many interpretations. Aristotelian and Thomistic logic is largely a system of classifications of word usages generally using the *syllogism* as its basic form. Consider the following example:

> All bachelors are unmarried.
> John is a bachelor.
> Therefore John is not married.

This kind of conclusion is not exactly dazzling in its revelation, and typically syllogisms are so obvious that it is useless to state them. Contemporary theorists have made much over an Aristotelian term, the *enthymeme*, which is supposedly "a rhetorical syllogism."[11] What this term generally means is that the communicator can omit the premise of the syllogism which everyone knows. The syllogism about John's marital status then becomes "John, being unmarried, is a bachelor." An enthymeme, like a syllogism, is hardly startling in its conclusions, but has the advantage of being a little more acceptable stylistically.

Another kind of logic that students may have used is *symbolic* logic. Symbolic logic is the basis of set theory, which springs from a mathematical system invented by Boole.[12] Symbolic logic is quite complex and very useful to researchers as a shorthand notation for relationships between events. Most of the relationships spring from the "if—then" relationship, like the following: "If my car won't start, I have either a bad battery or a faulty ignition system. If I have a faulty ignition system, then a red light will show up on my dashboard indicator, or the dashboard indicator light bulb doesn't work. No red light shows. The car won't start." What can be concluded from the above is that there is a bad battery, or a bad ignition system *and* a faulty bulb, or both. What is valuable about the symbolic logic system is the casting of statements into mathematical notation and the development of the problems from the manipulation of symbols alone. However, most symbolic logic systems are too complex to be of much use to a communicator

---

[11] Lloyd F. Bitzer, "Aristotle's Enthymeme Revisited," *Quarterly Journal of Speech*, (XLV, 1959), p. 399.
[12] Who gave this kind of analysis the term "Boolean Algebra."

who is intent on making a point to an audience and may be limited as to time and material. Symbolic logic is highly useful to communicators prior to communication, but, generally speaking, they need to place the relationships between variables in a much simpler light for the average receiver.

Toulmin's Model of Logical Relationships

Stephen Toulmin, in his *Uses of Argument* has set out a logical model that provides a very useful guide to communicators who are attempting to go from evidence to general conclusions.[13] Toulmin's model has several elements and the basic structure begins with *evidence*, and proceeds to a *claim* by means of a *warrant*. The structure can be graphically described like this:

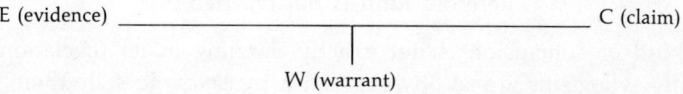

E (evidence)   C (claim)

W (warrant)

Toulmin's diagram doesn't seem to fit the actual manner in which we go from evidence to warrant to claim—the diagram seems to show a straight connection between evidence and claim. The warrant plays an extremely important part in this interaction, since it is the *means* by which we get from the evidence to the claim.

The evidence is only indicative of the claim if the warrant is true. Let us look at an example to see how the model works. Suppose that you have as evidence some FBI statistics that indicate that the rate of violent crimes is rising in the United States. You conclude from this that the general moral tone of our society is not what it should be. You can do this if and only if you can establish the warrant that a society with a high rate of crime is a society with poor moral tone. The structure of your reasoning looks like this:

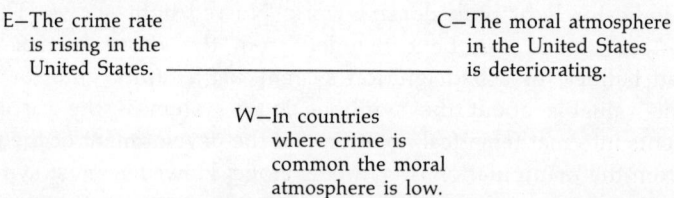

E—The crime rate is rising in the United States.   C—The moral atmosphere in the United States is deteriorating.

W—In countries where crime is common the moral atmosphere is low.

---

[13] Stephen Toulmin, *Uses of Argument*, (Cambridge, Mass., 1958).

When we first examine the warrant in this chain of reasoning, we probably accept it without too much reservation. But no warrant is an absolute, and the acceptability of the claim would only be as good as the strength of the warrant. Let's look at the warrant in the example—that in countries where crime is common, the moral atmosphere is low. Is it always true? In France in the early 1940s, there was a great deal of crime—thirty or forty times as much as we have in the United States today. The cause? The French were committing crimes against their established government, the occupying Nazi army. The moral atmosphere may have been extremely high to produce this kind of resistance. Since "crime" can mean any kind of violation of the law, does it follow that all laws are moral? Many laws in our country are unjust and repressive—and resistance to them seems highly moral. So the communicator in this case needs to establish and support his warrant as well as his evidence before he can arrive at his claim.

Let us look at another example of the structure in action. Here is an argument appearing in a nationally syndicated newspaper column: some years ago, American college students were asked the question, "If you were given the choice, which would you choose—surrender to the Soviet Union or nuclear war?" In spite of the difficulty of the choice (this is a little like responding which one would like to have cut off, an arm or a leg!) the students responded and the following table of preferences was prepared:

COLLEGE OR UNIVERSITY	PERCENT OF STUDENTS RESPONDING "SURRENDER"
Reed	60
Brandeis	48
Sarah Lawrence	45
Williams	39
Harvard	33
Stanford	27
Howard	21
Boston University	17
Yale	16
Davidson	14
Indiana University	7
South Carolina	4
Marquette	3

The author of the column concluded that "A striking aspect of the poll was the tendency of the poorer students to be more firmly anti-Communist, more gratefully American than the richer students. This tendency, as we see, crystallizes in the near-identity of the five poorest schools in the survey (Howard, Indiana, South Carolina, Marquette, and

Davidson, in that order) with the six schools most willing to go to war rather than surrender to the Communists."[14]

The results of the poll are in—and there is no arguing with them. What is hard to understand is the warrant in this argument. Let's look at the structure of the argument.

```
E—The five poorest              C—Poor students are
   schools in the poll             more "American" and
   were among the six most ——————— Anti-Communist than
   willing to go to war.           rich students.
                         |
              W—Being willing to go
                to war is a sign of
                Americanism.
```

This warrant is somewhat difficult to substantiate; being willing to go to war may be a sign of almost any kind of attitude about America. One possible interpretation would lead to a geographical explanation—of the four bottom schools in the list, three are far removed from potential targets. It is easier to be warlike from Davidson, North Carolina, or Bloomington, Indiana, than it is from New York City. The importance of the warrant in any argument should be obvious. Sometimes we cannot get from the evidence to the claim at all! What good warrants do is insure that the evidence that we have *really* leads to the claim we wish to make—if we see that it does not, then we should go out and get new evidence. Sometimes the structure is hard to see, as the ideas are usually wrapped up in many other considerations. But almost every procedure from evidence to a particular claim has an attendant warrant, and the communicator who wishes to reason this way must of necessity be aware of the process.

How does Toulmin's structure differ from typical syllogisms? Douglas Ehninger and Wayne Brockreide, in their book *Decision by Debate* have pointed out four major differences.[15] They are:

(1) In the Toulmin model, proofs are displayed in a spatial pattern, to help communicators see the *dynamic* relationship between the elements —while syllogisms are primarily a *static* kind of compartmentalization.

(2) The Toulmin model provides for the explicit support of warrants, emphasizing the importance of warrants in the total structure, while the syllogism seems to consider the premises of the process as a "given" that needs little attention.

(3) The Toulmin model emphasizes the relationship between the

---

[14] William F. Buckley's national column, January 21, 1968.
[15] Douglas Ehninger and Wayne Brockreide, *Decision by Debate*, (New York, 1963), p. 98.

evidence and external events—evidence has a *factual* cast in Toulmin that it may lack in the syllogistic reasoning.

(4) The Toulmin model provides explicit limitation on the force of a claim. The qualification of a claim is extremely important in this kind of communication, and does not necessarily take place in the syllogistic style.

As you might have guessed, we've only seen a part of the Toulmin model—there are three more important elements to add to the evidence, warrant, and claim structure: *support, reservations,* and *qualifiers*. To illustrate how these three elements operate, let us set up a typical evidence, warrant, and claim structure:

E—Grade school students who watch a lot of television are better readers than the grade school students who watch little or no television.

C—Television is a desirable part of our society because it creates good readers.

(Since) W—When two things are associated in this fashion, one causes the other.

Students will recognize immediately that the claim is actually a part of the structure, with a hidden warrant that reading is a positive good in our society. As we look at the basic structure, however, we see that the claim is not going to be an absolute one—no one would possibly state that all of the reading abilities that youngsters acquire could be due to television, and that sometimes television might even impair the student's reading ability. We should therefore qualify the claim, stating that in *general,* television creates good readers.

In addition, the warrant needs *support,* because not everyone believes that this particular warrant is true. In this warrant, support might be offered by stating that television viewing precedes reading practice and therefore has a time relationship that might support causative inference; and that Professor X from Y university has written that he believes that television has indeed caused the increase in reading ability. This all *supports* the warrant and makes it more believable.

The last element that is necessary in the reasoning structure is the *reservation.* We might think of many reservations to this particular relationship. Suppose, for example, that television exists only in those homes where a certain socio-economic level is in existence, and we might therefore believe that the association was due to the common cause, family background. Or we might also reasonably state that bright students tend to watch television more and therefore will also read better. These reservations are important in that their presence in the mind of the receiver of the communication might interfere with the attitude change that the communicator wishes to bring about. Let us look at the total structure:

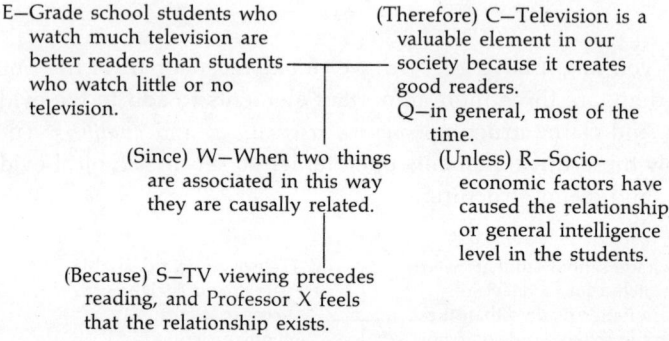

Now let's look at the relationships generally:

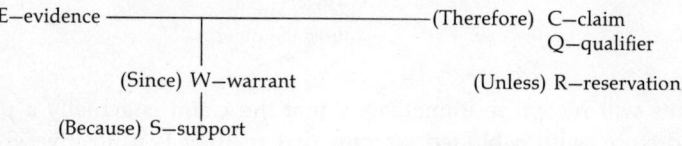

These six elements—evidence, claim, qualifier, warrant, reservation, and support—must be present if a communicator wishes to present a structured communication that can be said to be logically sound. The neglect of any of these elements leads to faulty thinking on the part of the source of the communication and/or lack of response on the part of the receiver. Mastery of the logical elements is as important as the gathering of evidence, because the evidence alone does not achieve the purpose of influencing receiver attitudes. Only in combination with sound reasoning can a communicator expect to achieve his purpose.

HOW ATTITUDES CHANGE—BALANCE

The study of evidence and logic is aimed at only one purpose—the modification of attitudes and values. Many different explanations have been offered to account for the process of change, but none of them are entirely satisfactory in that they do not all predict with perfect accuracy or explain all of the phenomena involved in the attitude modification.

Aristotle felt that "reason" was the principal causative agent in bringing about change, but we all have witnessed irrational factors which have had great effect in the modification of attitudes. Modern advertising is the best single example of the irrational argument and its efficacy in producing results. Until recently, we have tended to teach beginning students in communication that they should be "reasonable" because of the ethical question that irritational argument raises. And it is perfectly true that reasonable arguments are often effective and produce longlasting results. But if two diametrically opposed methods can both produce the same results, we ought to seek out the mechanism for this kind of occurrence. Many answers have been offered, and some of them are quite plausible. One very useful theory is the theory of balance, which holds that we attempt to keep our cognitions and knowledges in a sort of "balance" state and shift things around according to the tension this drive for balance creates. Let us attempt to see how such a process fits into the communicative attempt to change attitudes.

Basic Tenets of Balance Theory

The origin of balance theory has its roots in the writings of Heider,[16] Osgood,[17] and Festinger.[18] These three researchers have all proposed theories of balance which have many common elements. To illustrate what the concept of balance is, let us look at the processes involved when any of us makes a purchase. Let us suppose that we have bought a record player of considerable cost. Before we bought the player, we were involved in a decision-making process, comparing one model with another and weighing the alternatives. Each model has good points and bad points, and we make our choice for the one that has the most good points and the fewest bad ones. However, after the decision is made, we are committed to one of the models, and, despite its good points, we are still aware that we have committed ourselves to the bad points in the purchase. So here we have knowledge that we own the record player, but it still has some bad characteristics. In order to learn to live with this situation, we must emphasize the good points even more and bring our cognitive state into balance. By the very act of the purchase, we have committed ourselves to an unbalanced situation, and this of necessity means that we must seek behaviors that reduce this

---

[16] Fritz Heider, "Attitudes and Cognitive Organization," *Journal of Psychology*, (Vol. XXI, 1946), p. 107.

[17] Charles B. Osgood and Percy Tannenbaum, "The Principles of Congruity in the Prediction of Attitude Change," *Psychological Review*, (Vol. LXII, 1955), p. 42.

[18] Leon Festinger, *A Theory of Cognitive Dissonance*, (Evanston, Ill., 1957).

imbalance. This kind of behavior was graphically demonstrated by Leon Festinger in a now-classic experiment in buying behavior and choices.[19]

Let us consider another example. Suppose that one of us has an attitude that is quite different from the attitude that the rest of us hold. A teacher, for example, may have an attitude that is quite different from the members of the class. He may believe that Miles Davis is the only musician that deserves consideration when jazz is discussed. The class members will not necessarily go along with this opinion, depending on the manner in which they evaluate the teacher. To see how this illustrates balance, let us look at the diagram.

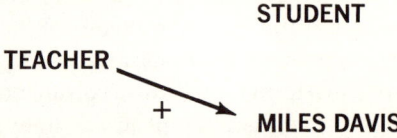

Notice that as yet there is no connection between the student and Miles Davis. Since we said that the teacher is positive about Miles Davis, we should put in a "plus" sign describing the relationship between the teacher and Miles Davis. Now let us suppose that the teacher is positively regarded by the student; thus a plus sign can be assigned here. The relationship between the student and Miles Davis will also have to be plus for the system to be in balance.

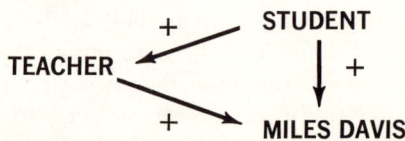

This is a good model for a communication to change attitudes—in that we as communicators need to have a positive bond between ourselves and the listener before we can bring about a positive effect in the listener concerning our subject matter. So far balance theory has not told us anything that we did not already suspect, however. Let us see what happens when a communicator approaches a receiver with a highly charged attitude for a subject and attempts to persuade the listener to change.

Let us suppose that a communicator wishes to enter a labor union and convince the union members that management is really their friend, and that the union members should vote a voluntary cut in pay to provide management with incentives for investment. To be sure, com-

---

[19] Jack W. Brehn and Arthur R. Cohen, *Explorations in Cognitive Dissonance*, (New York, 1962), p. 311.

municative attempts almost exactly like this one have been undertaken by management from time to time, and so the example is really not as farfetched as it might seem. But, to continue with our example, suppose a neutral source comes into the communicative interaction and attempts to do the same thing. Our interplay of forces will look something like this:

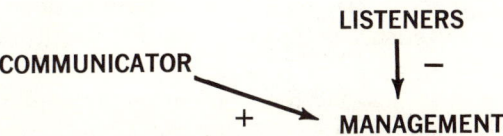

In this particular diagram, you will notice that no bond has been drawn between the communicator and the listeners, because this is the way the interaction begins. The listeners are against management, and the communicator is for management. The goal of the communicator is to move the listeners to change to be in favor of management. But unfortunately, if the attitude held is a fairly strong one, what is likely to happen is expressed in the following diagram:

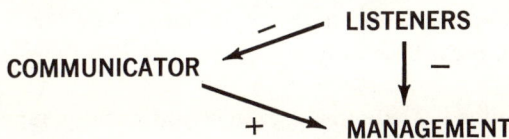

The system is still in balance, but the communicator has achieved the opposite of his desired effect; he has not only failed to win the listeners over to management, but he has failed to establish a positive relationship with them himself. If this speaker had expressed a negative statement about management, it is likely that the listeners' attitudes about him would have been quite favorable. It is important to notice that the diagram above is in balance for the listeners, but not for the communicator. This situation would be in balance if the negative link between the listeners and the communicator were mutual. If not, then the situation is not in balance for either side. Systems of this kind can be in balance for the communicator or in balance for the listeners, or both. But it is important to recognize which is which and to see what is considered important in the situation. Too many communicators convince themselves that they are really effective in situations like the above only because they are attempting to keep their own cognitions in balance.

The goal, then, in an attitudinally-oriented communication, is to bring about a state of balance by changing opinions—and this can only be done if the communicator is in a situation where the listeners cannot easily achieve a negative feeling about him. We then can see the utility of the evidential and logical strictures discussed at the beginning of this chapter. If a communicator presents a good deal of evidence in his case, then the listeners are aware that the source is well informed and is possessed of ample knowledge concerning the subject. This makes it more difficult for the audience to devalue the source by casting aspersions on his background. If the speaker presents an orderly, well thought out progression of ideas, the general impression is one of intelligence and method—characteristics that again make it difficult for an audience to value negatively.

Of course, it is possible for any listener to devalue almost any communicator. A good example of this occurred in the national press a few weeks after Dr. Benjamin Spock was arrested for counseling young men on methods of avoiding the draft. For years, Dr. Spock has been known as a humanitarian, a leader in his community, and the nation's most distinguished pediatrician. Following his stand on Vietnam, however, conservative editorial writers were referring to him as the "baby doctor" and cartoonists were drawing outlandish caricatures of Dr. Spock dressed in a Victorian baby's cap and waving a nursing bottle. Here is a classic case of a well-entrenched attitude turning the receiver against the communicator. If this can happen to Dr. Spock, it can happen to you, regardless of how well-prepared and well-informed you might be.

This chapter has attempted to give you some perspectives on the process of attitudes and opinion change as manifested in the oral communicative situation. It should be obvious to every reader that we have only scratched the surface. This is an enormously large subject and the student will profit a good bit from examining the list of readings appended to the end of this chapter. Communications that change attitudes are among the most difficult of human behaviors. It is not possible to be consistently successful in this endeavor, but experience, practice, and preparation will go a long distance in convincing your auditors to think as you do.

READINGS:

Erwin P. Bettinghaus, *Persuasive Communication*, (New York, 1968).
Martin Fishbein (ed.), *Readings in Attitude Theory and Measurement*, (New York, 1967).
Wallace Fotheringham, *Perspectives on Persuasion*, (New York, 1966).
Milton J. Rosenberg and others, *Attitude Organization and Change*, (New Haven, Conn., 1967).
Thomas Scheidel, *Persuasive Speaking*, (Evanston, Ill., 1967).

6 THE TRANSMITTERS OF ORAL COMMUNICATION

INTRODUCTION

Transmission in oral communication is accomplished through the use of the speaker's voice, articulation-pronunciation, and body—all of which help to convey a message to a listener or listeners. Obviously, man's refined abilities in the use of his vocal mechanism, coupled with his highly developed abilities to think and use symbols, make it possible for him to transmit information accurately and with a high degree of abstraction, using language as the tool. Voice and articulation convert "subvocal talking" into messages which can be picked up and understood by another person.

But the sender of a message has other resources which make it possible for him to reinforce the meaning which he imparts through oral language. The receptor of the message is capable of receiving and interpreting visual stimuli as well as auditory cues. In a face-to-face situation, the listener hears *and* sees the speaker. Thus, the control and use of bodily activity becomes an important aspect of transmission.

A speaker usually is motivated to talk by a strong desire to share an idea with another person. Obviously, he hopes that the listener will receive the same message which he sends. It is pointed out in another chapter that language is an important factor in accomplishing this goal. While voice and articulation are often considered merely the conveyors of the words, a more accurate view of vocal control recognizes that it adds to and enhances the message being sent in words. In addition, purposeful use of bodily activity may intensify the intent of the speaker and provide further guarantees against message distortion on the part of the listener.

Not many of us make full use of our potential vocal reinforcement. Improper use of the transmission system can easily distort the messages we send. But even more importantly, poor usage of the physical transmitters can mean serious loss of attention and subsequent loss of message. Thus, the communicator has at least two goals in developing skills of transmission—to avoid distortion of his message and to capture and maintain the attention of his receivers.

How is attention maintained? Most authorities agree that attention consists of two factors: the physical factor, and the psychological factor. The content of your communication furnishes the psychological factors, and the physical composition of your message furnishes the other attending habit. This form of attention is temporary and subject to change without notice, and is, additionally, easily distracted. These distractions may be external and apparent to the listener (noise, temperature) or internal (a private reaction to words or thoughts). They may simply result from that common activity, woolgathering!

We do know that some kinds of stimuli are more attention-getting than others. Let us look at some of the characteristics of attention-getting stimuli. The following list is adapted from Dashiell.[1]

1. **Intensity** A loud noise or a blinding flash of light is a fairly reliable stimulus for forcing the listener to reset himself. Other things being equal, the more intense the stimulation, the more likely it is to attract at least momentary attention.

2. **Extensity** This usually refers to visual stimuli, but might be applied to auditory stimuli in terms of the frequency or pitch, range from high to low. Other things being equal, the "larger" the stimulus, the more likely it is to be noticed. The wider the pitch range of the acoustic stimulus, the more apt it is to be attended.

3. **Duration and Repetition** By being repeated, a stimulus is more likely to be strengthened. Prolonging the duration of a stimulus will have effects which are very difficult to predict. It becomes a question of the attractiveness or the appeal of the stimulus itself to determine the point at which a prolonged exposure to the stimulus will beget attention or cause extinction.

4. **Movement** Just as electric signs produce the illusion of motion to attract the attention of a passerby, so the movement and gesture of the speaker will reinforce the set of the listener to attend.

5. **Change and Contrast** These are both closely related to movement. However, even without considering movement, the skillful speaker

[1] J. Dashiell, *Fundamentals of General Psychology*, (New York, 1949).

knows how to hold attention by judicious and meaningful changes in rate, loudness, and pitch. In a similar way, contrasts in language level and sentence length help to maintain the set to listen.

6 **Habits of Attention** Since set is, in part, a product of past experience, the listener's set will be created and will change in some measure according to his own constitution and background. Some listeners claim they pick up information faster in the presence of moderate noise or music, while others insist that for them the reverse is true.

It should be obvious that one way that we can utilize any of these attention factors is in the mastery of the transmitters of communication. In this chapter, an attempt will be made to help you to understand how the transmitters function, what interferes with their efficiency and effectiveness, and the complexity involved in the coordination of the various elements involved in transmission.

It is not enough for you—an individual interested in improving your oral communication—to understand the role of the transmitters in speaking. The ultimate goal is for you to develop the necessary skill and control in the use of voice, articulation, pronunciation, and bodily activity, in order that your messages will reach your listeners intact. Essential to the attainment of this goal is the need to understand how the vocal mechanism functions in producing speech.

In this chapter, an attempt will be made to explore the functioning of the transmitters, the conditions which interfere with their efficiency and effectiveness, and the complexity involved in the coordination of the various elements involved in transmission. Hopefully, this knowledge will be the basis upon which you begin a program of self-improvement.

THE VOCAL MECHANISM

Most species in the animal kingdom are capable of creating vocal sounds. Vocalization is produced by dogs, cats, birds, dolphins, cows, lions, horses, and bees, to mention but a few. The sounds produced by each of these creatures are vastly different—the quality of the sounds extends from the musical tones of some birds down to the "noise" of locusts; the loudness varies considerably from the trumpeting of the elephant to the weak signal of the bee; the duration of the sound ranges from short vocalization like the ultrasonic pulse or clicks of the bat to the prolonged howl of the wolf.

The human voice is one of the more flexible and musical. Yet basically it is produced in a manner which is common to all voice producing animals. Air is expelled from the lungs through the windpipe and larynx to the oral cavities and flows out or is forced out through the mouth or nose. Let us examine this principle of voice production in man.

There are four elements which are present in most sound producing systems. These elements are: (1) a source of energy, (2) a vibrator, (3) a resonator, and (4) obviously, air, through which the sound waves are propagated from the source to the receiver.

Musical instruments all require a source of energy to set their vibrators in motion. The specific nature of the force generated by this source varies from instrument to instrument. In the case of the tympanic family, a mallet or stick is struck against the skin, setting it in motion. In the string family, a slender strand of catgut may be stroked by a bow, initiating a vibratory pattern. A saxophone is representative of a number of musical instruments in which air is blown through the mouthpiece setting the vibrator in motion. This method of energizing a vibrator is not unlike the principle involved in voice production, which requires a steady stream of air to set the vocal folds in motion.

How is this continuous, steady air stream created for human speech? Let us look at the quiet life breathing cycle and the adjustments which must be made in order to utilize exhalation for the production of speech.

In order to maintain life, air laden with oxygen is taken into the lungs. It is usually inhaled through the nose and then flows into the lungs through the intake valve known as the larynx (sometimes referred to as the voice box) and then into the windpipe. The windpipe or trachea divides into two tubes in order to channel air into each lung. Each of these tubes subdivides into a maze of tiny tubules and minute chambers resulting in the spongelike tissues of the lungs. Here the oxygen is exchanged for body wastes in the form of carbon dioxide which saturates the blood stream. The process of exhalation makes it possible to discharge the carbon dioxide into the air; the air is squeezed out of the lungs at a slightly faster rate than that of inhalation, following the path of inhalation in reverse.

Observe your own breathing. Do not speak, but notice the gradual and steady intake of air and the slightly accelerated rate of expulsion. Now, say and prolong the sound "ah." Notice first that you inhaled more sharply and that the air is expelled slowly and steadily through your mouth. Now prepare to say "ah" again, but instead of producing voice, breathe the air out through your mouth which is in the position to say "ah." Now alternate the voiced "ah" with the silent one. Can you feel the difference? In the voiced sound you should feel a tingling sensation in your throat, the result of vibrations arising from the two ligaments that run from front to back in the larynx. Place your fingers on either side of your throat and repeat the voiced sound and feel the vibrations which are being produced by the vocal folds.

So the breathing pattern changes somewhat in preparation for vocalization. You inhale more quickly, and in connected speech you exhale much more slowly, conserving the outgoing breath stream in order to be able to say whole phrases or sentences without interruption. Control of the outgoing breath stream is extremely important. There must be a steady expulsion of air with force appropriate to the production of the kind of a sound you desire. The amount of air inhaled is of minor importance; the control of the exhalation pattern plays a more important role in determining the characteristics of the sound produced.

The vocal folds serve a similar function to the reed in a saxophone; both are energized by air pressure and both produce vibrations of sufficient frequency to be interpreted by the receiver as sound. In other words, both are vibrators which are essential to sound production.

The length and mass of a vibrator determine the pitch of the produced sound. For example, the heavy and/or short strings on a piano produce lower frequencies. These strings do not vibrate as rapidly and the sound is perceived by the listener as having a low pitch. Tension in the string also influences the frequency of the vibrations and the perceived pitch. The greater the tension in a vibrator, the higher the frequency and the higher the perceived pitch.

Typically men's voices are pitched approximately an octave below women's voices. This does not seem surprising when we consider the facts of sound production. Men's vocal folds tend to be more massive than women's, hence they are not capable of as rapid vibration. Therefore, they are perceived as having lower pitch.

If the vocal folds are fairly flaccid, the vibrations will be comparatively slow and the pitch of the resulting sound will be proportionately low. Likewise, if the vocal folds are stretched tightly, increasing their tension, the vibrations become very rapid and the perceived pitch of the voice is high.

The speaker should be able to exert control over the tautness of his vocal folds, thereby giving him the ability to adjust the pitch of his voice within certain limits. This control permits rapid changes and fine adjustments of pitch which help to reinforce the meaning of the language he is using.

Try this simple experiment. Find a two-inch rubber band and loop one end of the band around a tack fastened to the edge of a bulletin board or a notebook. Now stretch the band to a length of six or eight inches and pluck as you would a banjo string. First, notice the sound you have caused and then watch the movement of the strand of rubber. The band moves rapidly from side to side, displacing the air that surrounds it. The disturbance in the air reaches the ear of the listener and is interpreted as sound. Although the action of the rubber band in creating the vibrations is somewhat different from the action of the vocal folds, the resulting vibrations are similar.

Repeat the experiment, this time stretching the rubber band to twelve or fourteen inches in order to increase its tautness and decrease its mass. Pluck the string again. Notice this time that the pitch is higher and that the speed with which the band vibrates is more rapid.

In order to produce sound, then, a source of energy and a vibrator are essential. In the human voice, the outgoing breath stream provides the energy necessary to set the vocal folds (vibrators) in motion.

Resonators amplify and enhance the quality of the sound created by the outgoing breath stream which sets the vocal folds in motion. The sound produced by the vibrators is relatively weak.

You can perform another experiment with your rubber band which will illustrate the principal of resonance. Place the rubber band around a water glass—across the top, down the sides, and across the bottom. Now pluck the part of the band that is stretched across the open part of the glass and notice the change of the sound produced in your original experiment. The sound is richer and fuller; it also appears to be louder. This change is due to the effect of the resonator, in this case a space enclosed by the glass, open at the top. The vibratory motion produced by the moving rubber band sets the air in the glass in similar motion, thereby reinforcing the original sound and increasing its perceived loudness. Moreover, this type of resonator is capable of reinforcing particular frequencies, depending upon the shape and size of the cavity and the shape and size of its openings.

The vibratory motion which results from the action of the vocal folds is a complex one, and it produces a complex tone. In other words, the sound is made up of a fundamental vibration which is perceived by the listener as being the pitch of that particular voice, and a whole series of partials (vibrations of greater frequency). The listener does not identify these partials—he does not hear them as separate pitches. Rather the fundamental vibration and the partial vibrations merge to form a complex wave pattern which affects the listener's perception of quality. The partial vibrations are responsible for the overtones. Appropriate resonance may add great beauty and audibility to the human voice.

In human voice production, the major resonators are the mouth, the space at the back of the throat (called the pharynx), and, for certain sounds, the nasal cavities. The vibrations produced by the action of the vocal folds reverberate in these spaces and take on new complexity; a strengthened, richer, fuller, more musical sound usually results. The walls of the resonator cavities are also potential amplifiers of sound. However, they can have the opposite effect if the muscular tension of these walls is not properly adjusted; then they may act as absorbers of sound.

Man's vocal mechanism, then, permits him to produce full, rich, musical sounds at various pitches. In addition, man is able to exert conscious control over the degree of loudness he produces. Like the violinist who bows the strings with greater energy to produce a louder sound, the speaker first must increase the pressure of exhalation. In other words, the greater the pressure applied to the vibrator, the louder the sound.

Apply this rule to other vibrators. The drummer hits the head of his drum (the vibrator) with greater force in order to secure a louder sound; the pianist strikes the key which in turn raises the hammer to hit the strings with more force to produce intensified sound. In the case of your stretched rubber band, if you pluck it with more force, the resulting sound will be louder.

In order to demonstrate another aspect of loudness reinforcement, put the rubber band around the water glass again. Pluck the part of the band that is stretched across the open part of the glass. Then set the glass on a table or a chest of drawers and repeat the experiment. Now you will be aware of increased loudness due to increased resonance. The table and the glass are both serving as resonators; not only do they reinforce and improve the quality of the sound, but also they amplify or increase its loudness.

In vocal production, loudness is increased not only by exerting additional air pressure on the vocal folds, but also through the reinforcement provided by the resonators and their surfaces. The vibrations produced in the larynx find their ways into the appropriate cavities where they are *amplified* and *modified*.

The vocal mechanism is an essential transmitter in oral communication. For the best results, it must be structurally sound. In addition, the individual must be capable of controlling its use in the production of speech under any type of internal or external pressure.

At times, because of the multiple functions of the parts of the vocal mechanism, speech formation may encounter interference. In the first place, voice production makes use of structures which have been developed for more important purposes. The breathing process, which provides the energy for speech, is of primary concern in the maintenance of life; as it has been pointed out, it provides the means of exchanging oxygen for carbon dioxide formed in physiological processes. The larynx acts as a valve for inhalation and exhalation, and is constructed to prevent foreign materials from entering the windpipe. Other parts of the speech mechanism also have more important functions to perform which sometimes take precedence over voice production. Coughing to expel a particle of food or swallowing saliva are examples of urgent needs which can interfere with or prevent speech temporarily.

If the speaker has adequate control, he is able to produce speech in spite of the fact that it is a secondary function of the structures involved. He is able to coordinate the primary and secondary functions of the mechanisms involved so that there will be a minimum of conflict.

But the speaker not only must exert this type of control over his speech mechanism, but must also be able to modify his vocal characteristics so that voice, in addition to making speech possible, is used to enhance and clarify the message inherent in the words he uses. How is this achieved?

VOCAL CHARACTERISTICS

Any musical sound has certain dimensions which can be described by the receiver. Generally, we can talk about the *pitch, quality,* and *loudness* of sound. In a symphony, the composer uses these variable characteristics of sound to create an auditory experience which is capable of producing a somewhat similar response from the listeners. He makes use of changes of pitch to produce a pleasurable stimulus; he takes advantage of the fact that different musical instruments have vastly different qualities, and he indicates marked changes in loudness to assist him in creating the effect which he is trying to achieve. He also is aware of the importance of changes in rate and rhythm as another way of heightening the effect of his musical patterns.

The effective speaker uses these variable characteristics of sound to assist him in clarifying and enhancing the message he is trying to convey in words. He attempts to develop control of these elements so that his vocal characteristics, rather than arousing a negative or neutral response from his listeners, heighten his impact and further insure the reception of an undistorted message.

Pitch

Pitch, the first variable characteristic of voice, refers to the perceived place of the vocalization on the musical scale. Pitch is our interpretation of the frequency of the sound. It has been pointed out that the slower the vibratory pattern, the lower the pitch of the sound; the higher the frequency of vibrations, the higher the pitch. Hence, pitch is the psychological correlate of frequency.

The pitch of the voice is constantly changing in order to reinforce meaning and add color to speech. At the same time, there is a habitual basic pitch level which dominates in voice production and causes the listener to say: "His voice is pitched high," or "Her voice is lower than most women's voices," or "His voice is unusually low pitched." The habitual pitch and the possible range of pitch at the speaker's disposal are determined by the physical characteristics of the vocal mechanism, the tension in the mechanism, and the skill which the individual has developed in controlling the mechanism.

Both the speaking and singing ranges of pitch available to a person are determined first by the size, shape, and flexibility of the vocal folds. Similarly, in a stringed instrument, the lowest and highest notes possible are limited by the size, shape, and the flexibility of the strings. The violin, the smallest of the string family, has the thinnest and shortest vibrators and can be compared with the soprano voice in singing. The instrument is incapable of pleasant low pitch. The viola, similar in range to the alto voice, has strings somewhat thicker which cannot vibrate as rapidly as those of the violin and therefore cannot produce the high pitch of that instrument. The tenor voice is comparable to the cello, which has even thicker strings than the viola. And finally, the bass, with its very large, thick, long strings produces only relatively low pitch and could be compared to the bass singing voice.

Generally, a man's vocal folds are longer, heavier, and less flexible than a woman's; therefore, his possible pitch range is at the lower end of the musical scale, whereas the woman's is generally higher on the scale.

The range varies within the sexes, too. Consider for example, the singing ranges of typical vocal types, as indicated below:

DIAGRAM 1

```
        LOW         MIDDLE          HIGH
    C D E F G A B C D E F G A B C D E F G A B C D E F G A B C
                    '                                '
                                    soprano
                        '           alto         '
                '           bass        '
                            '           tenor        '
```

A soprano with a well-trained voice may be able to produce A below middle C with the same effectiveness that she can sing C above high C. This is a range of seventeen notes. The average alto voice has a much smaller range; in this case only ten notes. Moreover the range is concentrated around middle C. Likewise, the range of the bass voice is greater than that of the tenor, and while most of this range is below middle C, the tenor's range is concentrated about middle C.

Similar variances occur in the speaking voice. The usable speaking range may not be as great as that of the singing range, but there is a satisfactory, usable range on which the speaker can depend for variety to be used for the purposes of emphasis and color. This range is not the same for everybody, even for people of the same sex.

It has been pointed out that the male voice is usually an octave lower than the female voice. The average habitual pitch of the male voice is about 125 cycles per second. This frequency produces a pitch close to

B flat which is 12 tones below middle C on the tempered scale of the piano. The average habitual pitch of the female voice is approximately 250 cycles per second, which comes very close to middle C. Obviously, all male and female voices are not pitched at 125 and 250 cycles per second, respectively. The pitch distribution for each sex would approximate a normal curve and there would be an overlap between the two curves with some women's voices being lower pitched than some of the male voices and some men's voices being higher than some female's.

Although a speaker should use variety in pitch, his voice has a dominant or habitual pitch. In most cases, the individual's habitual pitch is the best in terms of the capabilities of his vocal mechanism. In other words, his habitual pitch is his optimum pitch—the pitch at which he can produce the best quality and loudness. However, there are some people whose habitual pitch is not appropriate and a slight shift in the basic pitch of the voice may bring about improvements in other characteristics of the voice.

According to most voice scientists, the optimum pitch is 25 to 35 percent above the lowest usable pitch available to the speaker. Various techniques have been suggested for determining this optimum pitch. Of these, the one which makes use of the piano as a guide is probably the best one for your experimentation.

Sing the sound "ah" and locate the pitch on the piano. Then sing from that point down the scale to the lowest tone you can produce easily and well. Mark this point on the piano; using this pitch as a starting point, sing up the scale as high as you can go and without entering the falsetto range. Mark the high point in your scale. Repeat this procedure several times on different occasions in order to determine your complete range of pitch. Be sure to keep track of the high and low pitch each time, and when you feel fairly certain that you have established your true range, count the total number of notes in this range.

Your optimum pitch is probably one-fourth above the lowest pitch you have produced. In other words, if your range was 12 notes on the piano, your optimum pitch would be three notes above the lowest pitch you produced.

If there is a significant difference between your habitual pitch and the optimum pitch as indicated in the experiment, your vocal folds are probably capable of the necessary adjustment to raise or lower your habitual pitch. You should attempt to narrow the gap by trying to make your optimum pitch more nearly your habitual pitch. Remember that your voice quality will probably be improved as a result and that you will be able to produce sounds of greater intensity more easily.

Hum the optimum pitch as determined in the experiment. At first, be sure to give yourself the proper key, by striking the pitch on the piano. Once you are producing the pitch accurately, begin to chant at the same pitch. Then stop and begin over again. When you feel you can produce the pitch at will, start humming and *then* check your pitch with the piano and make the necessary adjustment.

Practice this procedure for a few minutes every day until you can produce your optimum pitch without the help of the piano. Continue chanting impromptu speech and gradually shift to a more conversational type of delivery with natural, meaningful pitch changes.

If pitch adjustment is indicated for you, it is important that you make the effort to accomplish this change. An extremely high-pitched voice is unpleasant and tiring to an auditor. Likewise, the unusually low voice may blur articulation and make the transmission of your message difficult for the listener.

The inappropriately high-pitched speaking voice may be a result of imitation, habit, or tension. It may also be the result of a physical abnormality, in which case you should consult an ear, nose, and throat specialist before making the effort to change your basic pitch. Otherwise, there is no reason why you should not be able to do something about lowering the pitch of your voice. If the cause of your problem is imitation or habit, first you must recognize that your voice is inappropriately pitched; then you must hear your voice as others hear it; discover your optimum pitch next; then try to adjust your basic pitch so that it is at least closer to your optimum pitch. It will require concentration, practice, and a real determination to replace the old habit with the new one.

The problem of a high basic pitch is sometimes due to emotional tension in the speaker which is reflected in physical tension. Since we know that the pitch of the voice rises with increased tension in the vocal folds, it is easy to understand how increased tension due to fatigue, stage fright, anger, or frustration may sometimes raise the pitch of the voice to an irritating level. If this is the cause, it is necessary for the speaker to examine his whole attitude toward speaking in an effort to become more objective and matter-of-fact, thus eliminating that part of his tension caused by lack of adjustment to the situation.

In addition to assuming a more suitable basic pitch, the speaker should learn to make use of greater variety of pitch in his speech. There is nothing so tiresome as a speaker who has a monotonous pitch level. Lacking anything but the most minute changes in pitch, he drones on, adding no "voice coloring" to his language. True, the words themselves convey meaning to the listener, but how much richer the impressions would be if the speaker reinforced his words and sentences with "vocal meaning." For example, the simple sentence, "I am going downtown," means the same to every listener. However, by the way it is said, through changing pitch and using inflections, the meaning can be enhanced so that the auditor not only knows that the person *is* going downtown but is able to read more subtle meanings into the sentence. He may discover how the speaker *feels* about going downtown; he may realize that in spite of all barriers the speaker *will* go to town. In other words, the meaning of the sentence is made more exact through the use of variety in pitch.

At the same time, the speaker must avoid repeating the same inflections over and over again, thus establishing a "pitch pattern." In effect, the repetition of an inflection is just as monotonous as the lack of any inflection. The speaker should try to vary the pitch of his voice in accordance with the meaning. If he concentrates on the meaning, there is little danger of acquiring an undesirable pitch pattern.

Proper pitch level is important in the effective transmission of speech. Moreover, adequate control of pitch makes it possible for the speaker to attach color and meaningful reinforcement to the words of his message. Appropriate changes in pitch can clarify meaning, can aid in securing and holding the auditor's attention, may assist in building imagery, and will certainly add interest to the speech.

Quality

This is a somewhat confusing term, difficult to define simply. An analogy may clarify the meaning of the term. Most people can hear the difference between two musical instruments, even though they are producing the same note on the musical scale with the same degree of loudness. For example, it is quite simple to perceive the difference between middle C played on a violin and on a French horn; though more difficult, it would still be possible to differentiate between an oboe and an English horn. The element which makes this discrimination possible is the *quality* of the sound, and every class of instruments has its own individuality. Musicians can even detect the difference in the quality of the sound between two violins or two oboes or any other pair of instruments of a specific type. It is on this basis that musicians select their instruments, and this is one of the reasons that a concert pianist may transport his piano from one town to another while on tour.

So it is with the human voice. It is possible to recognize an individual voice because of its distinctive quality. In some instances that quality is unusually pleasing; it is rich and full and musical. In other cases the quality of the voice is disagreeable. These qualities are determined by the size, shape, flexibility, and condition of the vocal folds, the size and shape and condition of the resonators, and the use that the speaker makes of the entire vocal mechanism.

If there is no physical defect in the vocal folds, and the resonators are the appropriate size and shape with appropriate openings, and if the speaker uses the mechanisms properly, he should be able to produce

THE TRANSMITTERS OF ORAL COMMUNICATION   175

vibrations which will result in pleasant musical sounds. Fortunately, there are few people whose vocal mechanisms are incapable of producing voice of reasonably good quality. However, too many times functional problems interfere with the production of acceptable voice.

The most common fault is in the use of the resonators. Each sound produced requires that the speaker use the proper resonators and that he adjust the size and shape of the space resonators and the size and shape of the openings in order to achieve the proper reinforcement.

All sounds make use of the space at the back of the throat and all or part of the oral cavity for resonance; however, only the "m," "n," and "ng" sounds are properly resonated in the nasal cavities. This means that the opening into the nasal cavities must be blocked for the production of all other consonants and for the vowel sounds.

Look at your throat in a mirror. The bell-like projection you see hanging at the back of your mouth is the uvula as seen from the front. The uvula gives added flexibility to the soft palate so that it can completely block the opening to the nasal cavities. By pressing back against the wall of the pharynx, the soft palate can seal off this opening into the nasal cavities.

In all sounds except the three mentioned above ("m," "n," and "ng"), there should be a complete blocking off of the nasal cavities. However, if the speaker permits some air to seep into the nasal cavities on other sounds, the result will be that the voice takes on a *nasal* quality which is generally unpleasant to the listener. In these instances, the soft palate may have moved back toward the closed position, but the closure has not been complete and part of the vibrating air has found its way into the nasal cavities where nasal resonance is developed.

If you suspect that you are nasalizing sounds other than the "m," "n," and "ng," place your fingers lightly on the bridge of your nose and say the following words: *let, lay, crate, tall, spit, bed, dabble, every, frail, gobble, halo,* and other words containing non-nasal sounds. If you feel any vibrations such as those present in your nose when you say "m," you can be sure that you are using nasal resonance improperly.

It is difficult to control consciously the mechanism that blocks off the nasal resonators. However, you can produce the non-nasal sounds properly through trial and error. If you cannot hear the nasality yourself, you can always check for its presence by the method described above. In trying to produce non-nasal sounds correctly, try to force all of the air out through your mouth.

If your voice quality has marked nasality and you have been unable to make the necessary adjustments to eliminate it, you may have to seek special help from your instructor or from a speech therapist. Possibly a structural abnormality is responsible for your difficulty, or you may need intensive supervised practice to eliminate your problem.

Occasionally, instead of being nasal, the voice quality is *denasal*. In this case, the speaker lacks nasal resonance. In other words, the nasal reinforcement necessary for the proper production of the "m," "n," and "ng" is reduced or completely lacking. The resulting voice is flat, dull, and sounds as if the person has a bad head cold, as indeed he may. Generally, this problem is due to a structural abnormality or to temporary changes in the mechanism cause by infections, injuries, or irritations. Denasal speech is also present when the sinus cavities are filled as a result of a cold. Specifically, then, any growth, disarrangement, congestion, or swelling which reduces the size of the nasal cavities could cut nasal resonance to a point where the voice quality is impaired. An individual with this type of problem should seek the help of a physician, once it is established that his problem is not due to bad habit. He may also need the services of a speech therapist who may help him to compensate for the reduction in nasal resonance.

The *muffled* voice is also due to improper use of the resonators. With this type of voice quality, the speaker generally holds his jaws somewhat rigidly with few adjustments and changes from sound to sound. Voice quality is partly dependent for proper reinforcement on the adaptation of the size and shape of the resonator and the adjustment of the size and shape of the opening of the resonator for proper production of each sound. The "tight jaw" obviously interferes with the maintenance of proper resonance.

This is probably most true of the vowel sounds. For example, the sound "ah" should be made with the tongue in a flat, low position, with the mouth open wide, and with the lower jaw dropped. In order to produce this sound accurately and to ensure *proper resonance,* the mouth cavity and its openings must be adjusted for the sound. Say the sound properly and then raise your lower jaw so that there is no more than one-half inch of space between your teeth and produce the sound again. Notice the difference between the two sounds. The first one should have a richer, fuller sound, because it has been properly reinforced. The second sound is tight and flat and muffled, lacking suitable resonance.

Every sound requires a certain kind of resonance for its proper production. The oral cavity should constantly be adjusted in shape and size to modify the space which creates the resonance. Likewise, the space at the back of the throat must be used to the best advantage for each sound. If your voice is tight, flat, or muffled, try using a greater degree of jaw, tongue, and lip movements, remembering that all sounds require, first of all, different adjustments of the articulators, which may limit this jaw movement.

Breathiness, another problem of quality, is caused by a different lack of control. Characterized by a half-whispered effect, it gives the impression that the voice is being held back. It is a pseudo modulation which makes the speaker appear affected or uncertain of himself. Another type of breathiness is displayed by the speaker who has excessive exhalation before he begins to produce voice.

Poor breath control, inability to bring the vocal folds together for vocalization, inadequate adjustment to the speaking situation, or a combination of several of these causes may be responsible for the breathy voice. Once the cause has been established, the speaker must make every effort to change his speech production pattern in a way that will eliminate or reduce this excessive breathiness. Here are some general recommendations which may help you in learning to control your outgoing breath stream so that air is not wasted.

Inhale and count fairly slowly as far as possible on the air you have stored from this one inhalation. Be careful not to take short breaths between numbers. Now inhale again and try to conserve your breath as you count. Tighten up the diaphragm and the muscles in your chest and allow just enough air to escape for vocalization. Try to count further than you did the first time. Keep track of the highest number to which you can count on one inspiration. Be sure that you produce voice loud enough to be heard easily. Practice this drill several times each day, working to produce good full sound without the fuzziness of excessive breathiness.

In most cases, *hoarse* and *husky* voices are due to physical causes; that is, a person with such a problem may have strained his vocal mechanism yelling at a football game; he may have a cold which has "settled in his throat" and developed into laryngitis, in which the vocal folds are so swollen and infected that they are incapable of producing suitable vibrations; or in severe cases, the vocal folds may be so irritated over a long period of time that they have developed little growths which prevent vibrations capable of being interpreted as musical sound. These are all problems for the specialist. You should seek help from a doctor, preferably an ear, nose, and throat specialist (otolaryngologist) for evaluation and treatment. You may also seek the assistance of a speech therapist. The speech pathologist and medical specialist usually work in concert to help you to improve voice production.

Loudness

Loudness, the third variable of voice, refers to the degree of vocal loudness or softness. Any voice must be sufficiently loud to be heard easily and clearly without undue effort on the part of the listener. This means, of course, that a speaker must adjust the loudness of his voice to the size of the room in which he is speaking. If he is talking from the platform in an auditorium containing several hundred people he must speak louder than he would in a classroom with fifteen or twenty persons present. Conversely, in a small dormitory room, speaking with his roommate, much less voice is required.

The awareness of loudness on the part of the auditor is conditioned by his psychological state. Excitement, depression, preoccupation, or other attitudes or emotions affecting the auditor may decrease his sensitivity to sound. The speaker must be aware of this mental state of his auditor and must adjust the loudness level to compensate for his auditor's listening resistance.

The speaker must remember, too, that the carrying qualities of his voice are in part dependent on the physical composition of the voice. Equivalent loudness in various voices does not ensure equal carrying power, since the pitch and the resonance balance of the voice both help to determine its carrying power. The speaker will have to test the loudness of his voice in terms of audience reaction to his unique combination of vocal characteristics.

Speakers are sometimes careless about or unable to adjust their voices to the particular speaking situation, and do not realize that their voices are too loud or too soft for the size of the room or the "atmosphere" of the speaking situation.

Remember, in the case of the overly loud voice, that you are probably providing too much energy for vocalization. Conserve your air supply for sustained speech; don't waste it on too much intensity. Conversely, if people must strain to hear you, try to exert more pressure on the vocal folds by expelling air faster and with greater force.

In addition to producing voice suitable to the physical and emotional aspects of the situation, the good speaker varies loudness in order to emphasize important points, as a means of securing and holding attention and interest, and as a way of releasing his own tensions. He changes his loudness level as his material changes, using both increases and decreases for the reinforcements described. A very important or inspiring point can be emphasized either by greater loudness or softness. The technique should be selected on the basis of what kind of loudness has preceded the idea and the quality of the material itself. You generally don't *shout* when the subject is tender! But you probably would use a good deal of volume urging your favorite team on to win! Yes, you might even shout!

The meaning of even a sentence can be changed substantially by shifting the maximum or minimum loudness from word to word. For example, it is possible to transmit seven different ideas with the sentence, "I never said he stole the money," by changing the loudness stress on the words.

Try reading the sentence aloud, using your maximum loudness on the first word. "*I* never said he stole the money," suggests that *you* weren't the one who said he took the money. If you shift the maximum loudness to the "never," you change the message to, "At *no* time did I ever accuse him of stealing the money."

With each change of loudness emphasis, you change the meaning. Try reading the statement all seven ways, continuing to shift the loudness stress one word at a time. Note that the messages are different.

In your use of loudness as a reinforcement of your speech, avoid loudness patterns whereby you repeat the same sequence of changes over and over again. The most common of these is the gradual fading of the volume in each sentence spoken by the person. By the end of the sentence the voice is so soft that it is almost impossible to hear. The repetition of this pattern may attract as much attention as what the speaker is saying. Moreover, it is exasperating to the listener to miss the last part of every sentence.

ARTICULATION-PRONUNCIATION

Vocalization is sometimes used to transmit information. A baby cries because of discomfort; he makes cooing sounds to signal comfort and contentment. Birds communicate with their mates and babies with a variety of musical calls. Some adult birds "scold" audibly when their nests and young are threatened by the presence of squirrels. Many of the sounds produced in the animal world are purposeful, produced with the intent of conveying a message to another of the species. It is apparent that this vocalization, then, can be controlled and that signals which are sent, reflect a reaction to the elements in the environment.

But the extent of the differentiation that can be achieved with vocalization seems limited in human infants and in nonhuman species. Variety can be achieved by changing the pitch, the loudness pattern, the quality of the sound, the duration, and the manner in which the vocalization is released.

As far as we know, man's abilities to modify vocalization to create individual sounds in an almost unending combination is unique. This ability seems to set man apart from most species of the animal kingdom and provides him with the potential for a systematized code with which he can communicate. This code, *language*, is so extensive that man may relay reactions to the immediate environment, but he can also deal with the most abstract concepts and ideas. In a very real sense, man's ability to articulate has made him superior in the realm of oral communication.

In order to produce musical sound, four elements are necessary, including a source of energy, vibration, resonance, and a medium through which sound waves travel. Intelligible speech cannot be achieved without the addition of *articulation* and *pronunciation*. The term *articulation* refers to the formation of individual speech sounds and the word *pronunciation* relates to the fitting together of these sounds into words. These two processes are largely responsible for man's ability to communicate with an extensive and precise code.

Upon analysis, we find that the smallest unit of language which conveys meaning is a *word*. A word is made up of a sequence of sounds, in a particular order, divided into convenient syllables, with a pre-established accent. Since the ability to form individual sounds is the first prerequisite to the production of a word, let us examine this phenomenon.

Articulation

The modification of the outgoing breath stream which is essential to the formation of individual sounds is achieved through changes in the positions of the articulators. The lips, the teeth, the tongue, and the hard and soft palates are utilized in different combinations and positions to produce a variety of sounds which are recognizable and accepted in a particular language. For example, to create the initial sound in the word "let," the tip of the tongue is lifted and touches the back of the upper teeth, the ridge above the teeth, or the front part of the hard palate. The air is then expelled over the sides of the tongue and out through the open mouth. This manipulation of the articulators, together with the vocalization produced by the vocal folds and amplification provided by the resonators, produces a sound with peculiar acoustical characteristics which are identified with the printed letter "l."

Thus, intelligible speech is dependent upon the articulator's modification of the outgoing breath stream to produce recognizable sounds. Sometimes the exhaled air is set in motion by the movement of the vocal folds as in the case of the sound *l*, described above, or the sound *v*. In the latter sound, the vibrating air is resonated (reinforced and amplified) largely in the space at the back of the throat and in the mouth and is forced out through small openings between the upper teeth and the lower lip. Say the sound *v*; place your fingers on your larynx and feel the vibrations; notice also the tingling, tickling sensation that the vibrating air creates as it passes over your lower lip.

At other times, the voice mechanism does not operate in the same way. The air escapes from the windpipe, through the larynx, without being set in motion. But the sound can be created largely by the articulators in this case. This type of sound is dependent upon the nature of the expulsion of the air from the mouth. The *f* sound, for example, depends for its individuality upon the fact that a friction noise is created by the air being forced out through the small openings between the upper teeth and the lower lip.

Each sound is then partly dependent for its individuality on whether or not there is vocalization, on the position of the articulators, and on the way the air is expelled from the mouth or nose. These characteristics vary slightly from person to person. Sounds may be produced differently by different persons, but as long as the acoustic result is the same, the manner of production is unimportant. But if the sound is acoustically deficient, it is incorrect. For example, in the case of the *l* sound, if it is produced with the tongue halfway between the upper and lower teeth, a vowel-like sound is produced. Experiment with the sound: first say it correctly, with contact between the tip of your tongue and the upper teeth, teeth ridge, or hard palate. Now try to say the sound with your tongue in the other position. Compare the resulting sounds. There is a considerable difference, isn't there? And only the first one is acceptable.

There are four types of articulatory problems: sound substitutions, sound distortions, omission of sounds, and the addition of sounds. The latter two seem directly related to pronunciation since identification of the deficiencies cannot be made without words and/or connected speech. However, a brief explanation of the four types of problems may be helpful in helping you to assess your own articulatory effectiveness.

Sound substitutions, with one known sound being substituted for another, are particularly common among young children. Since some sounds are more difficult to identify and produce, a child may substitute a similar and easier sound for the troublesome one. For example, a "w" may be substituted for the more difficult "r" in words like radio (wadio), run (wun), and rabbit (wabbit). Such substitutions are not unexpected in the speech of a child. However, when a young adult persists in substituting "w" for "r," "th" for "f" (thine for fine), the voiced "th" for "v" (thiolin for violin), "th" for "s" (thunny for sunny), and the like, an effort must be made to modify his production of the incorrect sound. This is particularly important if there are multiple sound substitutions.

There are other common substitutions which are a result of imitation, regional influences, and the relative ease of producing the substituted sound in comparison to the desired sound. Many persons have difficulty in attaching the proper sound to the "e" in words such as g*e*t, *a*ny, *e*ngineer, wh*e*n, and p*e*n. Habitually, these persons say "git" for "get," "iny" for "any," "ingineer" for "engineer," and so on. Another substitution occurs in the word "just" which is often pronounced "jist" or "jest"; and yet another in "for" which becomes "fer."

Problems of sound distortion are probably not as common as sound substitutions. However, many times the former are more distasteful to the listener. For example, some persons produce the "s" sound with the articulators in the position for the "l" sound; the noisy, unpleasant, slushy sound resulting is called a "lateral lisp" and is particularly unpleasant from the auditor's point of view. In a sound distortion, no recognizable sound is substituted; rather, the individual produces a new sound—one that deviates too far from the accepted form to be acceptable.

Problems of omission and addition are highly individualized. Sometimes, the omissions are due to an extremely rapid rate in speaking and therefore do not follow any pattern. However, occasionally the omissions are consistent; that is, the same sound or sounds are omitted in every word. The latter problem is of more concern because it often indicates a physical cause. For example, an individual who has a hearing loss may find it difficult if not impossible to hear the acoustic pattern of a particular sound and therefore is unable to produce it. In such a case, the troublesome sound may be omitted from his speech.

Inconsistent omissions are usually due to carelessness and, strictly speaking, should not be classified as articulatory problems. It is not unusual, for example, to hear "probly" for "probably," "cause" for "because," "libary" for "library." Again imitation and carelessness are probably the primary causes.

Additions, which are also infrequent, are often due to imitation of another person and may reflect foreign background and dialectical differences. For example, you must have heard the word sing pronounced "sing-g" with a hard "g" tacked on to the word.

Sometimes overpreciseness results in sound additions. The word "often," which is correctly pronounced without the "t," is produced sometimes just the way it is spelled. Many people, in an effort to be very correct, say "elum" for "elm," "filum" for "film," and even, occasionally, "sword" for "sord," including the sound "w."

The average person has few of these marked deviations. However, it is the exceptional person who has consistently careful and accurate sound production. To begin with, many speakers are careless in the production of final plosive sounds such as "p," "b," "t," "d," "k," and "g." For example, the final "t" in the word "script" may be omitted or improperly exploded. The word may now sound like "scrip." The "pt" combination is a difficult one and the result is an omitted sound. Other difficult combinations include "sts," "sks," "fth," and "ngth." In the following words, which pronunciation is easier: "asts" or "asks"; "fift" or "fifth"; "lenth" or "length"? Notice the marked adjustment in the position of the articulators that you must make to say the word correctly. Many of us take the easier way and create a sound substitution or omission.

The inability of some people to combine certain sounds in sequence is reflected in the pronunciation of "library." It is not uncommon to hear "libary," which is much easier to say. Also, "Febjuary" is easier than "February" and so the former has become the more common pronunciation.

In some instances we hear rather marked deviations. It is not unusual to hear "mgonna," "gimme," "pleasta meetcha," "wherejago?" These are examples of common, inconsistent substitutions, omissions, and/or distortions of sounds we hear almost every day.

In an earlier section of this chapter, it was pointed out that a muffled voice quality is often due to oral inactivity. A rigid jaw also may have an effect on articulation. The articulators cannot perform their appropriate functions in the production of some sounds if the lower jaw movements are restricted. Many sounds are distorted as a result of oral inactivity and the over-all clarity of the resulting speech is diminished. This particular problem seems to be common among students; indeed, Americans in general are often criticized for speaking with a "lazy jaw."

Clarity of articulation is a necessity for effective and swift transmission of words which carry at least a part of your message to your listener. In a way, it is too bad that so many of us "get by" with inaccurate and/or careless formation of speech sounds; this fact decreases motivation which is essential to changing a habit.

Another complication often encountered by a person with substandard articulation is his inability to identify his own errors. If no one calls his articulatory problems to his attention, chances are good that he will not recognize his inadequacies. So, accept the help of your teacher in identifying your errors as the first step in improving your articulation.

Identification is only the initial step in modifying your formation of speech sounds. This must be followed by a program of ear training in which you learn to differentiate between the right and wrong sounds so that you will be able to recognize the error when it occurs in your own speech. Finally, after you have learned to produce the new sound at will, you must make a concerted effort to use it consistently in connected speech.

It has been suggested that articulatory problems may be due to physical causes. Among these would be brain damage, hearing loss, cleft palate and lip, improperly occluded teeth, and a variety of other organic problems. Persons whose articulatory differences are traceable directly to such causes should be referred to a speech clinic where they will have access to well trained therapists who in turn may refer them for additional help to the medical profession, to psychologists, or other specialists who may be of help.

Fortunately, the majority of articulatory deficiencies are functional problems and should be more readily modifiable. The most common causes of articulatory problems are bad habit, imitation of a model with poor speech, poor sound discrimination, foreign background, lazy articulators, and carelessness. Because the speech mechanism is capable of producing the correct sound, the prognosis here is favorable.

In spite of the difficulties associated with what appears to be a rather simple task, you can improve your articulation. In the absence of physical causes, your improvement will be limited only by lack of recognition of your problem, practice, and persistence. Any efforts that you make to cultivate more accurate formation of the speech sounds will contribute to the over-all objective of improving your ability to transmit facts, ideas, feelings, and beliefs to another person.

Pronunciation

Assuming that we have established consistent production of accurate speech sounds, we still face another related problem—that of putting the sounds together in proper sequence and with appropriate accents. The finest articulation does not guarantee that words will be pronounced according to accepted standards.

The English language is far from being a phonetic language. Unlike the Spanish language in which the letters signal a specific sound, in English the spelling of a word often does not give clues for its pronunciation. The letter "a" in a Spanish word is always articulated "ah." In English, the letter "a" can represent several sounds. Pronounce the words "comma," "cat," "made," "claw," "calm" and "aisle." In each of these words, the letter "a" represents a different sound.

We also pronounce identical letter combinations differently in different words. Consider, for example, "rough," "through," "hiccough," "though," "bough," and "cough." If letter combinations always represented the same sounds, the "ough" in each of these words would be pronounced alike. Yet none of these words rhymes with any other; the last part of each word is pronounced differently.

To further complicate pronunciation, a single sound may be represented by several spellings. In "lie," "climb," "buy," and "aisle" the vowel sound is represented by four different spellings.

How do we learn what sounds and accents to use in a word? Our first pronunciations were imitations of the patterns used by our parents, brothers and sisters, friends, and anyone else with whom we came in contact. With our entry into school, teachers began to influence our pronunciation more and more, making a special effort in the teaching of reading to provide us with an accurate production of each word. As we were introduced to radio, television, movies, and other forms of entertainment, we found new sources of information concerning the formations of words.

The bulk of the spoken words we used as models in our formative years were accurately formed. However, at times we were exposed to inaccurate models which we copied. In the absence of any corrective measures, these mispronunciations become a part of our habitual speech pattern. Children, hearing a teacher refer to a "sandwich" as "sand-ridge" may copy her pronunciation, not realizing that the model is incorrect. If we live in an area where there are regional differences, obviously we will adopt the pronunciations of the area without any regard for dictionary guidelines. Thus, in some sections of the country where there are heavy concentrations of Scandinavian people, "pople" becomes the accepted pronunciation for "poplar."

Sometimes we are exposed to a new word in our reading, we guess at its pronunciation, and a new mispronunciation may be added to our spoken vocabulary. For example, in an earlier section of this chapter, the word "flaccid" was used. From the context, you probably knew or guessed that the word means "relaxed" or "limp." But do you know the proper pronunciation? It doesn't appear to be a tricky word and you might guess that it is pronounced "flassid." However, the correct pronunciation is "flak-sid." Many words are spelled in such a way that you really do not get clues for pronunciation.

Another problem which complicates our pronunciation is the fact that some of us do not have a high degree of facility for remembering a series of sounds in a particular sequence. We hear a word, but when we try to reproduce it, we simply cannot recall all of the sounds and their order. This inability, which accounts for the difficulty that many of us have in learning to speak a foreign language, also is responsible for inaccurate pronunciation of our own language. Children often have trouble learning the proper pronunciation of words such as "elephant," or "aluminum," and the blame may be placed on their inability to remember sound sequences. Even adults have difficulty, especially with a word such as "statistics," which is so frequently called "stastistics."

Man's ability to remember complicated sound sequences was really put to a test by the made up word, SUPERCALIFRAGILISTICEXPIA-LIDOTIOUS, which appeared in a song written for the movie, *Mary Poppins.* Amazing as it may seem, pronunciation of the word seemed to cause little difficulty for small children. The rhythm established by the song seemed to be of some help; the word fascinated people; it was considered a rare accomplishment to say the word properly. In other words, there was strong motivation to learn the word properly, using the pronunciation presented in the film and reproduced on records as the standard.

Granted that we have the desire to cultivate consistently good pronunciation, where do we turn for models? Who determines what is right or wrong? Is there only one pronunciation that is acceptable? All of these questions focus on one problem: what is correct pronunciation?

In this book, *Voice Training for Speaking and Reading Aloud*, Paul Heinberg suggests that "it is essential that you acquire a philosophy—meaning a belief in certain principles—of pronunciation if affectation is to be avoided."[2] He goes on to point out that unlimited freedom of pronunciation is not desirable because a speaker's words might not be recognizable for the listener.

Hence, some sort of standard of pronunciation is necessary. The question becomes one relating to a choice of standard. Heinberg continues his discussion of pronunciation standards saying that a word should communicate the same meaning to as many persons as possible with as little distraction as possible. In other words, "good pronunciations are those with maximum intelligibility and minimum distractability."[3]

Heinberg then proposes and evaluates five possible pronunciation standards to assist the reader in the development of a pronunciation philosophy.[4]

1. The Majority Standard—that pronunciation used by the majority of the people in the country. Heinberg concludes his discussion of this standard by saying, "When a person who argues for the majority standard realizes the extent of uniqueness of pronunciations within each region (of the country), he tends to forego his adherence to such an artificial standard, preferring instead what is called the regional standard."
2. The Regional Standard—different standards would be established for different regions of the country. Mr. Heinberg points out this standard "is practically unwise because it contravenes interregional communication, which in the United States is increasing daily in both quantity and importance."
3. The Authoritarian Standard—pronunciation imposed by an officially sanctioned council, such as L'Office du Vocabulaire Français in France. Mr. Heinberg vetoes this standard saying, "To construe democracy as a system that should encourage conformity in anything is but a mockery of the Anglo-American meaning of the term."
4. The Audience Standard—the pronunciation of one's audience. "The audience standard . . . is abhorrent to some because of its implicit appeal to conform, to ingratiate oneself at any cost, to have no standards other than socially determined ones."

---

[2] Paul Heinberg, *Voice Training for Speaking and Reading Aloud*, (New York, 1964), p. 253.

[3] Heinberg, *Voice Training for Speaking and Reading Aloud*.

[4] Heinberg, *Voice Training for Speaking and Reading Aloud*, pp. 256–259.

5. The Elite or Cultured Speaker Standard—the pronunciation used by "those persons who have considerable prestige, engage in important oral communication frequently, and are respected for their ability to communicate effectively. . . ."

Ultimately, each person must decide on the standard of pronunciation he will adopt. However, it would seem logical that college students might select Mr. Heinberg's fifth choice—the elite or cultured speaker standard, since most of them will find their place in this social stratum after graduation. Also, this is essentially the standard that dictionaries use in their annotation of pronunciation.

In the preface to Webster's *Seventh New Collegiate Dictionary*, the editors state, "The standard of English pronunciation, so far as a standard may be said to exist, is the usage that now prevails among the educated and cultured people to whom the language is vernacular."[5]

The dictionary, then, is a good source of models if one adopts the cultured speaker standard. Its pronunciations ". . . reflect large file transcriptions from actual educated speech in all fields and in all parts of the United States."[6]

However, "since somewhat different pronunciations are used by the cultivated in different regions too large to be ignored, we must admit the fact that uniformity of pronunciation is not to be found throughout the English-speaking world, though there is a very large percentage of practical uniformity."[7] The most obvious differences are those that exist when American and British English are compared. Most Americans find it quite easy to identify British pronunciation. Likewise, Britains would rarely confuse American English with that spoken by their compatriots.

Not only are there national pronunciation characteristics, but within a country, dialectical differences will also exist. For example, pronunciation varies greatly in England, and it is quite easy for an Englishman to identify the geographical origin of a fellow countryman by hearing him talk. A similar situation exists in the United States. Most of us can recognize people who come from the general area of the south by their pronunciation.

However, we are not always able to identify the specific area by pronunciation clues because there are so many regional differences in the United States. According to Kenyon and Knott, "Recent studies and records of American speech have made it clear that there exists far

---

[5] By permission. From Webster's *Seventh New Collegiate Dictionary* © 1967 by G. & C. Merriam Co. Publishers of the Merriam-Webster Dictionaries.

[6] Webster's *Seventh New Collegiate Dictionary* © 1967 by G. & C. Merriam Co.

[7] Webster's *Seventh New Collegiate Dictionary* © 1967 by G. & C. Merriam Co.

greater variety than was formerly supposed in the speech of Americans of unquestioned cultivation and importance."[8]

Fortunately, the regional differences which exist are outweighed by the similarities that are found in the pronunciation of English in the United States. We can understand most cultured people regardless of their geographical origin. This point of view is stressed by the editors of the Merriam-Webster Dictionary who state that "At present all cultivated types, when well spoken, are easily intelligible to any speaker of English, and there is a very large percentage of practical identity in the speech sounds used."[9]

Jean Malmstrom and Annabel Ashley in their book, *Dialects USA*, identify three major dialect bands in the United States.

> These dialects are named Northern, Midland, and Southern. They are defined by means of differences in pronunciation, vocabulary, and grammar. On the Atlantic Seaboard, they reflect the patterns of original settlement. Farther inland, they reflect later migrations of people. The more recently settled the area, the less clearly defined are its patterns of dialect distribution.[10]

The recognition of these three areas suggests the possibility, then, of three "standards" of pronunciation in the United States. It seems a certainty that the pronunciation of the educated and cultured people in each of these areas would be sufficiently stabilized to consider it standard for that particular area. In other words, we can conceive of a standard pronunciation in the northern dialect area which includes New England, the Hudson Valley, up-state New York, the northernmost strip of Pennsylvania, and Greater New York, Michigan, Wisconsin, the northern counties of Ohio, Indiana, Illinois, Iowa, Minnesota, North Dakota, the northern-third of Iowa and the northeastern-half of South Dakota, part of Utah, Washington, northern and eastern Idaho, and to some extent California, Utah, and Colorado.

Likewise, a standard must exist for the Midland and southern areas. The pronunciation of educated people should be sufficiently stabilized to provide good models for those seeking to improve their pronunciation.

Dictionaries generally do not include the pronunciations of all three dialectical areas. In most instances, the editors record a pronunciation if it represents the speech of the greatest number of educated people.

---

[8] By permission. From *A Pronouncing Dictionary of the American English* © 1953 by G. & C. Merriam Co., Publishers of the Merriam-Webster Dictionaries.

[9] By permission. From Webster's *New International Dictionary*. Second Edition © 1959 by G. & C. Merriam Co., Publishers of the Merriam-Webster Dictionaries.

[10] Jean Malmstrom and Annabel Ashley, *Dialects USA*, (Champaign, Ill., 1963), p. 41.

And the editors of Webster's *Seventh New Collegiate Dictionary* warn that, "The function of a pronouncing dictionary is to record as far as possible the pronunciations prevailing in the best present usage rather than to attempt to dictate what that usage should be. Insofar as a dictionary may be known and acknowledged as a faithful recorder and interpreter of such usage, so far and no farther may it be appealed to as an authority."[11]

It would appear, then, that we can rely on the dictionary for pronunciation patterns. However, we should be aware of the limitations of a pronouncing dictionary. It does not attempt to provide us with standard pronunciations for all dialect areas in the United States and people living in the south or the north will probably be most aware of this fact. Neither does it exclude as "correct," pronunciations which are not included.

Another advantage of the dictionary is the policy of periodic revision; revisions reflect observed changes in pronunciation. The history of the English language is peppered with modifications of words. Not too many years ago, the dictionary indicated the first pronunciation of "contractor" (a builder) was kən-trak′tər with the accent on the second syllable; it also indicated djū′tĭ as the pronunciation of "duty." The first pronunciation we rarely if ever hear and the dictionary no longer lists it. We sometimes hear djū′tĭ but it is usually in the theater or some other formal meeting.

Poor articulation and inaccurate pronunciation may reduce your communication credibility. It has been pointed out that the standard of pronunciation for most countries is that used by the majority of the educated people who are native to the country. Of all people then, college graduates should assume some responsibility for insuring the continuance of uncontaminated pronunciation.

RATE AND RHYTHM

Coordination of the vocal and articulatory mechanisms is essential to the smooth and controlled production of the symbols of oral communication. These verbal symbols—words—must be discharged at a rate of speed suitable to the occasion, to the auditors, and to the subject matter. Generally, if the situation is formal or serious, the rate of utterance is relatively slow. If the listeners are young, immature, or unfamiliar with the subject matter, the performer should likewise speak slowly. If the subject being discussed is solemn and impressive, difficult or relatively obscure, the rate of speech should be moderate.

[11] From Webster's *Seventh New Collegiate Dictionary,* © 1967 by G. & C. Merriam Co. p. 18a.

However, there are situations in which the speaker should speed up his rate. Sometimes this increase in speed is a deliberate effort to add excitement; often it is a result of the heightened emotional state of the speaker. If the talker is dealing with familiar, relatively simple material, he may instinctively speed up the transmission of his ideas.

It is important that every speaker should develop a maximum of control over his rate of utterance. An understanding of how rate can be regulated is the first step in developing this control. You can slow down your speech in two ways: first by increasing the silent intervals between word and thought groups, and second, by taking more time with the production of individual sounds, specifically the vowel sounds.

For example, the sentence, "Now is the time for all good men to come to the aid of their country," can be said rapidly in about three seconds. In addition to being too rapid for easy reception by a listener, this rate prevents adequate changes in pitch, loudness, and quality. The meaning of the sentence certainly cannot be enhanced by desirable vocal variety if it is said at such a fast rate. Moreover, in many instances, this rate induces a problem called "cluttering." Because of the very fast production of sounds, they may not be given their true value and may even be omitted. This problem in speech is similar to the mistakes a typist makes when she accelerates her speed of typing to a point where she strikes two keys simultaneously; thus only one of the two letters is typed and the word "ten" appears in place of "then."

To slow down the reading of the sentence above, take more time in forming the vowel sounds, particularly; and in addition, pause briefly between words. These pauses will be of different duration: very short between words; longer between thought groups and ideas. Instead of "nowis" as if "now" and "is" are one word, say "Now-is–." Then, "Now-is the time—for all-good-men—to come—to the aid—of their-country." This reading of the sentence with the slower formation of certain sounds and the minute pauses as indicated by the hyphens and dashes takes at least five seconds to read. Without exaggeration or overpreciseness, you have taken almost twice as much time for a sixteen-word sentence.

Of course, this slower rate is not always suitable. You need faster rates, at times, and even slower ones, as determined by the situation, the message, or the listeners. Moreover, these adjustments in rate may be made throughout speech.

Occasionally, a speaker's rate in speech is too slow, with the result that the auditors are likely to lose interest and become preoccupied with other things. A person with a very slow rate is probably prolonging some sounds so that they are overemphasized in the word. Moreover, the silent intervals between the words may be disproportionate. This speaker should speed up sound and word production, but never lose sight of the fact that variety in rate is also important.

Control is the all-important word. You must be able to speak at an appropriate rate, in spite of habit or emotion. At the same time, your utterance must be smooth and rhythmic. Organ music is an example of sound production which is generally very smooth. The organist varies his speed of playing but usually holds on to one note until the next note is produced; the resulting music is continuous and fluid. In speech the individual sounds of a word and the succeeding words should flow together in much the same way.

The interruption in the rhythm of speaking is often a result of unusual types of pauses between words or phrases. Sometimes the speaker, pausing to think, attempts to compensate for the silent period by saying, "ah" or "and-ah." Instead of de-emphasizing the unnaturally long pause, he calls attention to it.

Pauses also can be distracting and can interfere with meaning. If the pause is in an illogical spot in the sentence, it breaks the flow of speech and the continuity of the idea. For example, if the sentence, "I threw the ball to the child," were said, "I threw—(pause)—the ball to the child," the rhythm of the sentence would be affected. Also the meaning might not be immediately clear. The object of the verb—"the ball"—must be said as a continuation of the subject and verb, "I threw the ball," in order to assist the listener.

Hesitations on and repetitions of a sound, or sounds, or words, also break up the rhythm in the same way that ill-timed or vocalized pauses do. If the word is repeated in a meaningful way, for a purpose, then the repetition will be useful and desirable. Otherwise such a habit certainly breaks up the continuity of speech.

If the speaker's rate of speaking is unusually rapid, his resulting speech is likely to be staccato. The successive sounds pop out in a machine-gun-like explosion. In addition to being excessively fast, this speech pattern probably lacks smoothness and continuity. If you have ever played a musical instrument, you can see the similarity between the staccato production of a musical note and of a word. Both are short, lacking richness and full resonance. In music this technique is sometimes used to add variety or a special effect of a type not generally desirable in speaking.

To improve the rhythm of your speaking, first make sure that your basic rate of speech production is slow enough so that you are not losing sounds or obscuring meaning. Time your pauses to reinforce meaning. If you must pause to reorganize your thinking, avoid any vocalization. Use pauses for verbal punctuation; use pauses, too, to emphasize important points in your discussion. Try to establish continuity in the production of the successive words.

The rate and rhythm of speaking compares favorably to that in a musical composition, with all the breaks, accelerations, retardations, and repetitions included consciously for the purpose of beauty, interest, and emphasis. In speech you can aid yourself to gain and hold the attention of the audience through the use of similar variations of speed.

CONVERSATIONAL STYLE

Any discussion of voice and articulation which breaks down and analyzes each aspect of vocal reinforcement and the various characteristics of sound and word production may overemphasize the *part* and lose sight of the *whole,* temporarily. This approach is defensible since any person who is trying to improve his oral communication skills must understand the purpose and function of each contributing part of his speech mechanism. However, in such an approach, the student may become so involved in the improvement of each function that he overlooks the importance of the coordination of all the parts in light of the only objective of speech—*communication.*

This is particularly true in the case of voice and articulation. The student of speech, in an effort to use his voice with maximum effectiveness, sometimes plays it like a pipe organ, with fantastic changes in pitch, inflections that cover his complete musical range, incredible changes in loudness, and unusual modifications in quality.

Superimposed on these vocal gymnastics will be overprecise, overarticulated sounds and words. Each consonant is given the same emphasis and care of production. Not a single sound is slighted, and the most discriminating ear hears not one slight distortion of sound. This type of delivery in its extreme is stilted and uncommunicative. The vocal changes seem to be motivated by a desire to demonstrate the flexibility and versatility of the instrument—the speech mechanism—rather than by a need to reinforce the meaning of the message. In such cases, the auditor feels that the speaker is *performing* rather than *communicating.*

This type of delivery may be a result of concentration on each of the parts of speech without adequate consideration of the whole. Or it may be a result of thoughtlessness concerning the real purpose of speech.

The primary purpose of speech is to transmit as effectively as possible a message to a listener or listeners. And this transmission can best be accomplished through a natural, conversational style of delivery. Your voice should reflect the intellectual and descriptive content and the emotional overtones of your message through its pitch changes, loudness and quality variations, and its rate and rhythm modifications. But these

THE TRANSMITTERS OF ORAL COMMUNICATION 193

variations must never dominate or detract from language, only reinforce it.

The way in which you deliver your message must be personalized in terms of your audience. Each listener (whether there be one or one hundred in the audience) must feel that you are talking to him in a man-to-man fashion. Your enthusiasm for your subject and your interest in your audience must be transmitted to him partly through your voice. Unlike some television salesmen imploring their listeners to buy their products, do not oversell yourself with false energy and exaggerated enthusiasm which is reflected in your vocal control. Be natural; be sincere; be yourself in all speaking situations. Don't misjudge your auditors and think that superficiality is a substitute for sincerity.

Above all, be communicative. If you concentrate on getting a message across to your listeners, you will instinctively avoid the so-called oratorical style of delivery and rely on a more intimate, direct vocal approach.

Like vocal gymnastics, overprecise articulation is a distraction rather than a reinforcement of speech. In connected discourse, all sounds are not given equivalent value, since each sound will be affected by others that precede or follow it. In an effort to be accurate, a speaker may pronounce each component part of a word as if it were an independent unit. Moreover, this speaker may pronounce each word as if it were not preceded or followed by other words. This type of articulation breaks up the natural flow of speech to some extent. It also allows for little emphasis of any type which will assist the listener with the meaning.

In the section of the book dealing with articulation and pronunciation, you have been urged to learn to produce sounds correctly and to pronounce words accurately. This advice must now be tempered with a warning. Do not let your concern with exactness cause you to be overprecise.

Conversational delivery is appropriate in any kind of speaking situation, from the intimate exchange of ideas between two persons to the most formal lecture situation. It is true, of course, that circumstances will modify your approach slightly, but it is important that you remember that most auditors are realistic, down-to-earth people who cannot be impressed by superficiality, who will not be fooled by false enthusiasm, who will actively resist artificiality.

Many speakers acquire and use the conversational style of speaking instinctively in all types of situations. Some will have to make a deliberate effort to transfer the informality of conversation to class discussions or recitations and to public speaking. However, any attempts in this direction will be well rewarded by the satisfaction obtained from greater auditor interest and attention.

THE USE OF THE BODY IN SPEECH

In addition to the vocal and articulatory mechanisms, the speaker's whole body acts as a communication transmitter. Not only does the speaker send auditory cues to the listener, but he supplements and reinforces his meanings by visual signals relayed by various types and degrees of physical activity. This visual reinforcement aids the listener by providing him with two avenues by which he may receive the communicator's message. It also helps the speaker to transmit his message more accurately.

Eye Contact

The speaker has four "levels" of physical activity which he may utilize to aid in the transmission of his ideas. The first of these is *eye contact*. While this direct contact with the audience is the least energetic of all of the levels of physical activity, it is probably the most essential. It is vital that the speaker look at the auditor or auditors during the transmission of any message, whether it be an informal conversation, a group discussion, a class recitation, or a formal speech. His eyes should meet the eyes of all members of his audience so that there is a feeling of directness and "all-inclusiveness." Every member of the listening group should feel that the speaker is talking *directly to him*.

Have you ever known a person who avoids looking directly at you during a conversation? You are his only auditor; yet he looks past you and his eyes never meet yours. Have you been aware of a feeling of embarrassment or uneasiness as you watch the speaker avoiding your gaze? You may even develop a feeling of distrust toward the person, suspecting, perhaps, that his motives are questionable. Even if you suspect that his extreme self-consciousness is the cause of his wavering eye contact, your awareness itself may be a distracting factor which interferes with communication.

These same listener reactions may be present in a formal speaking situation, but the problem is multiplied by many auditors reacting to the speaker's avoidance of them. As the speaker you must remember that you can inspire confidence in these auditors by talking directly *to* them, instead of over their heads, out of the window, down at the floor, or at the ceiling.

Moreover, the speaker should be watching his auditors for their reactions. He must be on the alert for any signs of misunderstanding, questioning, doubt, and so on, in order that he may modify his discussion in terms of this audience reception. If the speaker concentrates on continual observation of his listeners as a source of much-needed information and direction for his speaking, he will automatically establish satisfactory eye contact with his auditors! And the resulting concentration of both the speaker and his listeners will ensure livelier and more effective communication.

Facial Expression

Directly related to audience contact is the second level of physical reinforcement—*facial expression*. Not only must the eyes of the speaker meet those of members of his listening group, but also they should suggest an attitude or emotion which will be reflected in his face. There is no doubt that facial expression will do more to inspire and convince an audience than any other device available to a speaker.

Your facial expression must reflect an interest in what you are saying, if you expect an auditor to be interested. It must suggest the intensity of your feelings and must display an earnestness which the audience can interpret as a sign of sincerity and purposefulness.

Oftentimes a speaker virtually hides behind a mask. His face, instead of reflecting his personality, his attitudes toward the listeners and his subject, and his purposefulness, remains composed and blank. Thus, he denies himself one way of aiding in the transmission of his ideas.

This lack of reinforcing facial expression may be a result of uneasiness or anger or suspicion. Try to exercise some control over your facial expression so that it will not betray your lack of stability. Otherwise your negative facial expression may belittle the important facts you want your listeners to understand.

Concentrate on the message you are discussing. If you really want to convey it to another person or persons, if you are interested in the idea, and if you continually think about the real purpose of communication, you can hardly avoid reflecting your attitudes in your face. And then you will be substantiating the words of the poet who said that the face is the "mirror of the soul."

Gestures

The use of *gestures* opens up another possible way of supplementing language. At the same time it reopens an old argument as to the extent and nature of the gestures which are necessary for oral communication. First of all, if we accept as our definition of a gesture "any movements of the head, shoulders, torso, arms, or hands, which tend to emphasize the spoken word," we have accepted the word in its broadest form. Too many people have been accustomed to using the more limited meaning of the word and have felt that unless they are using their hands, specifically, they are not making use of gestures.

Yet some of the most effective and natural gestures are movements of the head, shoulders, and torso. For example, a shrug of the shoulders will effectively indicate indifference or disgust; a nod of the head will emphasize a statement of fact; a straightening of the torso can imply a firmness of purpose; a lift of the chin may strengthen a question. All of these are gestures—gestures that many are using unconsciously; gestures which have developed out of what the speaker has said or felt.

Naturally, you will want to use your hands and arms, too, as a means of emphasizing important ideas. But be sure that you use them as effectively as you use other gestures. Let their movement be a natural outgrowth of what you are saying. Don't superimpose planned body movements on your speaking. It is only those gestures which seem natural, spontaneous, and unaffected that will actually reinforce what you are saying; forced and awkward movements of any part of the body will call attention to themselves and away from the ideas you are trying to impart.

No doubt many of you will find yourselves automatically using your hands and arms to emphasize or describe or locate. These movements are essential to vivid and exact explanations and descriptions. For example, directions for reaching a particular building in a city can be more specific if the speaker supplements his verbal instructions with gestures. If he says, "Walk two blocks north—", a pointing gesture toward the north clarifies his instruction. These movements and all others should be free, graceful, and coordinated with the ideas which they are meant to enhance. They include such movements as pointing, clenching of your fist, opening and closing of your hands, and other broader and more transitory movements.

Again, control of bodily activity is important. Some speakers develop distracting mannerisms of which they are unaware. These result from habit, nervousness, or preoccupation. But regardless of their cause, they are likely to distract the auditor and make him uncomfortable. Thus he may miss part of the message. If you have any such habits, it will take real concentration on your part to eradicate them. Try to substitute meaningful use of your hands; use the same energy for a positive effect.

Movement

Before discussing the fourth level of bodily action, *movement*, it would be well to consider posture standards. Most experts agree that there is no *one* correct way of standing. The posture you adopt should be one that is *comfortable* for you. Some people find it easy to stand with feet slightly apart so that there is a reassuring sense of balance. Others prefer to stand with one foot slightly ahead of the other, with the weight on the forward foot. With either of these positions there is a tendency to rock, either from side to side, or backward and forward. The speaker must try to avoid this unnecessary movement, which calls attention to itself. He should stand erect, shoulders back, but not stiffly as a soldier stands at attention. His chin should be up so that he can direct his speech out toward his auditors, not down to the floor. When his hands and arms are not being used to gesture, they may be held in a relaxed position at the sides, or in any other natural and comfortable position. In general, the speaker may assume any posture and stance which is comfortable so long as he does nothing to distract his audience.

There are standards of good taste that all speakers must consider in all aspects of speaking, including appearance. Some speakers rationalize that their informal postures are comfortable and therefore must be acceptable. They do not realize that they may appear awkward, stiff, careless, uncoordinated, and even ridiculous.

Gross movement of the body is very helpful in securing and maintaining the interest of your auditors, especially if the speech is very long or if the subject is difficult or abstract. Instead of standing quietly in one spot, the speaker should, under certain circumstances, move about the platform, punctuating his ideas or assisting in a transition from one idea to another.

This movement must be purposeful. Ill-timed or meaningless pacing, for example, will detract from, rather then reinforce the speech. Such movement gives the audience the impression that the speaker is restless, ill at ease, or undecided. Like all other bodily action, gross movements must be in harmony with what is being said by the speaker at the moment.

If the movement is coordinated with the thought, it can not only secure and hold attention, but can also further emphasize what is being said by the speaker. Moreover, any kind of movement helps relieve some of the tension in the speaker, and if necessary, will siphon off excess energy.

VISUAL AIDS

Now that we have examined all of the ways in which speakers can capture attention by use of their voice and body movement, we are ready to look at another means for holding audience attention—the use of visual aids. Visual aids are not very complicated. They are simply devices other than the speaker's voice and body that are used to assist in the presentation of the speaker's message. Research has consistently shown that communications presented with visual aids are more effective in terms of knowledge retention. The reason is quite simple: the communicator who uses visual devices adds to the stimuli available to his audience.

Let us consider the most common type of visual device first. This is the acutal physical use of an object about which the speaker is communicating. For example, if you were to present information to an audience about the important elements to look for in the construction of a new shoe, you might use an actual shoe to illustrate your points. The problem with this device is that many kinds of things are not easily manipulable. It is hard to bring large objects into most settings. The authors have had experience with students who have used automobiles in classroom speeches, and in one extreme instance even a dairy cow was brought into a classroom communication. Most of the time, however, this device should be confined to the small and easily manipulated objects such as frogs, cake pans, and neckties. It is quite possible for communicators to use hand-held objects even when the subject may not seem to call for it. A communication about the Chicago city water purification system may seem at first glance to be a little unwieldy to bring into the classroom. However a student might bring a sample of the intake devices that are used in the system, or some other small part of the whole process. A small object that is part of a larger system of the communication is always a welcome addition.

By far the most common type of visual aid is the physical representation of an object which cannot actually be present. We usually call this sort of visual aid a *chart* or *diagram.* The principal reason for its popularity is that charts and diagrams are much more flexible. They are capable of expressing a broader range of material than an actual object brought into the communicative situation. For example, if something is quite small and the parts of it are complex, a chart or diagram can expand and magnify the essential elements in the object so that the receivers of the communication can get a clear picture of it. If, for example, you would wish to demonstrate how the timing mechanism in a watch was built, it would be absolutely essential that you magnify the parts so that they were visible to the members of the audience. In addition, a series of charts or diagrams can express changes that take place in time, by showing all the positions of objects or transformations that happen. A communication that was designed to show how beer is brewed might use a chart or diagram expressing the various conditions of the mixture as it travels through the brewing process, explaining what happens to the raw material as it is transformed into a drinkable beer. In a communication that is designed to show how a vacuum tube operates it would be possible to show the vacuum tube in a state of rest, and an additional chart might show the tube under various switching positions and various amplification states.

THE TRANSMITTERS OF ORAL COMMUNICATION 199

Another important use of the chart or diagram involves the visual presentation of main points or important facts to remember in the communication. Someone who was communicating to an audience concerning the Army's use of combat intelligence might choose to construct a chart listing the words, "Strength, Equipment, Location, Disposition, Organization, and Movement." Devices such as this type are reinforcing in that they remain visual for the audience throughout the presentation and serve to fix the content of the communication in the auditors' minds. And, of course, communicators often can utilize both of these principles together, using explanatory words and sentences together with the visual or pictorial elements in their charts or diagrams.

If equipment is available to you, you may want to make use of a device called a *flip chart*, in which visuals are bound together, allowing you to change them rapidly. This is an effective device, since you can go back to illustrations previously used and emphasize various points by moving back and forth.

Although in the typical class, students are not expected to make use of complex audio-visual devices, all students of communication should be aware that there are many types that are very useful to a communicator. One of the most useful is the *overhead projector*, in which one can project slide transparencies and write on them with a grease pencil. These transparencies are projected on a screen behind the speaker which usually makes a very effective presentation.

Another commonly used device is the *opaque projector*, which projects opaque material. Pages of books or manuscripts and other pictures can be used with this device. And, of course, students should not overlook the possible use of slides, filmstrips, and even motion picture projectors.

One visual device that students should not overlook (since it exists in most classrooms) is the chalkboard. Effective use of the chalkboard requires planning and imagination. Part of the problem with its use is that the speaker must draw or letter as he speaks, and normally the two processes are not compatible; the attention of the communicator should be focused on his audience rather than on the material that he is attempting to draw or letter. But when the material is carefully prepared and has been tried out in advance, speakers can use chalk drawings to emphasize important elements in the communication. Often the communicator will hang a chart or diagram on the chalkboard and accompany the chart or diagram with chalk drawings or chalk lettering.

The real key to effective use of visual devices is the active interaction of the communicator with the visual device. To this end, the speaker should plan to interact physically with his visual aid, using hand and arm gestures to emphasize important parts or elements on the chart or diagram. Student communicators should plan to place their visual aid at some point convenient to the speaker's stand and then plan to move physically from point to point, emphasizing the visual aspects of their presentation. It should be clear that rehearsal is essential to the use of visual aids. There is no more sorry spectacle than a beginning communicator who has not planned exactly how his chart will hang (or stand up) in the particular room which he uses, and who must spend all of his time desperately clutching the chart to keep it from falling down. Nor is there anything more frustrating than a well made visual aid which is too small to be seen from the rear of the room. Only careful planning and rehearsal can eliminate these difficulties.

A good rule of thumb to remember in the planning of visuals is that almost every communication can be improved by the use of visual aids but that the degree of improvement is entirely dependent upon the speaker's willingness to plan carefully and exercise strict control over the presentation of the stimuli to his audience. Careful preparation will reap great benefits in receivers' understanding and retaining of the content of the communication.

7 LISTENING

INTRODUCTION

For centuries, our emphasis on communication centered on the source and the message—particularly the speaker and his preparation. In almost all of the classical works on rhetoric, the speaker and his ideas take the central role in the study. This classical emphasis is still very much with us in the humanities today, and we still find most communication and related disciplines emphasizing the origin of communication. Responsibility for transmitting a message was assigned to the speaker and if he was unsuccessful in influencing an audience, the fault was his. During the last twenty-five years or so, we have developed a greater awareness and understanding of the entire communication cycle, not just the portion concerned with the sending of messages. Many scholars are putting communication to microscopic tests in an effort to discover improved methods for sending messages *and receiving* them. In addition to continuing work on the role and responsibilities of the speaker, we are beginning to see greater attention focused on the listener—his role, responsibilities, and problems. According to one report, for example, there were only two doctoral dissertations written in the general area of listening during the 1920s. The 1950s, however, produced eighty-eight studies in various aspects of listening.[1]

The research done as a partial requirement for advanced degrees is only part of the total literature. A great deal of research is being carried on by university and college teachers and by people in business

---

[1] Sam Duker, "Doctoral Dissertations on Listening," *The Journal of Communication*, (Vol. XIII, No. 2, 1963), p. 106.

and industry. Our knowledge of the field of listening is increasing year by year.

The breadth and depth of the research in listening are also increasing. Early studies dealt primarily with fairly general questions. As our knowledge increases and our techniques for measurement become more sophisticated, new and more definitive questions are challenging the researcher.

As teachers and students *and* communicators, we must be aware of the vital role which listening plays in our civilization. If we are to perform well as speakers and listeners, we must understand both roles. Generally, at least, most of us have some concept of the former; however, many of us have not perceived the importance of listening and the responsibilities and problems of the listener.

Listening is one of our most important avenues of learning. Much of our knowledge comes to us through our ears; in fact, our earliest learning is a result of exposure to auditory stimuli. The infant begins to recognize that there is order in speech sounds and that with those ordered speech sounds he can achieve a response. After listening to repeated samples of speech, he begins to imitate oral examples, putting together sounds which, up to this time, he has produced by chance as he indulges in "vocal play." His learning has been dependent upon his ability to hear and discriminate.

From a very early age, then, the child makes use of listening in the accumulation of knowledge and the development of vocal skills. It is interesting to note the interdependence between all the tools of communication. Speaking and listening complement each other, and each is employed in the learning or development of the other. In turn, speaking and listening are essential to the development of the other two communication skills—reading and writing. Together, these four provide us with universal tools of learning, teaching, advising, enjoying, and evaluating, *ad infinitum.* Each of them must be developed to operate with maximum efficiency and effectiveness.

Unfortunately, as we grow older and learn to read and write, and as we begin studying a variety of subjects, we tend to forget the importance of listening and rarely, if ever, make any specific attempt to understand its complexities; nor do we make much of an effort to improve our listening skills as a way of reducing receiver errors. Researchers have demonstrated that, contrary to expectation, our ability to receive oral messages intact does not automatically improve with added years and maturity or with greater knowledge and discrimination. Instead, our listening efficiency seems to diminish almost systematically from childhood to adulthood.

It does not follow, however, that this apparent loss of efficiency reflects a deterioration of listening skills. Instead, it may indicate the individual's bewildered reaction to his own developing complexities and to an increasingly complex environment.

The area of listening, then, should be the concern of educators at all levels. Specific programs designed to improve listening comprehension, discriminative listening, appreciative listening, and/or critical listening should be expanded. The individual must make every effort to insure that his listening abilities are capable of dealing with increasingly difficult materials and situations with which he will come in contact. The youngster in the first grade is faced with a comparatively simple communication environment; the adult's environment is much more complex and demanding, and the decisions based upon his reception of messages are much more critical.

According to Ralph G. Nichols, "Perhaps the most dramatic recognition of the importance of ability to listen has been by management personnel in American industry. A somewhat sudden realization a few years ago that there are clear-cut dollar values in having employees who listen well has resulted in the institution of a number of training programs designed to achieve that end. Among the first firms to take such action have been American Telephone and Telegraph, The Methods Engineering Council, General Motors, The Dow Chemical Company, The Wood Conversion Company, Minnesota Mining and Manufacturing, and many others."[2] Mr. Nichols goes on to predict that "within a few years, one of the first steps an employer will take when considering a new employee will be that of verifying the latter's listening index."[3]

While educators particularly in higher education have been somewhat slow in recognizing their responsibility for providing training in listening to college students, they have not hesitated to use the oral method and particularly the lecture as one, if not the most frequent, way of transmitting information to students. In the school setting, at all levels, it cannot be denied that listening is a significant medium of learning. It would seem reasonable, then, that we make every effort to do it well.

Listening skills facilitate the acquisition of knowledge. Each of us is exposed to rich learning opportunities every day of our lives. These opportunities exist in the home, in the school, in the church, and in the incidental, everyday contacts outside the formal structures of society. Modern communication systems such as radio and television provide another valuable source of knowledge. Since these contacts are *communication contacts*, we must be not only expert speakers but also effective listeners. According to the late Edward R. Murrow, radio and television commentator, his decision to take a year's leave of absence from his

---

[2] Ralph G. Nichols, "Listening Ability and Success," *Minnesota Medicine*, (Vol. 39, 1956).

[3] Ralph G. Nichols, "Listening Ability and Success."

position at the Columbia Broadcasting System was to provide an opportunity for "traveling, *listening,* reading, and trying to learn." Apparently he did not overlook the potential of listening as a great source of knowledge.

Listening becomes increasingly important as one matures and takes on a more responsible role in family living and as one moves from a formal educational setting into a vocation. In business, industry, or in the professions, the ability to listen plays an important role in the efficiency and effectiveness and eventual success of every person. An essential characteristic of the manager of a small business, of the factory foreman, the union steward, of the psychiatrist, of the engineer, of the priest, minister, or rabbi is the ability to listen well—to receive information intact, without distortion or elaboration, and to retain the important facts as a basis for giving advice, decision-making, and understanding.

A federal mediator in labor-management disputes, for example, must be adept in listening as he sits at the head of the conference table and pays close attention not only to the issues presented by both sides but also to the undercurrents revealed in vocal inflections and facial expressions of the speakers. He is, by careful listening, able to read what "is between the lines." He should be able to listen calmly and unemotionally, receive and retain key issues and ideas, separate the important from the unimportant. He must resist the propaganda techniques used by both sides. In other words, he must be competent in the area of listening.

In a family situation, both the children and the parents must be good listeners if they are to get along satisfactorily, solving the mutal, complex problems of family life. Too often parents end up talking to themselves; the children don't listen because the message being sent is not what they want to hear. Parents sometimes encourage children to talk, but because of preoccupation with more pressing matters, pay little attention to the comments of the children.

Listening, then, is crucial in learning; it is also a critical factor in a vocation and in human relations. It also plays an important role in our leisure-time activities. The pleasure of poetry, of the drama, of television, and of the movies is partly auditory. Unfortunately, some people have not developed appreciative listening skills and therefore the potential of these sound-centered activities do not serve the needs for relaxation that are essential to the individual.

The amount of time you spend in listening should be reason enough to motivate you to improve your listening skill. A study done by Paul Rankin[4] in 1926 revealed that the average person spends 70

---

[4] Paul Rankin, "The Measurement of the Ability to Understand Spoken Language," *Dissertation Abstracts,* (Vol. XII, 1952), pp. 847–848.

percent of his waking day engaged in some form of communication activity; 9 percent of this time he is involved with writing; 16 percent is spent on reading; 30 percent is used for speaking activities; and 45 percent is devoted to listening. One cannot help but be impressed by the fact that the average person spends almost one-half of his waking communication day engaged in *listening;* anything that takes up this much of our life and energy should be done well.

Because individuals with normal hearing are not "taught" to listen initially, most people take this skill for granted. They assume that because they can *hear,* because the sound waves are successfully conducted to the brain, that they have nothing to be concerned about as listeners. For too long educators had somewhat the same view with the result that little attention was given to listening in the classroom. As a matter of fact, most of the attention in the elementary and secondary schools was focused on "silent" communication tools—reading and writing. Far less attention was given to speaking and listening.

We should not be too critical, however, of this early lack of concern about listening. Little information was available about the process of listening. There was no standardized measurement tool available which would give an estimate of listening ability and therefore, no way to measure improvement.

But during the past twenty-five years, researchers have focused on the problem and useful information about listening has resulted from their efforts. According to Isabella H. Toussaint,[5] researchers seem to be concerned with these questions:

1. What is listening?
2. Is listening important?
3. What factors influence listening?
4. Are listening and reading related?
5. Can listening be taught?
6. Can listening be measured?

Obviously, we do not have all of the answers; there are even other questions which must be asked and answered. However, a good beginning has been made.

Several of the research projects were concerned with the efficiency of our listening. H. E. Jones[6] discovered that college students had an average immediate recall of about 60 percent following a lecture. After

---

[5] Isabella H. Toussaint, "A Classified Summary of Listening—1950-1959," *The Journal of Communication,* (Vol. X, 1960), pp. 125-134.

[6] H. E. Jones, "Experimental Studies of College Training," (The Effect of Examination on the Permanence of Learning), *Archives of Psychology,* (Columbia University, Vol. LXVIII, 1923).

two months, students could recall about one-third of what they recalled immediately following the lecture and only one-fourth of the important points emphasized in the lecture. Later studies have substantiated these findings that after two months, the average listening efficiency is not more than 25 percent. The implications here are even more revealing when it is pointed out that these findings were based on tests given over relatively short lectures.

Fortunately, we can do something about this situation. Experimentation has demonstrated that listening efficiency can be improved by systematic training.

THE LISTENER

As a first move toward better listening habits, let us consider the various aspects of listening. Figure 12 from Chapter 1 is repeated on this page for your convenience.

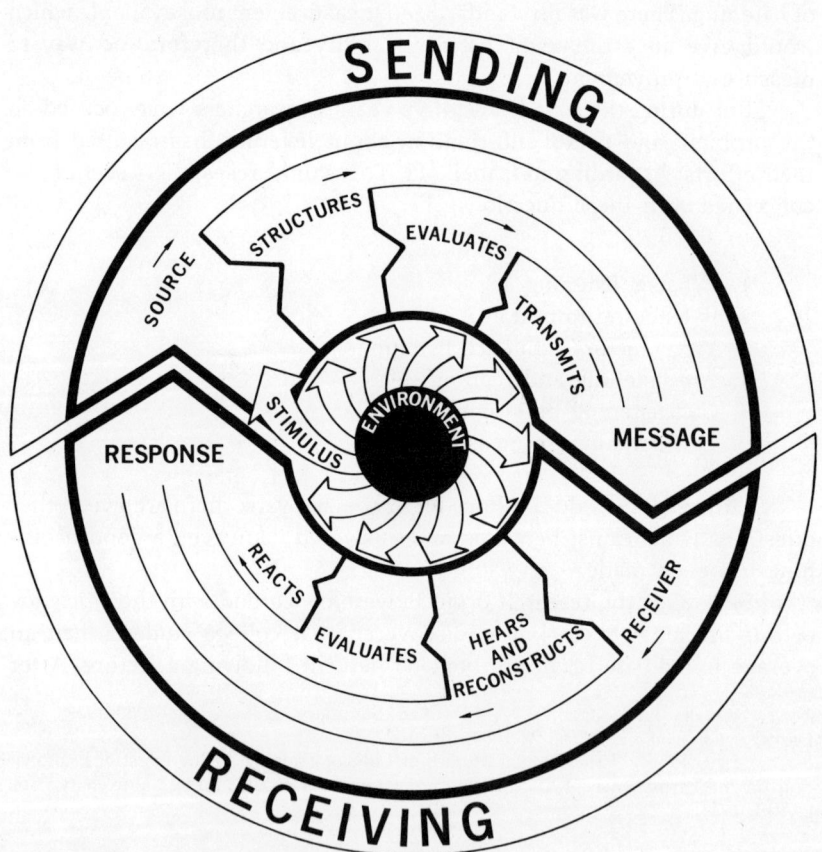

Each element indicated on the diagram is of equal importance and is essential to good listening. To begin with, there must be a person—the listener. Each listener is an individual in the truest sense of the word. While there is no need or desire to try to mold every listener into the counterpart of other listeners, it is important for you to understand how your individuality affects you as a listener. You must recognize that your age, your sex, your interests, your attitudes toward the speaker or his subject, your feelings about the speaking situation, and your pattern of thinking will influence and control your listening behavior. This uniqueness may act as a deterrent to good listening or may be a positive factor which heightens and improves your listening skill. It all depends on the nature of your attitudinal structure.

The Listener Hears and Restructures

The Listener Hears If the listener's auditory mechanism is normal and functional, the sound waves created by the speaker are captured by the listener's outer ear and are transmitted to the brain through the middle and inner ear. At this point, the listener is aware of stimuli but he may not have attached meaning to them. Most of you have experienced or observed *hearing* without comprehension. For example, have you ever watched a child recounting the day's events to a tired father who is trying to read his evening paper? The parent hears the sounds, even punctuates his son's account with "Hmmmm," or "Uh-uh," but he could never repeat what the child has said because he has not attached meaning to the stimuli arriving in his brain.

The same thing happens when you try to carry on a conversation or read a book while you "half listen" to a radio or television program. You attach no meaning to the sound coming from the set. Occasionally, you may "tune in" on the sounds, interpret and reconstruct them in a meaningful way, and as a result understand what is going on. Part of the time, then, you are hearing; part of the time you may be listening.

The Listener Reconstructs Hearing, then, is the first process or step in listening. But *hearing* is not the same as *listening*. Hearing is the conversion of a mechanical operation to nerve impulses which stimulate the brain. These stimulations must be interpreted or decoded and reconstructed into meaningful units.

Restructuring simply means that the listener begins to place the sounds he hears into categories that approximate the categories that the sender intended to use. For example, the sender may articulate the word "self-determination" and have used it in a framework of international politics. The listener will categorize the sound into the same kind of framework, carrying with it the same structure. This means that he not only places it into its language structure (compound noun), he finds a place for it in the sentence that the speaker was using, and finds a place for it in his (the listener's) knowledge and attitude structures. These, of course, may not be even vaguely similar to the structures of the sender, so the listener has "restructured" the term according to his own frames of reference.

In a very real sense, the ability to listen is no more than a potential. Because you possess the necessary mechanism for listening does not guarantee that you will listen effectively. Some of the conditions and attitudes which will improve your chances for effective listening may be helpful to you in your efforts to improve your role as a receiver of a message.

"You must want to listen" Your mental "set" determines whether the second stage of reception is achieved. *You must want to reconstruct a message.* Too often we approach a situation with a negative attitude, assuming that it will be boring or unrelated to our interests; we are indifferent about receiving the communication. We may acknowledge a responsibility by being present in the speaking situation, but we feel that we have met our obligation by being there. We have no interest in the message and therefore make no effort to reconstruct it.

If one has a positive attitude toward the situation, he will make the effort to attach meaning to the sequences of sounds, will perceive the relationships in the word sequences, and will make an effort to reconstruct the sender's message as faithfully as possible. The listener without determination to listen finds it easy to slip into a half-conscious state in which comprehension and reconstruction are not possible.

Regardless of our feelings toward a speaker or his subject, we must make up our minds to reconstruct his message or our presence in the communication situation is a fraud. The good listener keeps looking for values in the speaker's message. Even if he considers the delivery of the speaker poor and the subject dull, he must try to understand and refuse to be diverted by his own subvocal criticisms of the speaker's failings.

"Listen for ideas" Dr. Ralph Nichols, on the basis of an extensive research project, was able to isolate habits which differentiated the good listener from the ineffective listener.[7] Out of this study came ten suggestions for improving listening skill. One of these is of particular importance in connection with the listener's reconstruction of the message. He suggests that you *listen primarily for ideas* rather than for facts. He points out that the listener who concentrates on isolated facts becomes so involved in the effort to remember details that he may miss the real substance of the discussion. Dr. Nichols found in his research

---

[7] Ralph G. Nichols, "Ten Components of Effective Listening," *Education*, (Vol. LXXV, 1955), pp. 292–302.

with college students that if they listened for ideas they also were able to retain more details.

"Adapt your form of note-taking to the speaker" According to Dr. Nichols, note-taking in outline form can interfere with your listening at this level, too. It can trap the listener in such a way that it decreases his efficiency. For example, in a classroom lecture, the student may try to fit the professor's speech into a particular outline form; in so doing, he wastes time which should be directed toward understanding the meaning of the lecture. Adapt your form of note-taking to the speaker. Wait for him to develop a complete idea and then record the essence of his message.

"Wait for speaker to develop an idea before reacting to it" Another distraction which can interfere with your listening efficiency is a preoccupation with a speaker's point of view before it is fully explored. This preoccupation is frequently a result of the mental activity of the listener as he prematurely considers and reconsiders an isolated detail and prepares to challenge the speaker. Meantime, he misses the explanation. The listener should wait until an idea has been fully explored before questioning it. The auditor's signal reaction to a small part of the message may be neutralized by the speaker's more intensive discussion of the issue.

"Put the time difference between thinking speed and speaking speed to work" According to Dr. Nichols, there is a marked difference between thinking speed and speaking speed. "Whereas the typical lecture is given at about 100 words per minute, there is evidence to indicate that if their thought rates were similarly measured, most students normally think at a pace about five times that fast."[8]

This time differential makes it easy for the student listening to a lecture to go off on a tangent in his thinking—anticipating a date that evening, worrying about a test to be taken during the next hour, and so forth. Instead of drifting into thoughts about unrelated topics, he should be concentrating on the subject under discussion, and he should be using the time differential to his advantage to reinforce his comprehension and restructuring of the message. This activity will assist him in understanding and retaining the message.

"Develop an adequate listening vocabulary" Vocabulary plays the same vital role in listening that it does in speaking or learning a foreign language. It seems obvious that the more limited your storehouse of words, the more difficult your listening tasks will prove. If many words do not have associations or meaning for you, you will have

---

[8] Ralph G. Nichols, "Listening Instruction in the Secondary School," *Bulletin of the National Association of Secondary School Principals*, Washington, D.C.: Department of Secondary School Administration of the National Education Association, Vol. 36, No. 187, p. 169.

problems attempting to understand a speaker's message. Repeated failures due to an inadequate vocabulary may discourage you from participating in activities which have the potential for enjoyment and stimulation.

Development of an extensive working vocabulary is one way to help you understand what you hear and read; moreover, it will make it possible for you to become a more interesting, more precise, and a more colorful writer and speaker.

"Listen in spite of distractions" It is possible to discipline yourself to listen selectively. In other words, even though there are several auditory sources, you can develop the ability to filter out those sounds which are potential distractors. In reality, this ability is a necessity in a world which is so filled with noise. We are literally bombarded with sounds of all types; some of them are meaningful and pertinent; others are undesirable at any time; still others are pleasant but not always appropriate at a particular time.

You can train yourself to listen to and comprehend that which is of significance to you, screening out the noise which you do not want to hear. When you are listening to someone who is trying to send you a message, ignore extraneous noises; discipline yourself to listen intently to the primary message. Good listeners can achieve this type of selective listening.

The Listener Evaluates

Frequently, the listening process is terminated at the level of comprehension and reconstruction of the sender's message. The listener accepts without question all of the information, all of the evidence, and all of the conclusions presented by the speaker. This is the same as saying, "I believe everything I hear!" Or it may mean, "I'm too lazy to think about it!" Although you have been advised to be patient and listen to everything a speaker has to say, this does not mean that you should store away in your mind as truth all of the information fed to you by the speaker.

"Do not allow external characteristics of the speaker to mislead you" There are many ways in which listeners may be trapped into accepting unquestioningly all of the speaker's ideas. You should be aware of certain subtle dangers which may cause you to be *too receptive*.

1. In the first place, *the listener must not be unduly influenced by the speaker's status in society*. Even in the case of the President of the United States, his position is not sufficient proof of the soundness of his ideas. His facts must be accurate and his point of view undistorted by politics or personal prejudices before his ideas can be fully accepted.

Sometimes important leaders in society may take advantage of their positions to impose unsound policies on a gullible public. By virtue of their status in political, economic, or educational circles, these people may lead naïve listeners into a passive acceptance of a course of action disastrous to the majority. Hitler's leadership in Germany is a good example of this type of practice.

Unethical speakers have always traded on the fact that people can be influenced by other things besides what the speaker says. The fact that the speaker is a celebrity frequently seems to carry more weight than the importance or truth of the ideas that he conveys. Skillful propagandists have capitalized on this situation, sometimes to the advantage of the listener, but more often to his disadvantage. Through language, these persons may distort the truth in various ways; they may becloud the issue, bypass the vital arguments, exaggerate the unimportant, and minimize the important. And they may get away with it because they seem to be somebody. The listener must take measures to protect himself against these methods.

2. *The listener must be on guard against being too easily moved by the character of the speaker.* Even a "good" man can be mistaken or misinformed. He is not infallible. An auditor should not agree with the speaker merely because of his reputation for honesty and sincerity. Good intentions are not a substitute for facts. Listeners, then, must try to protect themselves against any "halo effects" in the comprehension and evaluation of a speaker's message. They must not allow the talker's integrity to *substitute* for concrete, credible information or evidence.

3. *The listener must not be carried away by a magnetic or forceful personality.* Sometimes a speaker is so likeable that we are swept into agreement with him. At other times, we reject the speaker's message because he does not appeal to us. The listener cannot help but be aware of personality differences; however, decisions regarding the speaker's message must not be made on the basis of our personal reactions to him. Instead, what the speaker *says* or *implies* should be carefully weighed by the listener before he is influenced to accept the ideas.

4. *The auditor must not be misled by the appearance of the speaker.* Remember that attractive clothes and faultless grooming are not a substitute for sound reasoning and thorough analysis. Neither should the listener close his mind to the speaker whose appearance is not up to the standards of the auditor. It is possible that this speaker may have an important intellectual contribution to offer, or he may have information that is essential to his auditor's health and safety. Or the listener may find such a speaker delightfully entertaining.

"Do not allow preconceived attitudes toward the subject to distort the message" *Misevaluations on the part of the listener may also be a direct result of his preconceived attitudes toward the subject being discussed or the material* *which the speaker uses to explain his key idea.* If a listener enters into a communication situation with fixed ideas, marked prejudices, or strong emotional attitudes, he is likely to cause the communication system to break down; he prevents the intent of the speaker's message from reaching him; he refuses to consider the possibility that the speaker may be right. A fanatical Democrat, for example, may reject any praise of a Republican. The strong pro feelings for his own party make it difficult for him to acknowledge merit in the other political group. He resists listening to constructive or complimentary statements related to his opponents.

Instead of listening to all the evidence presented by the speaker, the auditor spends his time brooding over the fact that he has been trapped in this speaking-listening situation. Or he may occupy himself by trying to devise troublesome questions for the speaker, reciting to himself silently various ways of presenting his challenges. He ignores completely what the speaker is saying in defense of his point of view. If the subject itself is charged with emotional implications, the auditor may deliberately remove himself from the situation by thinking of other things. Occasionally, he may attend to the speaker, and because he hears only fragments of what the speaker says, he may get a distorted picture. But usually, especially when the subject is unpleasant, the listener simply stops the reception of the message.

The subject may evoke a multitude of reactions, including distaste or revulsion, indifference, suspicion, or anger, among others. Each of these, if not properly controlled, may reduce the effectiveness of two-way *communication.* The father whose son has been arrested for careless driving may be so angry with the boy for breaking the law that he never hears the son's explanation which indicates that there were mitigating circumstances.

"Try not to allow the multimeanings of words to interfere with message" There is another way in which both the comprehension and the evaluation of a message by the listener can be inadequate, and the responsibility for this breakdown may have to be shared by both the speaker and the listener.

The multimeanings of words may interfere with communication. It has been pointed out in earlier chapters that, unfortunately, a word may not mean precisely the same thing to everybody. Because of attitudes resulting from past experiences, a word may mean one thing to one person and something quite different to another. For example, upon hearing the word "car," a young man may conjure up a mental picture of a sleek, speedy, low sports car which he covets; he may even see it in gleaming white. The fifteen-year old, close to the time when he is allowed his first driver's license, dreams of the fifty-dollar jalopy he has been promised on his sixteenth birthday. Dad, on the other hand, reluctantly thinks of his five-year-old car and its worn tires that should be replaced. But the six-year-old baby of the family thinks only of his $2.50 racer. Mother, who recently saw a head-on collision between a truck and a passenger car, sees only the flaming heap of wreckage of the two vehicles. Thus, if the speaker uses the word "car," he may evoke responses that he had not quite expected, since the exact meaning that he intended to convey is different from all the rest.

In the case of the word "car," even though different images of a car may occur among various people, probably no serious misunderstandings would occur. However, if the word represents a controversial issue and if it inspires strong emotions, its use is more likely to prohibit or impede the transmission of an idea intact.

Take the word "trade-union," for example. It is probable that this word will take on meaning in terms of the past experiences of each individual. For example, to some members of a union, the word will conjure up a picture of a paternal organization, watching after its members in a fatherly, protective way. To others, it suggests an impersonal, somewhat ethereal organization which collects a given amount from their wages each week. Some will picture a large army poised to fight management at any moment, under capable, eager generals—the union officers.

On the other hand, a congressional investigator steeped in testimony concerning union racketeering, may think of a union as a group governed by dishonest, corrupt, greedy, and ruthless leaders. The manager of a large industry may think in terms of a grievance committee, which is continually making demands on management. Thus the meaning of the word varies in terms of the person's relationship to the union.

The word "trade-union" then becomes one with which it may be difficult to communicate exact meanings, especially if the listener is unwilling or unable to be objective, unemotional, and realistic. If the speaker is using the word ethically, the listener must attempt to receive it in the same form in which it was transmitted. He must obliterate from his listening mind, at least, his own connotation of the word which may obscure the real and original meaning of the word, which according to *The American College Dictionary* is "organization of workmen."

And so it is with many words in our language. These multimeanings are likely to becloud the issue unless the speaker carefully defines or explains his real meaning, and the listener tries to receive the precise meaning of the word.

Evaluation of a speaker's message is not an easy task. It is complicated by the unique reactions of the listener to the speaker and toward the subject and the message. Every listener's problem of evaluation is different, and the listener's reaction is highly individualized for each speaker.

The difficulty of the process is increased because words do not always have a common meaning for both the sender and the receiver.

So far, the following advice has been given to the listener to aid him in future evaluations:

1. Do not allow the external characteristics of the speaker—his status in society, his character, his personality, or his appearance—to mislead you in your evaluation of his message.

2. Do not permit your preconceived attitudes toward the subject, or the material used to develop the idea, distort the message for you.

3. Try not to allow the multimeanings of words to interfere with accurate reception of the speaker's message.

Throughout this discussion it has been pointed out that in the evaluation of the message the listener must consider the facts. It has also been suggested that speakers often trade on the known weaknesses of listeners. They recognize that a speaker's "position" carries authority; his spotless character inspires belief; his charming personality wins admiration; or his boyish appearance brings out the protective instinct. These and many other things the speaker knows about the listener, and he capitalizes on this information in his effort to gain approbation.

But sometimes these and other clues to listener behavior are the bases for more insidious means of persuasion. Techniques have been developed to *control* listener reaction and behavior. By various means, and often without conscience, the speaker sets out to appeal to the known weaknesses, foibles, and peculiarities of a listener, or more often of listeners in a group.

These methods lead to exaggeration, camouflage, and dishonesty. The facts are altered to suit the needs of the speaker and may be obscured or deliberately concealed. In the place of reason and evidence, the speaker substitutes appeals based on knowledge of the insecurities or ignorance of the auditors.

As a listener, you should be aware of these propaganda techniques so that you will not be "taken in" by them. If you succumb to these tricks, you will be unable to evaluate the speaker's message and his intentions properly. Here are some of the common devices which speakers may use to mislead listeners:

1. Of the many propaganda techniques, one of the most insidious is the *half-truth* used as an explanation or in place of legitimate support and evidence in behalf of a particular point of view. The speaker does not say anything that is not true, but he suppresses carefully selected, related material, and deliberately misleads his auditors.

For example, when arguing against fluoridation of drinking water in a city, the speaker says: "It is well-known that in communities where natural fluorine exists in the water supply, much discoloration and mottling of the teeth occur." This statement is true; what the speaker neglects to add is that the discoloration of the teeth is due to the large amount of fluorine that is present in the water supply. When fluorine is artificially added, amounts are carefully metered and it does not affect the color of the teeth.

Sometimes a speaker, seeking support for a particular point of view, will use the statement of an authority in an article, book, or newspaper. He may select one sentence which substantiates his thesis. Close inspection of the paragraph from which the statement was extracted may reveal that the author is really defending the opposite point of view. In other words, if the whole section had been quoted by the speaker, he would have challenged his own cause. Knowing this, he has chosen to use material out of context in an attempt to validate his argument, using a well-known and respected name to assist him.

2. The half-truth is a device which the defunct Institute for Propaganda Analysis classified as *card stacking*, a broader category which includes all types of distortions of the truth, even the outright lie. The deceptions employed in this type of propaganda are meant to prevent the truth from reaching the auditors or readers.

Probably the most skillful advocate of this device in the history of the world was Adolph Hitler, who made extensive use of this and other devices in building his empire. Apparently he had no conscience where truth was concerned, as seen in the following quotation from *Mein Kampf:*

> Propaganda—does not have to seek objectively for the truth so far as it favors an opponent . . . but exclusively has to serve our interests. (It must adopt every device of slander that ingenuity can suggest.) Whenever our propaganda permits for a single moment the shimmer of an appearance of right on the other side, it has laid a foundation for doubt in the right of our cause . . . especially among a people that so suffers from objectivity-mania as the Germans.[9]

3. In some instances, a speaker submits *hasty generalizations* as logical proof in support of a proposal or idea. Because one student has cheated on a final examination in mathematics, one cannot conclude that there is a very serious problem developing in the mathematics department; or that all mathematics students are dishonest; or that there must be a reason for all of the cheating going on in the mathematics department.

A generalization must be based upon sufficient evidence before it is acceptable as proof. A speaker says, "Look at Watts! Detroit! Harlem! Newark! America's Negroes are rioting, burning, defying law and order

---

[9] "Propaganda Techniques of German Fascism," *Propaganda Analysis,* (New York: Institute for Propaganda Analysis, Inc., Vol. 1), p. 41.

with impunity!" No one in his right mind would attribute all of the rioting in the slums to all American Negroes.

4. In addition to the hasty generalization, another device, the *glittering generality*, may trap the listener and trick him into thinking as the speaker *wills* him to think. This is "a device by which the propagandist identifies his program with virtue by use of 'virtue words' . . . like truth, freedom, honor, liberty, social justice, public service, the right to work, loyalty, progress, democracy, the American way, Constitution defender."[10] Because these words suggest *good*, they influence the listener to believe that the idea with which the word is associated is also good.

Hitler traded on the effectiveness of this device when he evolved the "official name of the party" which dominated during his rule of Germany. It was "a perfect example of the glittering generalities device —National Socialist German Workers Party. In Germany the great pre-Nazi program of public housing and public works and the higher living standards achieved through labor unions had given the word "socialist" favorable connotations. Hitler took full advantage of these connotations, though later his actual program drove socialists into concentration camps and abolished labor unions."[11]

5. In an effort to insure certain unfavorable responses from listeners, speakers sometimes employ *name calling*. Such words as "scab," "goldbricker," "honkey," "square," and "hood," are used in a deliberately derogatory way. Some auditors will be ensnared by the speaker and will share the speaker's reaction to the person or thing being alluded to, and in turn, to the idea which the speaker is denouncing. Instead of judging the idea or the person on a basis of evidence and truth, the listener is tricked by the speaker into sharing his attitude.

The White Citizen's Council shouts, "Nigger!" and H. Rap Brown feels called upon to retaliate with, "Honkey!" and the old labor song, "Which Side Are You On?" asks the question:

> Workers, can you stand it?
> Tell me how you can!
> Will you be a lousy scab
> Or will you be a man?

6. Another device, similar to name calling, has been described as the *transfer* device, with which

---

[10] "How to Detect Propaganda," *Propaganda Analysis*, (New York: Institute for Propaganda Analysis, Inc., Vol. 1), pp. 5–6.

[11] "Propaganda Techniques of German Fascism," p. 41.

the propagandist carries over the authority, sanction, and prestige of something we respect and revere to something he would have us accept. For example, most of us respect and revere our church and our nation. If the propagandist succeeds in getting church or nation to approve a campaign in behalf of some program, he thereby transfers its authority, sanction, and prestige to that program. Thus we may accept something which otherwise we might reject.[12]

This is a particularly useful device for the politician. Often a political party solicits support from a specific group and advertises the fact in newspapers and other publications, and over the radio and television, in order to transfer the prestige of the group to the proposal or the candidate.

For example, at national political conventions, nominating and seconding speakers are chosen who represent all kinds of institutions and who come from all walks of life. First will come a Protestant minister, then a labor union official, then a school teacher, then a priest, then a mother, then a farmer, and finally, a rabbi! Students enjoy convention speaking because of this kind of posturing. It is too bad that conventions occur only once in four years.

7. Similar in its purpose is the *testimonial* with which you must be familiar. Our national magazines are peppered with ads carrying the pictures and autographs of famous persons who have endorsed products or plans. Likewise, television advertising makes frequent use of endorsements of movie stars, sportsmen, and other well-known public figures. It is hoped that this type of testimonial will sell the item or promote a policy. If someone you admire is interested in the project or partial to the product, the propagandist feels sure that you will be influenced positively.

8. The *plain folks* device is another one which is frequently used

> by politicians, labor leaders, businessmen, and even by ministers and educators to win our confidence by appearing to be people like ourselves. ... In election years, especially, candidates show their devotion to little children and the common, homey things of life.[13]

Harry S Truman, running for president in 1948, used to start his "train-platform" speeches by declaring: "My name's Harry Truman. I work for the government, and I'd like to keep my job."

In Germany in the late thirties, an attempt was made to create a "plain folks" image of Hitler.

---

[12] "How to Detect Propaganda," p. 6.
[13] "How to Detect Propaganda," p. 6.

In this, the propagandists are greatly assisted by his habits; for he affects ordinary clothes, wears no medals other than his simple Iron Cross, eats plain food and that sparingly, and leads a quiet secluded life. He is pictured as a man of the people meeting plain folks in their ordinary walks of life, enjoying with them their simple work and pleasures.[14]

9. A final device is called by the Institute of Propaganda Analysis, Inc., the *bandwagon*. With this approach the speaker urges all of his auditors "to follow the crowd," the premise being that anything done by so many people must be right for you. A mild, undramatic form of this argument is used by children with their parents, wives with their husbands and vice versa, and bosses with their employees. Politicians often use a more colorful approach attempting to influence the voters. With all of the pageantry and color and excitement of a circus wagon, they employ theatrical methods to carry the crowd along with them. The dangers inherent in this device are many. First, it is a well-known fact that it is difficult for some people to remain individuals in a crowd. They are willingly and easily swept along with public opinion or pressure. Also, too often the impetus is so strong that it prevents a logical conclusion based on evaluation of the evidence. Finally, the pressures used capitalize on the listeners' vulnerable feelings of inferiority, apprehension, or insecurity.

The degree to which you are susceptible to the various propaganda techniques that have been discussed are based largely on the effectiveness of your defenses against them. If you recognize unethical propaganda when you hear it or see it and if you can remain objective and unemotional as you evaluate the idea devoid of all of the fabrications or trappings, you will not be so easily influenced by these devices.

Remember, too, that not all propaganda is spurious; it is not always meant to delude or confuse us. As Aldous Huxley explains in his article, "Tyranny over the Mind,"

> There are two kinds of propaganda—rational propaganda in favor of actions that are consonant with the enlightened self-interest of those who make it and those to whom it is addressed, and non-rational propaganda in favor of action that is not consonant with anybody's enlightened self-interest, but is dictated, directly or indirectly, by passions, blind impulses, unconscious cravings or fears.[15]

Propaganda can work honestly in support of a worthy cause. Local community chest drives, Red Cross blood programs, foreign aid plans such as CARE and the Foster Parents plan all employ propaganda tech-

---

[14] "Propaganda Techniques of German Fascism," p. 46.
[15] Aldous Huxley, "Tyranny Over the Mind," special supplement to *Newsday*, (Garden City, New York, 1958).

niques at one time or another. But their appeals are made on a *rational basis* for "the most good for the most people." Unlike dishonest propaganda which is inspired by greed, hunger for power or wealth or glory, this type of propaganda is stimulated by a concern for others' hunger, need of love, protection, friendship, and for other humanitarian motives. But more important, it must not make use of devious means to attain its objectives. Instead of *card stacking, glittering generalities,* or other devices of this type, the speaker bases his case on facts and evidence.

This discussion of listening has been punctuated with specific advice on how to be a good listener. So far, these suggestions have been made:

1. You should develop an understanding of and an appreciation for the process of listening and the part that it plays in oral communication, as a basis for your improvement.

2. You must be determined to listen in spite of lack of interest, of fatigue, suspicion, or any other physical, mental, or emotional factors.

3. You must listen primarily for ideas not details.

4. You must adapt your note-taking or your memory scheme to the individuality of the speaker's presentation.

5. You must wait until you have fully comprehended the speaker's complete idea before reacting to what he has to say.

6. You must take advantage of the difference in thinking and speaking time.

7. You must initiate and continue a consistent program of vocabulary improvement.

8. You must listen in spite of distractions.

9. You must not allow the external characteristics of the speaker to mislead you.

10. You must not allow your preconceived attitudes and prejudices to distort the speaker's message.

11. You must try not to allow the multimeanings of words to interfere with your reception of the message.

12. You must gain some insight into propaganda techniques in order to be able to resist succumbing to those that are used unethically.

The Listener Reacts

Listening involves a series of steps. The listener first hears, then comprehends and reconstructs, and finally evaluates the message. All of these processes may be reflected in the behavior of the listener and relayed to the speaker largely through refined or slight movements of the body. The auditor continues to send silent messages in a special kind of code through facial expression, eye contact, small but meaningful movements, and a unique kind of tension which is reflected in the way he sits or stands. These messages may be encouraging or discouraging to the speaker and should tell him whether or not he is getting through to the listener.

Nothing tells a teacher, for example, so much about his students and their listening ability as his observation of them as they listen to a lecture. It's quite a cast of characters! And yet, each in his own way stimulates the instructor. Let us look at some of the types to which the professor must respond:

1. "Eager beaver" keeps smiling and nodding as the teacher talks. Whether or not the message gets through to him is the real question. His eyes have a strange, slightly out-of-focus appearance. His energies are directed toward impressing the speaker with what a good listener he is—a real waste! The same amount of energy, if properly channeled, could result in effective listening.

2. The "sleeper" seeks a restful haven in a relatively quiet classroom. He has no intention of listening and is quite irritated if there are out-of-the-ordinary disturbances. His eyes are closed as he sits—rather, as he half reclines in his seat. A blissful repose is reflected in his face.

3. The "tiger" is ready to pounce on everything the speaker says. He is occupied with looking for trouble and shows it in his crouching position, leaning forward, eyes flashing, with the alertness of a big cat. He may silently "snarl" as he "hears" his first bone of contention.

4. The shy, "bewildered" listener has never quite found out what the class is all about. The pained, quizzical glances from this person are a constant reminder to the teacher that he must go slowly, repeating and reinforcing important information.

5. Occasionally, there is a "frowner" in the group. His forehead has a perpetual furrow and he seems always on the verge of a question. Sometimes his expression is an accurate reflection of his state of mind, but often it is a façade of attention.

6. The "relaxed" one seems to stay awake, but he slips down in his chair, rests his head on the back of it, and stares fixedly at some object or person. There is so little tension in him that there are no visible means of "reading" him. He never seems to react to anything that is said, either negatively or positively, and presents a real problem for the speaker.

7. One of the most resented listeners is the "busy bee" who not only does not listen but impresses the fact on everyone by writing letters, "buzzing" with his neighbors, sneaking glances at a magazine, cleaning his fingernails, combing his hair, and so on. Although he really is not a listener in the true sense of the word, he is a potential auditor in a captive audience. This person certainly will motivate the speaker,

causing him to try a multitude of devices designed to capture his attention.

8. There are probably many other types, but only one more is important in a discussion of effective listening—the "two-eared listener." He listens not only with his ears but also with his mind. This person, who actively participates in listening, who listens carefully for the sound cues, decodes them properly, evaluates carefully, and reacts objectively to the message, is the model that all of us should follow. This auditor has an eagerness which stimulates the speaker as he begins to talk. He watches the speaker so that he gets the full benefit of the auditory and visual clues; his alertness is reflected in his body tensions, in his standing or sitting postures. His face reflects agreement or disagreement, interest, questions, approval, and a host of other attitudes which result from thoughtful, objective consideration of the message.

His behavior is not static like that of the "sleeper." It may constantly change as ideas continue to get through to him. He encourages and discourages as he reacts; silently, he questions or reaffirms the points that are made; and he keeps sending out small, silent messages to the speaker which should aid the latter in his own evaluations of his effectiveness. Thus, the listener supplies the feedback which is necessary to complete the communication circuit.

If your ability to listen well is to grow and develop *with you*, you must consciously practice good listening. You must deliberately and frequently subject yourself to "difficult expository material." Exposure to materials somewhat beyond the individual is one of the best exercises for reinforcing good listening habits.

People shy away from listening to complicated speaking and as a result are unable to cope with complex subject matter when it becomes imperative for them to do so. Miss "Bewildered's" fate in her lecture class might have been quite different had she started listening to educational programs on television and radio when she was younger; if she had really listened to the sermon in her church on Sundays; if she had practiced listening to challenging material over a long period of time. All of this would have prepared her for the concentrated, somewhat difficult material with which she is faced in the college classroom.

This discussion of the listener may seem to overemphasize his role in a successful exchange of ideas. At this point, you as a listener may feel that you are solely responsible for fulfilling the purposes of effective communication. You may also feel that the function of the speaker has been relegated to a secondary role. In this chapter it has been, *but only in order to impress upon you the importance of listening.*

If oral communication is to serve its many purposes, both the speaker and the listener must perform to the best of their respective abilities. Previous chapters have stressed the talker's responsibilities. It has been pointed out to the speaker that if his auditors are continually subjected to second-rate, uninteresting, unstimulating messages, they have the right and privilege of "turning off" their receivers.

However, an auditor sometimes refuses to listen before he has given the speaker a chance. Because he anticipates being bored or because he is sure that he will not understand, the listener detaches himself intellectually from the communication situation and thereby misses what might have been an unusual opportunity.

This action on the listener's part can be most annoying to a speaker. Trying to talk to someone who is obviously not listening can be a most frustrating experience, and in this situation, there is no hope for the speaker and his message.

8 THE COMMUNICATOR'S RESPONSIBILITY

"FREEDOM OF SPEECH"

In the atmosphere that prevails today on most of our college campuses, it may be difficult for students to remember that at one time the open and free communication was not nearly as universally honored as it seems to be today. The "free speech" movement on the Berkeley Campus and similar movements at Michigan, Iowa, and other universities across the country tend to give the impression that the right of expressing oneself is conferred automatically with registration in college. At Ohio University, for example, students played an important role in implementing a nonacademic employees strike and participated in the decision making process concerning fee increases and other aspects of student life. In this kind of climate it may be difficult to realize that at many institutions and at many other times, students' rights of self expression have not been so freely given and so earnestly safeguarded. And in a society which prizes free expression, it is difficult to remember that many societies have repressive laws concerning communication. Even America's history is not unblemished in this respect. It is only a few short years ago that Senator Joseph McCarthy struck terror into campuses across the land by charging that American higher education was infiltrated with active members of the Communist party and Communist sympathizers. Senator McCarthy was greatly effective for at least two reasons: first, he played upon the anxieties and suspicions that most of our citizens felt about the Soviet Union, and second, he capitalized on the mistrust that many citizens feel for the intellectual activities at universities in general.

 The wave of suspicion that the so-called McCarthy era produced was still very much in evidence when the House Un-American Activities

Committee met in San Francisco in 1960 to conduct investigations of the possible influence of the Communist Party in the San Francisco area. At that time students from San José State College, University of California, San Francisco State College, and Sacramento State College staged a noisy and highly successful demonstration to call national attention to techniques and goals of this particular committee. It was in this protest demonstration that the so-called free speech movement was born in the California colleges.

In the ferment accompanying the war in Vietnam, strong protest movements have been greatly in evidence on university campuses. In addition the civil rights movement has received great support from students in general and has been combined with other kinds of protest. We work in an atmosphere of great communicative freedom in our nation's colleges and universities.

Those who were students during the McCarthy era and who suffered through some of the indignities of the loyalty oath and other restrictions on academic freedom, have generally felt that the relaxing of control and stress on academic freedom and student rights was an unqualified improvement. In the past few years, however, we have seen that students in the "free speech" movement may not be as committed to free speech as they seem to be. Speaking at one campus, George Wallace of Alabama was booed off the platform, and his speech was not allowed to be heard. Students raised so much din and created so much noise that Governor Wallace could not deliver his speech. In another instance, Robert McNamara, then Secretary of Defense, was barely able to be heard above the noise and shouting of the anti-Vietnam protestors among the students present. At the State University of Iowa, a large campus demonstration was arranged to prevent the appearance of a speaker whose opinions ran counter to the opinions of many of the students.

It is ironic to witness students who ostensibly believe in the freedom of speech advocating that someone with whom they disagree not be allowed to speak. This position is the same one that college administrators and Senator McCarthy took many years ago when they advocated that freedom of speech be restricted for the people with whom they disagreed. With this particular point of view, "freedom of speech" ceases to exist. Whether or not a student "free speech" movement or a repressive university administrator censors communication matters very little. Nor does the content of the speech matter. Freedom of expression as an ideal in our society has never been limited to a particular form or particular content. To have a free and open society, we cannot simply hear our own opinions expressed. And, unfortunately, to have a society at all, we must have some restrictions on the general communicative activity of individuals. The key word in the whole problem is "responsibility"—a regard for the rights of others, along with as much individual freedom as is possible. Let us examine some of the responsibilities that communicators face in a society which is dedicated to such freedom of expression.

Limitations on Communication

"Clear and Present Danger" The first thing we must admit to ourselves is that in no society is communication truly free. Nowhere are individuals completely at liberty to say anything that they wish. Our society has codified one of the important restrictions on speech under the "clear and present danger" test in our legal system. Robert M. O'Neil, in his excellent book, *Free Speech: Responsible Communication Under Law*, comments that the "clear and present danger" test has its source in a passage from one of Justice Oliver Wendell Holmes' opinions. In a 1919 case being tried under the Espionage Act, Justice Holmes wrote:

> The character of every act depends on the circumstances in which it is done. The most stringent protection of free speech would not protect a man in falsely shouting fire in a theatre and causing a panic. It does not even protect a man from an injunction against uttering words that may have all the effect of force. The question in every case is whether the words used are used in such circumstances and are of such a nature as to create a clear and present danger that they will bring about the substantive evils that Congress has a right to prevent. There is a question of proximity and degree.[1]

What this means is that when speech gives an effect of immediate evil or an intent to bring about an immediate evil, it warrants the constitutionality of a congressional decree which sets a limit to the expression of opinion where private rights are not concerned. The majority of the Supreme Court followed the "clear and present" danger test for a great period of time thereafter.

Confronted with the existence of the Communist party and one world crisis after another, the Supreme Court in 1950 held that a "conspiracy to overthrow the government" rather than direct advocacy of overthrow itself was an evil sufficient to warrant suppression of speech tending toward that result. The evidence in many cases presented to the Court proved a clear case of conspiracy, and the Court at that time rejected claims for the First Amendment in the defendents' cases.

This position of the Supreme Court gave rise to much criticism

---

[1] Robert M. O'Neil, *Free Speech: Responsible Communication Under Law*, (Indianapolis, Ind., 1966), p. 31.

within and without our society. Several years later the position was mitigated somewhat when the court held that they had not really meant to suppress mere discussion of violent overthrow of the government, but only such advocacy that actually urged the audience to do something or to take direct action toward subversion or treason.

That decision was made in 1957. Of late, the doctrine of clear and present danger has been invoked in the arrest of the chairman of the Student Nonviolent Coordinating Committee, H. Rapp Brown. In Cambridge, Maryland, in 1967, Brown advocated that Negroes take arms and fight the white community. The subsequent riot and disorder that followed was interpreted as evidence that Brown had overstepped his legal and constitutional guarantee to the freedom of speech and that his speaking constituted a clear and present danger to the community.

What exactly is a clear and present danger arising from any kind of a communicative act? Justice Holmes' example of shouting fire in a crowded theatre is an obvious instance. Several other examples come to mind. We might be driving along the freeway as a passenger in an automobile, and suddenly shout "look out!" at the driver—who could easily be panicked into causing an accident. If we were a passenger in an airplane and distracted the pilot at some critical moment, our speech could have grave consequences. It is more difficult, however, to decide what is a danger to our society.

In the first place, it is much harder to define a society. Our constitution specifies our form of government, and on the surface at least, it might seem that anything that tends to modify the constitution would be a clear and present danger to our form of government. But since the constitution contains provisions for amendment, it is hard to argue that modifying the constitution is a clear and present danger to our society. For example, Senator Dirksen of Illinois has recently advocated an amendment which would allow prayers in public schools. It is hard to imagine how this amendment could be a clear and present danger to our society, especially in the framework that Senator Dirksen has advocated the amendment.

Changes to a society cannot be clear and present dangers to it. What we need to do is to decide at what point a clear and present danger exists and under what circumstances freedom of expression and communication ought to be restricted to avoid the clear and present danger. Typically in wartime we believe that our society is in danger. But consider the situation of the individual living, for example, in Nazi Germany in 1944. The society is at war with other societies, is clearly in danger of being overrun and destroyed, and yet the individual may feel (as many Germans at that time did feel) that the defeat of the country would be the best thing that could happen. The dangers posed by wartime are not an infallible test, but are only part of the situation in which the citizen finds himself in judging acceptable standards of communication.

Similarly we have typically held that communications that led to violent actions or the destruction of property were a clear example of what we would call danger to our society. H. Rapp Brown's speech in Maryland, for example, brought about the destruction of much property, and most legal thinkers at the time were in agreement that this form of communication constituted a danger to the society. Yet it is the view of Brown and his followers that the society in which he found himself was an oppressive one, a society that felt that the Negro could never be given a position of equality in the processes of government. They felt that drastic measures were needed in order to bring about some new form of government.

In other words, the simple invocation of a "clear and present danger" doctrine is not enough to answer our question of whether or not freedom of speech is deserved in any given situation. Each situation must be approached as a separate and distinct entity and a decision of whether a communication is a clear and present danger must be answered on the merits of each individual case. Robert O'Neil's book provides a discussion of some of the typical thinking of the Supreme Court in this area and is and should be recommended for students who are interested in further reading on this problem.[2] The Supreme Court's thinking is, of course, far from the final word in this area. Our citizens often disagree with the Supreme Court, but the Court's reasoning is a good guide for stimulating thought in this area.

It should be obvious, then, that one of the things that every communicator should consider is whether or not his task in communication would constitute what could easily be defined as a clear and present danger to his society. It is not enough for laws and regulations to limit the behavior and limit the speech of our citizens. It is more important for citizens to exercise sober and reasonable judgment in governing themselves in this kind of a decision. Communicators therefore have a responsibility to their society and to their auditors to at least consider the question of clear and present danger before undertaking a communicative act.

Other Restrictions Another restriction on the freedom of expression of communicators in our society is made on the basis of whether or not their expression could be considered obscene, appealing to the prurient interests of the audience. In 1957 the Supreme Court took the question of obscenity out of the "clear and present danger" clause, holding that it was not necessary to prove that obscene material was a clear and present danger because it would incite antisocial sexual acts.

[2] Robert M. O'Neil, *Free Speech: Responsible Communication Under Law*, p. 36.

Since that decision several clarifications have been made about obscene materials and their acceptability in terms of expression. The standard finally given by the Court has been "contemporary community standards" which are quite difficult to find. Standards in some communities obviously are different than standards in others. Another factor posed by the Court is whether or not the material has "redeeming social importance." The Illinois Supreme Court (in the case of the late Lenny Bruce, a comedian whose remarks offended many) held that Mr. Bruce's acts were not obscene because much of what he had said had redeeming social importance.

Speakers and communicators generally are not faced with the problem of obscenity, but it is not hard to imagine a situation in which the material which a communicator might use might be objectionable to audiences. Once again, as in the clear and present danger test, the best guide to whether or not the material is obscene is to examine the writing of the Supreme Court. If a speaker takes the express purpose of shocking an audience out of its lethargy, the purpose of the communication might be of greater importance to the speaker than the possible legal consequences of the speech. Under that circumstance the speaker may be well advised to use any kind of material that he likes in order to achieve his purpose. A speaker who has long-range goals in mind and who is attempting to bring about attitude and opinion change may find that the use of this kind of material might damage his acceptability as a message-source. In other words, this kind of material could create obvious boomerang effects which the speaker ought to avoid.

There is another area in which communicators are not free. They may not, (under recent court decisions) use material that is offensive to racial minorities. In spite of all the so-called "polack" jokes that we have heard circulating throughout the country in recent years, any kind of utterance that is gravely offensive to any racial or religious minority comes under this particular legal restriction. A communicator who uses this sort of thing is liable to prosecution. It is hard to imagine any communicator legitimately needing either of the above kinds of material.

So there are several ways in which our society regulates expression. There are things that society will not tolerate and communicators must be aware of these. The existence of the laws is to act as a check upon irresponsible utterances that will be seriously damaging both to the majority and minorities in our society. We generally feel that reasonable people adhere to the legal framework of our societies.

When legal frameworks are not the best kind of guide to actions, individuals may choose to deliberately violate the law in order to bring about desirable social action. Constructive passive disobedience as outlined by Henry David Thoreau seems to be a legitimate force. But those who engage in such civil disobedience must be prepared to accept the consequences of their actions, which in many instances could even involve jail sentences. Many who misunderstand Thoreau seem to feel that laws can be violated with impunity, and this certainly is not the case. The untimely death of Dr. Martin Luther King reminded many of us that true civil disobedience involves suffering the consequences of the law as well as violating it. Dr. King's behavior was always in this framework. Whether or not a communication is justified can be answered only by the ultimate end sought by the communicator. There is no other source to seek justification.

Once again we are confronted by the means-ends justification controversy. In many social issues we can make a strong case for social ends which justify unfortunate means which bring us to the goal that we seek. On the other hand, it is difficult to visualize any social good which could not also be brought about by legitimate oral expression and communication that stays within the framework of the law as articulated by the decisions of the highest court of the land.

OBLIGATIONS OF THE COMMUNICATOR

So far in this chapter we have taken a fairly negative point of view examining some of the strictures *against* forms of communications that may be legally invoked against a communicator. Let us turn now to some of the obligations that communicators have in our society and some of the things that our particular society imposes on us in the form of communicative obligations.

As everyone knows, we live in a society that is dedicated to free and open expression by its citizens and its governmental officials. Representative government has been carefully preserved over the years by strict adherence to the guarantees of our particular constitution. However, for representative government to work means that those who are represented must communicate with the representors. The citizenry must communicate and express their wants, desires, and afflictions to the lawmakers who are expected to implement these wants and desires. It is obvious that representative government cannot succeed unless this is done. We may expect our representatives in Congress to seek information from us, and many do. Some Congressmen even send questionnaires to their constituency which are designed to keep the representative well-informed. But no matter how hard they try, it is extremely difficult for any one representative to collect this much information. It is therefore the duty of the citizenry to communicate with their representative, as well as they can.

Many of us are prevented from communicating with others by various reasons—we do not wish to appear unusual or to "rock the boat." Every such inhibition directly diminishes the effect of self government in our society. Every individual who fails to communicate to responsible officials information and attitudes about his neighborhood, his city, his state, and even himself damages democracy. It is not enough to have polling organizations (such as the Gallup or the Harris poll) which reflect public opinion. "Public opinion" is too varied and diverse to depend upon the few simple questionnaires these polls use. The power of such public opinion as expressed by the polls is enormous, however. President Johnson's decision not to run in 1968 may well have been the result of polling information which showed that his policies were generally disapproved of by the populace in April of that year. The national polls do not represent opinion in given areas, and do not report to each individual Congressman or Senator what his constituents are thinking.

Our local government is even more dependent on communication from the citizenry. Municipal and local governments affect our daily lives more than the federal government, and citizens who do not communicate with elected officials do great damage to the causes of their cities and states.

Our only conclusion can be that not only do citizens have the right to communicate (as guaranteed by constitutional provisions) but they have the duty to communicate in order to make our self government operate. No matter what unit we find ourselves operating in, whether it be student government, university self government, state, local, or federal government, our responsibilities are still the same. The existence of self-governmental forms in our particular society place upon us the burden and obligation of communication in order to make our institutions work. If we lived in a totalitarian society we would have no such burden. In Franco's Spain, for example, there is very little need for the citizens to communicate with the central government. If we lived in Red China, our desires about the outcome of the government's national policy would have very little interest for the national decision makers. But in our society these obligations assume tremendous importance. If we are to receive the benefits of our society we must also assume its obligations, both in its constraint of our communications according to constitutional provisions and in the obligation that our form of government imposes upon us.

PART TWO

COMMUNICATION THEORY IN PRACTICE

INTRODUCTION

Part One of this book was concerned with a detailed analysis of communication with special emphasis on speaking and listening. A knowledge of the interaction of the elements in a communication situation is essential to the individual who is concerned with the improvement of his communication skills.

However, reading about communication is only the first step in a program designed to help an individual to develop effectiveness, efficiency, and control in the communicative activities of speaking and listening. It is doubtful that many people have learned to speak effectively by reading about the techniques of good oral communication. Likewise, few people are capable of becoming competent communicators merely by *wanting* to improve.

To develop skill in the many phases of oral communication, the student must have help in identifying his oral communication needs, and supervised and controlled practice opportunities, structured to develop maximum improvement. Experience has demonstrated that an individual will learn to speak and listen more effectively if he approaches the learning situation with a positive attitude, if he is given expert guidance and instruction, and if he has the opportunity to participate in a series of carefully arranged and designed assignments.

Part Two of this book provides a sequence of assignments which are an essential part of a course dealing with the communication problems which we face every day of our lives. The projects have been designed to give you a variety of experiences. Moreover, they have been carefully planned to help you develop certain skills in the areas of structuring messages and in the effective use of voice and body as reinforcers of language.

It should be remembered that a communication class is a means to an end and not an end in itself. Its sole objective is to assist in the over-all improvement of communication skills which are so involved in our everyday living, and upon which we are so dependent for adequate adjustment to our total environment. In a very real sense, the test of the effectiveness of this course can only be judged by the degree of improvement in your daily communication contacts with people.

But you probably will be more interested, at this point, in your teacher's evaluation of your progress in class. To keep you fully informed on this matter, Communication Evaluation forms have been provided in your Workbook.

Note that these forms are in duplicate. The first copy when properly completed will provide you with a teacher evaluation of your communication effectiveness on a particular assignment. The carbon copy is kept by the teacher for reference and for tracing your progress throughout the semester. Save your criticisms for every performance, so that you too will have a cumulative record of your work in this course.

If you will look at one of the criticism blanks in the workbook, you will note that the evaluation form is divided into two sections: one is labeled "message composition" and the other "delivery." Your instructor will write helpful comments relating to the construction of your speech in the first space, with particular emphasis on choice of subject, selection of material, structure of message, and language effectiveness. In addition, he may give you a numerical score on each of these items using the rating scale on the right side of the criticism blank. The numerical evaluation will be assigned on the following basis:

> 7—Definitely Superior
> 6—Approaching Excellence
> 5—Better than Average
> 4—Average
> 3—Below Average
> 2—Poor
> 1—Definitely Inferior

The second part of the criticism blank deals with "delivery," and your instructor will record in this space constructive suggestions concerning your vocal reinforcement, articulation, pronunciation, and physical reinforcement in addition to giving you a numerical score for each item.

Finally, on the criticism blank there are spaces for the instructor's rating of the general effectiveness of your communication and for a letter grade.

Each time you receive one of these evaluation blanks from your instructor, read it carefully. As you prepare your next speech keep in mind the advice your instructor has given you in the past. Try to eliminate the weaknesses that have been pointed out to you; try to capitalize on the strengths which he has heard in your speech. Following this procedure should assist you in developing the skills of oral communication.

In the second part of this book, you will also find a list of listening devices. Some of these have been suggested by people interested in the problem of developing better listening skills. Some of them have been created by the authors. Your instructor will select the most appropriate one for each speaking performance. He will ask you to perform certain tasks which should direct your attention to the improvement of your attitude toward listening, toward your comprehension of the speaker's message, toward your evaluation of materials which are utilized by the speaker, or toward the important problem of listener reactions.

Your instructor may use one device repeatedly. If he does, you should know that he is attacking a problem which seems to be prevalent in your class. Or he may use a different device for each performance. Work at accomplishing the goals he sets for you. Remember that speaking and listening are closely related and that you must take every opportunity to improve not only your speaking, but also your listening. Work at becoming a good speaker *and* a good listener.

ASSIGNMENT OUTLINE

Drills
1. Key Idea Evaluation
2. Scrambled Outlines
3. Conclusion Identification
4. Introduction Identification

Projects
1. Observation of a Formal Speaking Situation
2. Observation of a Group Interaction
3. Propaganda Analysis
4. Observation: Emphasis on Vocal Effectiveness
5. Observation: Emphasis on Physical Reinforcement

Diagnostic Performances
1. Introduction of a Classmate
2. Group Discussion on the Subject, "What is Effective Communication?"
3. "Communication Breakdown"
4. Three-minute Speech
5. Voice and Articulation Test

Communication Problems
1. Demonstration
2. Demonstration with Chalkboard

3. Explanation of a Process
4. An Introduction
5. Review of Book, Play, Movie, or TV Show
6. Explanation of an Abstract Idea
7. "This I Believe"
8. Presentation of a Problem
9. Sales Talk
10. Defense of Status Quo
11. Advocacy of a Change of Policy

DRILLS

AND PROJECTS

DRILL 1

KEY IDEA EVALUATION

Listed below are some examples of key idea statements which beginning students have used in speeches. Using the answer sheet provided for this drill in your Workbook, rewrite the statements which do not comply with the characteristics of a good key idea.

1. An educated person should have a basic knowledge of how to write a clear and concise business letter in an acceptable form.
2. Citizenship in this country may be obtained through birth in the United States or by a naturalization process.
3. I find Japan very interesting and quite different from all the knowledge about it I had gained from textbooks.
4. The political philosophy of Charles de Gaulle is expressed in his book, *The Sword's Edge*, which he wrote in 1932; this philosophy still guides his policies now that he is the President of the Fifth Republic.
5. Among the most noteworthy things in Israel today are her people, her new and modern buildings, and the apparent fertility of the countryside.
6. The preamble to the charter of the United Nations sets up certain ideals that a country must live up to in order to be a member.
7. There are numerous steps in our federal lawmaking process from the origin of an idea for a legislative proposal through its promulgation and publication as a statute.

8. Young men of America should realize and take advantage of the many benefits derived from affiliation with the National Guard.
9. The gimbaled motor in relation to Newton's laws of motion.
10. The Polaris missile is superior to all other long-range missiles which have been produced by the United States.
11. How a reciprocating steam engine works.
12. Hobo signs on fence posts and telephone poles.
13. The system of interstate highways will provide faster, cheaper, and safer travel by cars.
14. To inform the class in using an exposure meter.
15. The split-T offense in football has a great scoring potential.
16. My key idea is—three types of complicated-looking card tricks.
17. Archery today is completely different in the type of equipment used in the early ages.
18. The motto of Junior Achievement is "Learn by doing."
19. Basically, there are two single-wing formations in football with variations run off of each.
20. The leaf, its arrangements, structures, and functions.
21. In manufacturing paint, one follows three main steps.
22. The cooling effect of evaporation is utilized in most modern refrigerators.
23. An artesian well is a natural spring of water. The word artesian comes from a province in France where these natural phenomena were first discovered.
24. How to execute a football play.
25. Television programs should be critically examined by parents before permitting children to view them.
26. The importance of obeying the speed laws in school zones.
27. Support the March of Dimes!
28. We don't listen.
29. Jaywalking, a frequent cause of traffic accidents, can be prevented.
30. Elementary and secondary teaching conditions need improving.
31. A brief history of printing from its beginning until now.
32. By using known techniques with a leadstrap and other equipment, I can show you how to win first place in exhibiting cattle.
33. The American public would not gain by adopting a policy of free trade.
34. To inform people about some of the qualifications and adventures of a stewardess.
35. The tradition of Christmas tree trimming.
36. Parachute jumping is probably the greatest emotional test that a man can force himself to face.

37. Today, I would like to tell you the different meanings of words.
38. The California Junior College—its history and significance as it relates to modern education.
39. I would like to tell you about some strange occupations.
40. People make many wrong decisions in their lives.
41. The application of certain techniques is one of the most important principles of becoming a good pianist.
42. I have been especially interested in Mohammedanism because I have a friend who is a Moslem and until I met this friend my ideas were completely wrong about this religion. This friend explained to me that the Mohammedans believe in God and only in God, and that Mohammed was only a prophet—a teacher of God's word.

DRILL 2

SCRAMBLED OUTLINES

Listed below are several scrambled outlines. Put the items for each outline in the proper order and form. Select the key idea and put it in the proper space on the answer sheet provided in your Workbook. Next, arrange the main points of the body of the speech in the proper order. Indicate the type of order which you have made use of in each case. Finally, indicate the purpose of each speech.

1. He will reduce taxes.
   Elect John Brown mayor.
   He will improve your city government.
   He will build much-needed public buildings.
2. Abraham Lincoln's reputation as a speaker is based largely on several important speeches.
   The Lincoln-Douglass debates helped to establish Lincoln as a public speaker.
   His Gettysburg Address won new admirers for Lincoln.
   In spite of bitter antagonisms, Lincoln's Second Inaugural Address went down in history as great oratory.
   The simplicity of the First Inaugural Address appealed to the masses.
3. Salt brine is pumped from wells.
   Salt is obtained by a process of evaporation.
   Crystals are formed in a settler.
   The brine is boiled off by evaporation.

4. Weapons
   Fencing is an interesting sport to watch if you understand it.
   Tactics and techniques
   Stances and movements
5. *In this scrambled outline, the introduction and conclusion have also been included.*
   Remember the next time someone in your community asks you to donate money or time to your community, that your community gives you protection, education, and social life. Any one of these is worth more than all of the money or time you have or you will ever have.
   Each person should donate his free time as much as possible.
   You should help your community in any way possible.
   Your entire community is the hub that your whole life revolves around. Your community may be part of a great city or just a small village. But no matter how large or how small it is, your community helps you in many ways.
   Your community helps you in many ways.
   Your community helps you, so you should help your community.
   Protection is offered to everyone in the community.
   Each person should donate money as often as he can.
   Your community offers social life.
   The entire community is protected against fire.
   The entire community has police protection.
   The entire community is protected from a health standpoint.
   Your community offers education for everyone.

DRILL 3

CONCLUSION IDENTIFICATION

Listed below are examples of different types of conclusions. Read each one carefully and decide what type each is most like. Indicate your answer on the answer sheet provided for this drill in your Workbook.

1. My plea is that we practice the principles in which we glory; that we not only believe in equality, but determine we shall have equality. American patriotism is admired throughout the world and there is no battle we should refuse to fight in the defense of principle. But not alone the sight of the American

eagle and the sound of the fife and drum corps thrill the patriot, but the marvel of our country's founding, the fundamental right of our principles, the freedom of our people—these are the things that stir American blood. Let us once again determine that those rugged men who built our country shall not have lived in vain; that those brave fathers who fought to defend it shall not have died in vain; but that the ideals of humanity are the practices of the United States; that every American citizen is indeed an American citizen; that in the final test, democracy shall prevail.—E. M. LIVINGSTON

2. As for me, give me liberty or give me death.—PATRICK HENRY
3. In conclusion, may I quote part of President Roosevelt's book *Looking Forward:* "I hope that in all states we shall be continually decreasing the number of prison guards and wardens and increasing the number of our parole and probation officers."

    Even if that might mean that prison administrators like myself would become as obsolete as horsecars, I fervently say, "God speed the day."—A. H. MACCORMICK
4. There is a story attributed to Colonel House about the visit of Balfour to this country in 1917. The story goes that after the conclusion of his business in Washington, Balfour had five days before his sailing. He asked House how he could most profitably spend those five days in acquiring the fullest possible knowledge of American public opinion for his future use as a member of the British Government. The Colonel is said to have replied in substance: "You have, I know, friends in the so-called upper classes in New York and on Long Island. Spend all your five days with them and listen to their views. Then you will know what the great mass of American men and women think, for they will think just the opposite of your Long Island friends."

    That story has not lost its point today. You know as well as I, the very limited and narrow understanding of public movements possessed by too many of the so-called educated— the products of our colleges and universities—who have had all the leisure and advantages that ought to make for real distinterestedness, detachment, and imaginative understanding.— ROBERT H. JACKSON
5. With malice towards none, with charity for all, with firmness in the right as God gives us to see the right, let us finish the work we are in, to bind up the nation's wounds, to care for him who shall have borne the battle and for his widows and orphans, to do all which may achieve and cherish a just and lasting peace among ourselves and with all nations. [Abraham Lincoln's Second Inaugural Address.]

6. This evening, I come back to you only as one with some experience in war and peace, of some acquaintanceship with our friends of Western Europe, to bring you what is in my heart and mind. I shall go about my own task in this undertaking with the unshakable confidence that America will respond fully when the basic issues are understood. We know that 150 million united Americans constitute the greatest temporal force that has ever existed on God's earth. If we join in a common understanding of our country's role today and wholeheartedly devote ourselves to its discharge, the year 1951 may be recorded in our history in letters as bright as is written the year 1776.—DWIGHT D. EISENHOWER, February 2, 1951.

7. I am closing my fifty-two years of military service. When I joined the army, even before the turn of the century, it was the fulfillment of all of my boyish hopes and dreams. The world has turned over many times since I took the oath at West Point, and the hopes and dreams have all since vanished, but I still remember the refrain of one of the most popular barracks ballads of that day which proclaimed most proudly that old soldiers never die; they just fade away. And like the old soldier of that ballad, I now close my military career and just fade away, an old soldier who tried to do his duty as God gave him the light to see that duty. Goodbye.—DOUGLAS MACARTHUR, April 19, 1951.

8. Now, a second time, our life as a free nation is in grave danger. Now, a second time, brute force of magnitude bears down upon us. Once more we call upon you to help us resist the aggressor. Our fight is your fight—more so now than ever. It is the fight of free men anywhere and everywhere in the world, to preserve liberty and to destroy tyranny! It is a struggle which can never be encompassed by any single geographical area, no matter how seemingly remote. We share a common cause, a holy cause. You did not fail us in the past. I know you will not fail us now.
—BEN C. LIMB

DRILL 4

INTRODUCTION IDENTIFICATION

Listed below are samples of different types of introductions. Read each one carefully and decide what type each is. Indicate your answers on the answer sheet provided for this drill in your Workbook.

DRILLS AND PROJECTS 243

1. In 1946, we lost 110,000,000 man-days of labor through 5,575 major strikes. Think of it! 301,397 man-years of labor in one year. Isn't there something which could be done to curb this unbelievable loss? [From a student's speech.]
2. During the fifteenth and sixteenth centuries the rhythm and beat of music was measured by means of a pulse beat, the pendulum of a clock, or the "tick" of an ordinary clock. Now, we have a simple instrument designed specifically for this task. [From a student's speech.]
3. It is very simple to count to five. Try it over and over again. Just remember that each time you reach five—somewhere in this world—an old man, a middle-aged woman, a small child, or a baby has just died from starvation. Yes, every five seconds someone dies from starvation. Today there are 500 million people all over the world starving. One-half of these face death—death from hunger alone—unless help is given immediately.—ROSEMARY ARNOLD
4. Imagine, if you can, a horde of gold greater than that of Fort Knox, vast stores of jewels worth more than the combined wealth of all the Indian Princes, and myriads of articles of worth more precious than the iron ore of the Mesabi Range! This is but a small part of the treasure guarded so jealously and well by King Neptune, in the hulks of sunken pirates' vessels, modern ocean liners, and slow-moving cargo boats. [From a student's speech.]
5. Imagine the national horror if a strange plague were to wipe out the entire population of a city of 15,000. Such a plague actually has struck all over America. In the first six months of 1946, 15,750 persons were killed in highway traffic accidents; the automobile accounted for one out of every five deaths from all causes. [From a student's speech.]
6. During my high school days, I earned spending money and had a glorious time acting as stage assistant for a magician. From my position behind the footlights, I saw how gullible audiences are. Without revealing too many of the magician's professional secrets, perhaps I can show you how easily he fools the public. [From a student's speech.]
7. A little more than a year ago today, on April 16, 1947, there occurred in Texas City, Texas, probably one of the worst disasters ever known in the United States. The people of Texas City at last had an idea of the damage caused by the atom bomb dropped on Hiroshima, for their town was almost completely demolished. An atom bomb, however, was not the cause of the damage. The cause was blamed on a nitrate-laden

ship that had exploded in the harbor, thus causing a series of disastrous explosions. After the holocaust was over, the citizens of Texas City took count of the damage. Result—there were 462 persons dead, 50 persons missing, 3000 injured, 3382 homes and 130 business structures destroyed or damaged, and a $55,000,000 property loss. If Texas City had thrown in the sponge one year ago, not even the most boisterous Texan would have blamed it; instead the people rolled up their sleeves and went to work. [From a student's speech.]

8. I plan to become a social worker upon graduation from college. My main field of interest is working with children, preferably those who have been placed in a children's home. I lived in an orphanage myself at one time. I wasn't there very long, but, nevertheless, my stay there affected me profoundly. Although this institution was thought to be well organized, there were many things missing which are necessary to children. Among these essentials were love and security. The administrative staff did not have time to see to it that we were surrounded by the warmth and security of a real home. [From a student's speech.]

9. On August 6, 1945, a bomb was dropped on Hiroshima, Japan. This was not an ordinary "Grand Slam" bomb equal to eleven tons of trinitrotoluene, better known as TNT. This new bomb was equal to twenty thousand tons of TNT. It killed outright sixty thousand persons, injured one hundred thousand more, and left two hundred thousand homeless. This was the first use of the atomic bomb in warfare. [From a student's speech.]

10. Shortly after the school bell had rung for the dismissal of afternoon classes, six-year-old David came running down the street on his way home. It was pouring rain and Little David forgot to look both ways before he ran out into the street. Out of the haze came a car speeding along at about fifty miles an hour. The driver couldn't stop quickly enough, and after the car hit David, it skidded sixty feet, dragging the child on its bumper. [From a student's speech.]

11. The National Guard has served our nation with honor and distinction in every emergency from pre-Revolutionary War days through the Korean emergency. Actually, it is older than our country, with one guard regiment going back to 1636. In World War I, of the eight divisions rated by the German High Command as superior or excellent, six were National Guard divisions. The Guard made a brilliant record on every fighting front in World War II—eight divisions and twenty-two Air

Guard Wings—more than one hundred and fifty thousand guardsmen served with distinction in the Korean emergency. [From a student's speech.]

PROJECT 1

OBSERVATION OF A FORMAL SPEAKING SITUATION

Attend a formal speaking situation such as a convocation, a political meeting in which at least one speech is presented, a meeting of a service organization where a speaker is scheduled to speak, and so on. Using the report blank provided in the Workbook for this project, write a short commentary on the effectiveness of the speaker's performance. Follow the suggestions outlined on the answer blank in making your report.

PROJECT 2

OBSERVATION OF A GROUP INTERACTION

Observe a meeting in your dormitory, sorority or fraternity; or a meeting of the city council or any other organized group discussion. On the report blank provided in the Workbook for this project, write an analysis following the guidelines suggested.

PROJECT 3

PROPAGANDA ANALYSIS

1. Using the blank provided in your Workbook for this exercise, discuss five advertisements which have made use of one of the many propaganda techniques discussed in Chapter 7, pages 214 to 219. If the ad has appeared in a magazine or newspaper, cut it out and paste it on the report blank; if this is not possible, reproduce the ad. Then explain the appeal which the copywriter has attempted to achieve. Also, explain how he has achieved his end and whether or not his approach violates any ethical principles.

Some of your ads may have had their source in radio or television commercials. Try to write the ad out in full. Comment on it following the above suggestions.
2. Does the advertisement make use of imbalance? Does it create imbalance? What are the elements involved in the imbalance? Explain each. What result do you think it will have? How will the system get back into balance?

PROJECT 4

OBSERVATION: EMPHASIS ON VOCAL EFFECTIVENESS

While listening to a speech, fill out the check list that is provided in the Workbook for this assignment. You may use a member of your speech class as your subject; or you may use a convocation speaker, a minister, a politician, and so on. *Be sure to read the check list on pages 25–26 of your Workbook before undertaking this assignment.*

PROJECT 5

OBSERVATION: EMPHASIS ON PHYSICAL REINFORCEMENT

While listening to a speech, fill in the check list that is provided in the Workbook for this assignment. You may use a member of your class as your subject; or you may use a convocation speaker, a minister, a politician, and so on. *Be sure to read the check list on pages 27–28 of the Workbook before undertaking this assignment.*

DIAGNOSTIC PERFORMANCES

PERFORMANCE 1

INTRODUCTION OF A CLASSMATE

A. *Purpose of assignment*
   1. To initiate each student into the class speaking situation.
   2. To introduce students to each other and to the instructor.
   3. To provide an impromptu sample of each student's speech as the first step in the evaluation of the individual's speaking ability.

B. *Procedure*
   A partner will be assigned to you, and the speaker-member of the team will be given from five to ten minutes to interview his partner in preparation for introducing him to the class. The interviewer should question his partner about his educational objectives, his hobbies, his home town, his high school, highlights in his life, his reasons for coming to this school, his ambitions, and so on.

C. *Performance*
   1. Each speaker will introduce his partner to the class. As the speaker, try to present your partner so that your listeners will want to know this person better. Avoid just listing facts about him.
   2. Repeat the whole process, with newly assigned partners.

D. *Directed listening activity*
   Try to associate one important fact and the first name with each individual as he is presented to the class. Following the introductions of the first half of the class, the instructor will ask ques-

tions about each individual; or he will ask someone to name every person in the class; or he will ask someone to mention one interesting item about each student.

PERFORMANCE 2

GROUP DISCUSSION: "WHAT IS EFFECTIVE COMMUNICATION?"

A. *Purpose of assignment*
   1. To analyze the subject of communication.
   2. To set up some criteria of effective oral communication.
   3. To describe some goals for this class.
   4. To place each student in a group communication situation.
B. *Procedure*
   Based upon your reading and your broad experience with communication, prepare to discuss the questions in the outline below.

OUTLINE

   I. What are the important elements in your everyday communication?
   II. What is there about some communicators that makes you want to listen?
   III. Exploration of the problem
      A. What brought you into the communicative interaction in the first place?
      B. What did you expect from it?
      C. What ideas were involved?
      D. What extraneous factors helped or hindered in the interaction?
   IV. Describe, from the above points, the "effective" communicator.
C. *Activity in the class*
   During the discussion, take an active part in helping to describe the characteristics of good communication. When the chairman, your instructor, presents a question, volunteer to answer it in terms of your own experiences and beliefs, illustrating as often as possible with personal examples.
D. *Directed listening activity*
   It is important in a group discussion that you listen attentively to each speaker. Do not attempt to interrupt anyone's discussion with rebuttal. Wait until the person has finished speaking, since he

DIAGNOSTIC PERFORMANCES 249

may clear up the point which caused you concern. Evaluate each speaker's contribution as objectively as possible, and, after this consideration, if you desire amplification or justification, secure recognition from the chairman and direct your questions to the proper person.

PERFORMANCE 3

COMMUNICATION BREAKDOWNS

A. *Time limit:* 3 minutes

B. *Purpose of assignment*
   1. To introduce you as a speaker to your classmates and your instructor.
   2. To increase your awareness of everyday problems in communication.

C. *Preparation*
   Try to remember a situation in which you and someone else failed to communicate when you should have. Look into the situation in terms of the model presented at the end of Chapter 1. Analyze whether your failure was due to relaying, externalizing, or manding. Present the situation to the class as simply and directly as you can.

D. *Directed listening activity*
   Listen to the various breakdowns as they are presented. Is there a tendency for the individual to blame "the other guy" when communication breaks down? Be ready to respond after each presentation with a similar analysis from your point of view.

PERFORMANCE 4

THREE-MINUTE ORAL COMMUNICATION

A. *Time limit:* 3 minutes

B. *Purpose of assignment*
   1. To aid your instructor to assess your speaking debits and credits.
   2. To further initiate you into speaking before a group.
   3. To give your classmates and instructor further opportunities to become better acquainted with you.

250 COMMUNICATION THEORY IN PRACTICE

C. *Preparation*

For this speech, you may choose any subject. If you are having difficulty thinking of a topic, consider one of the following: "My Home Town," "The One City in the World I Would Like to Visit," "My Favorite Teacher," "The Best Speaker I Have Ever Heard," "A Person I Have Admired." Prepare your speech carefully. Your instructor expects you to utilize all of your present knowledge concerning effective speech in order that your performance will reflect your present skill in speaking. Prepare an outline, using one of the forms that are provided in your Workbook.

D. *Directed listening activity*

Try to comprehend and retain the central idea which each speaker presents. After the speech, you may be asked a question by your instructor, such as, "Why does this speaker have such admiration for his home town?" "What characteristics did the speaker seem to admire in the discussion of his favorite instructor?" and so forth.

PERFORMANCE 5

VOICE AND ARTICULATION TEST

A. *Purpose of assignment*
   1. To discover consistent inaccuracies in articulation.
   2. To evaluate your vocal characteristics, including
      a. Your vocal quality
      b. Your basic voice pitch
      c. Your loudness control
      d. Your use of variety in quality, pitch, and loudness
   3. To evaluate the rate and rhythm of your speaking.

B. *Preparation:* none necessary.

C. *Activity in class*

You will be asked to read the paragraph just below this assignment. This material contains all of the sounds of the English language as we use it. Read it naturally.

D. *Directed listening activity*

Your instructor is listening primarily for voice, articulation, pronunciation, and rate and rhythm problems. You, too, should attempt to discern inaccuracies or inadequacies in the performances of your classmates.

Test Material[1]

In September there is increased activity on all college and university campuses as new classes of Freshmen prepare to enroll. These students are entering a new phase of life. They now find themselves thrust into a type of environment in which they should exercise greater responsibility together with skillful management of their own affairs. Through group and club functions in which they participate during leisure time, they learn cooperation and loyalty. In planning programs, students must choose various fields of emphasis. Among these are music, agriculture, drama, medicine, zoology, mathematics, theology, psychology, journalism, architecture, speech, languages, economics, engineering, and botany. Such courses of study form the foundation upon which future lives are built.

[1] This test is one which is used widely in colleges and universities for testing voice and articulation.

COMMUNICATIVE PROBLEMS

On the following pages you will find a series of communication problems, arranged in a sequence of increasing difficulty. Your instructor will select a reasonable number of appropriate assignments for his particular course.

Most of the materials which will facilitate the preparation of these projects may be found in Part One of the text. However, specific instructions or reminders of special importance are included in the instructions provided for each assignment.

You are expected to provide your instructor with a copy of a carefully structured outline for each communication task. You may want a second copy of the outline for your use while speaking. If you do, put it on 3 × 5 index cards which you can hold comfortably in your hand without calling attention to them.

In the diagnostic performance assignments you will remember that there were "Directed Listening Activities" included. Since this course is concerned with communication generally, it is important that you make an effort to improve not only your speaking abilities but also your listening skills.

The following "Listening Improvement Devices" will be used at various times during the term in an effort to direct your attention to the reception of messages and to assist you to sharpen your listening abilities. Your instructor will select those exercises which seem to meet your particular needs.

LISTENING IMPROVEMENT DEVICES
(To be used at the discretion of the instructor)

1. Following a speech, your instructor may ask one of the listeners to summarize the speech which he has just heard.

2. The instructor will pass out 3 × 5 cards to each member of the class at some point in the hour and ask the students to record what has happened in the class during the preceding ten minutes.
3. The members of the class may be asked to record the central idea of each speech. No writing is to be done during the speech. Do not attempt to remember the exact wording of the key idea.
4. List the main points in each speech presented in class.
5. You will be asked to give a critique for a speech. However, you will not be warned in advance of the speech that you are expected to evaluate. This assignment may be used in different ways. On some occasions, your instructor will ask you to comment on the whole speech. On other occasions, he may ask you to discuss speech composition, content, arrangement, language, or some other aspect of speaking.
6. You may be asked to give a critique for a speech. However, in this instance your evaluation will be delayed one or more speeches. For example, three speeches may have been given in the class when your instructor calls upon you to criticize the first speech that was given.
7. You may be asked to participate in a compliment and razz session. Following a speech you will be asked to tell the speaker all the things he did well and those things he needs to improve further.
8. The instructor may ask the speaker to be particularly observant of his listeners. Following the speech, the instructor will ask the speaker to discuss the listeners. In this case, the speaker should discuss the listeners primarily from the standpoint of the effectiveness of their feedbacks.
9. As you go to the front of the room to speak, your instructor will whisper the name of a listener to you. During your speech note whether or not this person is actively participating in the speaking situation. Following your performance, your instructor will ask you to discuss the listening of the individual whom you observed.
10. As a variation of listening device 9, you may be asked by your instructor to observe two or three listeners and report on their listening behavior.
11. Your instructor may ask you to discuss the various types of support used by a speaker in developing his speech.
12. During the persuasive speeches, your instructor may ask you to cross-examine the speaker. That is, he may expect you to challenge the case presented by the speaker in defense of his point of view. He may ask you to perform this chore with or without advance warning.

13. You may be asked to take notes on a speech; following this, you will be asked to summarize the speech from your notes.
14. After a speech, you may be asked to evaluate the total effectiveness of your whole audience. Did they motivate you positively or negatively? Why?
15. Your instructor may test you over the content of the speeches on a particular day or on a particular speech.
16. The subjects for some of your impromptu speeches will be drawn from speeches which have been given in your class. In other words, following a group of informative speeches you may be asked to give an impromptu informative speech. The subject which you will be given will be one that has been discussed in class.
17. Your instructor may ask you, following your speech, to name the two or three best listeners. You should explain why you make the choice that you do.

PROBLEM 1

DEMONSTRATION

A. *Time limit:* 5 minutes
B. *Emphasis:* In this speech you will be challenged to use controlled and purposeful bodily activity as reinforcement of the message you relay in language.
C. *Preparation:*
   1. Locate an object which you can use in a demonstration speech. It may be a piece of machinery, an unusual musical instrument, a household gadget, a model, a map, scientific equipment, or any other thing which meets the requirements of a good speech topic. Be sure that it is worthwhile talking about, that it is suitable for your auditors, and that you can do a satisfactory job of explaining or using it.
   2. Plan your speech, using the four-part plan of organization. In your introduction try to arouse the interest and curiosity of your audience by giving an historical background for the subject, or by relating how you happened to secure the object, what it means to you, or by using startling facts which may be associated with your subject.

   Plan to conceal your object from the audience during your introduction. Bring it to class in a sack or a box or hide it by placing it in an inconspicuous place in the classroom. Be sure to

state the intent of your speech clearly and concisely, following your introduction. The body of your speech should involve an actual demonstration of the object in which you show its uses, its construction, and/or its operation. In the conclusion, re-emphasize the points which you have made by summarizing, or reinforce the idea of your speech by using any of the other types of conclusions.
3. Prepare an outline, using one of the blanks which have been provided in the Workbook for this purpose. This is to be handed to your instructor as you go to the front of the room to give your speech. Pay particular attention to the planning of your introduction and write it out in its entirety.
4. Be sure to practice your speech several times before giving it in class. Ample preparation and practice will help to give you greater self-confidence and will ensure a more effective performance in class.

D. *Delivery:*
When you present your speech in class, be sure to make the best possible use of your object. Hold it so that every member of the audience can see it easily. If necessary, move about the front of the room and hold the object for all to see. In your demonstration, be sure that you explain what you are doing. Check to make sure that your auditors are able to see what you are doing. Try to determine from their responses whether or not they understand. If they do not, try to reinforce your explanation with reiteration.

E. *Purpose of communication:* While it is impossible to anticipate all of the dimensions of a personalized and highly individualized message, the primary purposes of this assignment should be to relay and externalize. You will be providing your listeners with information which they probably do not presently possess and you will be sharing with your auditors your attitude toward the subject which you choose to discuss.

PROBLEM 2

DEMONSTRATION USING CHALKBOARD

A. *Time limit:* 5 minutes
B. *Emphasis:* In this speech you have another opportunity to use bodily activity in a meaningful way to clarify and reinforce the message which you structure in language. The problem of coordination will

probably prove more difficult than in the demonstration speech. You must draw or write on the blackboard while you are talking and at the same time you must maintain contact with your listeners.

C. *Preparation:*
1. Select a subject which will lend itself to picturization. It should be a topic which would be difficult for your listeners to understand without the visual aid which you provide on the blackboard. Students in the past have explained processes, inventions, trends in design, unusual architecture, garden design, farming methods, sports and games, ship design, military strategy, and so forth.
2. Plan your speech in the accustomed way. Provide an interesting and attention-getting introduction. State your key idea concisely and clearly. Explain your central idea thoroughly in the body of your speech. Round out your speech with a suitable conclusion. Reread the discussion of the various types of conclusions which you might use.
3. Prepare an outline, using one of the outline blanks from the Workbook. Pay particular attention to the planning of your conclusion and write it out in full in your outline. Hand the outline to your instructor as you go to the front of the room to speak.

D. *Delivery:*
The diagram may be drawn on the board during your introduction. Or it may be more convenient and effective for you to put it on in parts as you proceed through the body of your speech. Under certain circumstances, it is effective to put the outline of your diagram on the board during the first part of your speech, filling in the details as you discuss them in the body of your speech. The following suggestions may be of help to you:
1. Talk as you put your diagram on the board. It is awkward for both the listeners and the speaker when there are long pauses interrupted only by the squeaking of the chalk on the slate.
2. Face your audience as much of the time as you can conveniently do so. Be sure to face them during your explanations.
3. Be sure to handle your drawing in such a way that you do not have to talk over your shoulder to your listeners. If you are right-handed and plan to use your preferred hand to point to the board, stand to the right of your diagram. If you are left-handed, stand to the left. You will not have to fight to talk across your shoulder if you follow this plan.
4. Make the diagram an important part of the speech. Draw it so that it can be seen by all members of the audience. Make your

chalk lines bold and heavy. Finally, make use of the diagram throughout your explanations.

E. *Purpose of communication:* relaying and externalizing.

PROBLEM 3

EXPLANATION OF A PROCESS

A. *Time limit:* 5 minutes
B. *Emphasis:* Clear, concise, and accurate language is of prime importance in this communicative situation. Your outline must provide a substantial framework around which to build an accurate and comprehensive *verbal* explanation.
C. *Preparation:*
   1. Select a subject which requires your explanation of a process such as the steps in the adoption of a bill or resolution in a state legislature; or the principles involved in writing a good news story; or the procedure used in the selection of a jury for a murder trial; or the criteria and methods used by a play director in casting a show; or the way a football coach plans his strategy; or how stocks are bought and sold; or how an advertising agency obtains sponsors for various television shows; or how some of the new office machines work for a secretary. Note the emphasis on the word "how" in these suggested topics. In each case the speaker will explain how something works or operates. This is the type of subject you should choose.
   2. Plan your outline, using the regulation four-part plan. Be sure that the points in the body of the speech are arranged in the proper order. Select your facts carefully and word them in exact language. The wording of your speech is extremely important. Keep asking yourself as you plan, "Am I making this idea clear and easily understood?"
D. *Delivery:*
   Do not hurry your speech when you give it in class. Take your time with your explanations. Watch your listeners because they'll reflect their comprehension or lack of it. They'll provide you with the answer to whether or not you are getting through to them. If you suspect that you are not, try to reinforce the idea by restating it in another way which may be clearer to more of your listeners.
E. *Purpose of communication:* relaying.

PROBLEM 4

AN INTRODUCTION

A. *Time limit:* 2 minutes

B. *Emphasis:* The introduction of a speaker is helpful to both the listeners and the speaker. The person making the introduction gives the background of the speaker and helps to prepare the audience for him. The introduction often helps to make the listeners more receptive to the speaker. Occasionally these introductions are highly entertaining. On other occasions, they are highly informative. In this assignment, the introduction must be of the latter type—highly informative.

C. *Preparation:*
   1. For your introduction, set up an imaginary situation. Decide on the type of occasion and the name of the speaker. Choose a person who, you feel, would be interesting for a college group to hear. For example, you may select a well-known person from the entertainment world, from the world of government, from industry, from educational circles, from the ministry, politics, the military world, or from the sports field.
   2. In many instances, it will be necessary for you to do research regarding this person in order to present interesting and vital facts concerning him.

D. *Delivery:*
   The introduction should be performed in such a way that the auditors know that the introducer is genuinely interested in the speaker and his proposed subject. There must be animation and vitality in the presentation and a real sincerity of purpose.

E. *Further suggestions:* Briefly, the speech of introduction should acquaint the members of the audience with the speaker, give them a knowledge of his background and accomplishments, render them favorable toward him and create within them an interest in his speech.

   In presenting a speaker to an audience, try to avoid the trite or too casual type of introduction. Usually, it is wise to say more than, "We are glad to have Mr. _____ with us tonight to speak on the subject '_____.'"

   At the same time, the introductory speaker should avoid being too extravagant in his remarks. It is embarrassing for a speaker to listen to highly complimentary remarks. His discomfiture may result from his own comparison of himself with the picture being painted by the introducer.

The person performing the introduction should avoid speaking too long. A minute or two is considered adequate under normal circumstances. Don't seize such an opportunity to put yourself on exhibition. Remember that the main speaker should be allowed the greater part of the time and the spotlight. Therefore keep your introduction brief but to the point.

Tact is a necessary part of handling introductions. Lack of it has embarrassed and even angered many speakers. In one instance, a superintendent of schools was introducing the commencement speaker. He spoke as follows: "Ladies and gentlemen: This is not the speaker I wanted to present to you. I tried my best to secure the services of Dr. _____. However, he was unable to be with us tonight. He recommended Professor _____ who is beside me on the platform. Now, I don't know much about Professor _____, for I have never met him before tonight. But we will soon find out whether he is as capable a speaker as Dr. _____ says he is." With such an introduction, is it any wonder that the speaker was in an irritable frame of mind as he approached the speaking situation.

Happily, there are many examples of very fine introductions which accomplish their purposes. Probably there is none more famous for its appropriateness than the one used first by Shailer Mathews. He introduced President Woodrow Wilson by saying, "Ladies and gentlemen: the President." Apparently this has become somewhat standard form for introducing the President of the United States. The television networks all rely on this simple form.

In most cases, however, the introducer needs to say more about the speaker. He feels he has a responsibility to acquaint the listeners with the speaker, to pave the way for the subject matter, or to break the ice for the speaker. You will find a sample of an introduction in the Appendix. Read this to see what other people have said in introducing a speaker.

F. *Purposes of communication:* relaying and externalizing.

PROBLEM 5

REVIEW OF BOOK, PLAY, MOVIE OR TV SHOW

A. *Time limit:* 6 minutes

B. *Emphasis:* This assignment represents a real challenge for the speaker. In it you should attempt to share the enjoyment that you have experienced from your contact with the subject of your speech. For example, reading a novel may have afforded you a good deal of pleasure. It had a compelling plot, interesting characters, and vivid descriptions. The author was able to make his characters real, and the situation believable, and the setting vivid and appropriate. Reading this book was a delightful and/or moving experience. Now you have the opportunity to share your feelings with your listeners. Try to avoid the typical book-report approach. Try to do more than summarize what you have read. Share your amusement, concern, admiration, or other feelings which were stimulated by the story. Help your audience to enjoy what you did in the original reading.

C. *Preparation:*
   1. You ought to spend some time recalling plays you have enjoyed; novels you have read; television shows which were memorable; movies that you still remember vividly. Select as the subject of your speech one of these which made an impression; one that you remember with affection because of the warmth of the story; one that even recalling causes you to smile or chuckle, or one that still haunts you and at the same time intrigues you.
   2. Review the story of the plot which you will include as a part of your speech. Analyze the effect it had on you. Then try to determine how the author or director achieved this effect. Was it primarily in the plot, the characters, the dialogue, or in the atmosphere and mood?
   3. Decide on the most appropriate and effective method of presenting your review and outline your speech in the usual way. Devote only a portion of your speech to the recreation of the story. In addition, you will want to analyze the approach of the writer or the director to show how he achieved effectiveness in his work. In the case of a play, movie, or television show, you certainly will want to comment on the skill of the performers. Try to be original in your presentation. Throughout all of your planning remember the purpose of your speech: to transmit your enjoyment and/or your intensity of feeling to your listeners.

D. *Delivery:*
   Try to recreate the mood and atmosphere of the story through appropriate language and vocal and physical reinforcement. If you really enjoyed the story, you cannot help but share this same experience with your listeners. Let your reaction to it be reflected

in your vocal control and in your facial expression and bodily activity. Above all, get some personal satisfaction from your discussion.

E. *Purposes of communication:* Relaying and externalizing will be the primary purposes in this speech. However, there is an element of the esthetic involved, since the subject matter is primarily esthetic.

PROBLEM 6

"THIS I BELIEVE"

A. *Time limit:* 5 minutes

B. *Emphasis:* In this problem, the student is attempting to externalize an idea, an attitude, or a point of view that he holds. His main goal is to achieve understanding with his auditors. He has to present a point of view without all of the rationalization that usually accompanies this kind of utterance.

C. *Preparation:*
   1. The first major problem in the preparation of this kind of communication is to find out what the idea is. Many of us have half-formed thoughts on many subjects, but in order to express them well, a clear and definite picture is needed. The first thing that the student needs to do is to look within himself and discover his own feelings.
   2. In planning the outline, the student may wish to proceed chronologically, using the same basic outline that he had used in the other communications. Show how the events in your life and your environment have brought this idea into being.
   3. Carefully avoid attempts to convert the audience to your way of thinking. It is sufficient that they understand what your position is, without necessarily agreeing with it.

D. *Delivery:*
   Keep your delivery conversational and direct. You can discuss emotional ideas without becoming emotional about them.

E. *Purpose of communication:* In this problem, your only purpose is externalization. Your goal is for the audience to have a clear understanding of your inner state.

PROBLEM 7

EXPLANATION OF AN ABSTRACT IDEA

A. *Time limit:* 5 minutes

B. *Emphasis:* In this communicative situation, you face the challenge of explaining a subject of a theoretical nature. You will not be able to depend upon visual aids for assistance in clarifying your ideas. Instead, you will have to rely solely on words and bodily reinforcement for the transmission of your message. Your problem is complicated by the fact that your central idea is going to be more general and abstract than those which you have communicated in previous speeches.

C. *Preparation:*
   1. There are many interesting and challenging abstract subjects which need to be explored and discussed. Too often much is left unsaid in regard to "friendship," "patriotism," "loyalty," "spiritual needs," "standards of ethics," "justice," "cooperation," "initiative," "success," "failure," "ambition," "faith, hope, and charity," and so on, as they apply to our daily lives. Admittedly these are difficult subjects to discuss. But it is important that we explore them in order to determine what these attributes are and how they function in our society.

      Any speech concerning abstract subjects is bound to be highly personal and rightly so. With such a topic you may rely heavily on the use of personal experiences and illustrations in order to clarify your ideas.
   2. Plan your outline carefully, using the same basic outline that you have used in other speeches. Remember that your primary purpose is exploration and explanation. In order to rid your abstract subject of generalities and obscurities be as specific as possible in your applications. Show how the principle you are discussing has touched and affected people or situations in different ways. Use vivid illustrations of actual experiences to aid in your explanations.

D. *Delivery:*
   Keep your delivery conversational and direct.

E. *Purposes of communication:* Relaying and externalizing probably will be your prime objectives in this speech. However, there may be suasory purposes, in addition. It is likely that you will also attempt to relay your feelings in a particular way in order to achieve an emotional response on the part of your listeners. You may upset them, stimulate or excite them, and/or jar them out of their state of lethargy. The intensity of your own attitudes will determine the degree to which you make use of the suasory approach.

PROBLEM 8

PRESENTATION OF A PROBLEM

A. *Time limit:* 5 minutes

B. *Emphasis:* In this speech your auditors must *feel* the impact and challenge of your message. Therefore you must be concerned with their values and attitudes as well as their intellects. Sound and logical explanations must be supported by evidence and testimony in order to satisfy the listeners' intellectual comprehension and acceptance. But you must further reinforce your logical message with deftly created images which will disturb the complacency of your listeners and stimulate them to take some type of action.

C. *Preparation:*
   1. Certain problems exist in society. These are a result of disinterest, boredom, lethargy, and laziness, rather than of negative feelings. If you are aware of such a problem and have a strong desire to stir your listeners out of their complacency into action, you have a potential subject for this speech.
   2. Outline your message using the four-part plan. The addition of supporting materials to your basic outline will be of prime importance. Your plea must be based on a sound, logical analysis of the problem. This plea may be strengthened and reinforced by the use of well-selected illustrations which have emotional overtones. For example, a plea for donations of plasma for the blood bank can be enhanced by describing a young victim of leukemia who is the picture of health but actually on the brink of death. Find *real* and moving illustrations and describe them vividly.

      Your introduction and conclusion will be of particular importance. Be sure to use material in these parts which you feel would guarantee audience attention and interest. In your conclusion, hit your audience hard with material that may propel them into action.

D. *Delivery:*
This speech calls for artistic delivery. It must be animated, dynamic, and forceful. At the same time it must be sincere, earnest, and natural. Unfortunately, the nature of the material often tempts the speaker to be bombastic and overdramatic. The speaker must be careful not to become maudlin, pseudo-oratorical, or condescending. In other words, do not lose your sense of communication. Remember, you are talking to people like yourself. Let them feel your desire to share this message with them.

E. *Purposes of communication:* This message will be largely suasory, though, as it has been pointed out, in most communications there will be some relaying and externalizing. In this communication, however, the primary objective will be to prick your listeners' feelings, to change their understanding of a particular condition. So there are affective and cognitive dimensions to the multiple purposes of this communicative task.

PROBLEM 9

SALES TALK

A. *Time limit:* 5 minutes

B. *Emphasis:* In this speech you are to assume that you have only one chance to make this presentation to this particular group of listeners. Thus, if you hope to make a sale, you must present a strong case for your product. It should be based on demonstrable facts, presented in an ethical manner. In other words, you must not mislead or overpower your listeners for the sake of a sale. Make a logical and valid appeal to your prospective customers.

C. *Preparation:*
1. First, select an object which you have used and appreciated or one that is used in your home. This is important because only familiarity with and acceptance of the object or product can provide you with the necessary background for this speech. If you have used the product, you know its advantages, its uses, and its values.
2. Once you have decided upon the item you wish to sell, analyze it in terms of its uses, its values, its distinguishing characteristics, its comparative cost, its reliability, and so on. Write down your findings. Talk with other people who have used the product, in

order to collect additional evidence which may strengthen your case.
3. Using this material, organize your message. As with any subject, you may have more material than you require. Select only that which will help to build a substantial, positive case for the product.

D. *Delivery:*
There is only one warning in connection with this project. Do not be a "phony"—a super-salesman whose main concern is to charm the potential buyer into the purchase of an item which he really may not want. Sincerity and honesty must be reflected in the content of the message *and* in the manner of the salesman.

E. *Purposes of communication:* Obviously, part of your job will be to relay information about the product you are attempting to sell. However, you are relaying with the intent of changing the prospective buyer's cognition or understanding of the product, with the ultimate objective of a particular kind of behavior—namely, the purchase of your product. Therefore, this communication is more concerned with suasory purposes of a cognitive and behaviorial nature.

PROBLEM 10

DEFENSE OF THE STATUS QUO

A. *Time limit:* 5 minutes

B. *Emphasis:*
The phrase "status quo" is defined as the existing state. For example, at the present time, we have committed ourselves to a program of substantial foreign aid for the "have not" nations. In referring to this program it could be described as the "status quo." In this speech you are asked to defend the "status quo" of a policy in effect in the university, in your home community, in the state, or in the nation.

C. *Preparation:*
1. There is a policy now in effect which you heartily endorse. You believe it is the proper way to handle the problem involved. However, you may have heard rumblings of discontent from your acquaintances. They condemn the program and begin talking about other ways to handle it. Your defense of the present policy is the subject of this speech.

2. Think about and write down the reasons why you believe this policy is sound. Do the necessary research for other material which will support your point of view. Then select the three reasons why your point of view is sound and make these the main points in the body of your speech. The material which you use to support these three main points is extremely important. Testimony, statistics, specific instances, and explanations will be essential to the development of your case.
3. You will find that the introduction serves a double purpose in this speech. It can be used for the usual reasons—to secure attention and interest. In addition, you can use the introduction to provide the necessary background. Historical events may be of special importance to an understanding of the problem.

D. *Delivery:*
Be careful not to show any antagonism in presenting your subject. You may be quite indignant that people have been trying to disturb the status quo which you consider appropriate and effective. But you must not risk irritating your auditors if you want them to listen to your views. Be objective, sincere, and friendly.

E. *Purposes of communication:* This communicative activity is concerned primarily with suasory objectives. The sender, feeling that the "status quo" is desirable, attempts to relay sufficient material to convince his auditors that "no change" is the most desirable course of action. He solicits the continuing support of some of his listeners and enlists the endorsement of others. Thus, he is concerned with all of the suasory objectives.

PROBLEM 11

ADVOCACY OF A CHANGE OF POLICY

A. *Time limit:* 5 minutes

B. *Emphasis:*
In this type of speech you reveal and support your dissatisfaction with the status quo. If, for example, you believe and recommend that we reduce the extent of our foreign aid, you are advocating a change in policy. Or if you advocate an increase in this aid, you are likewise recommending a change of policy.

C. *Preparation:*
   1. Again your choice of a speech topic is determined by your beliefs. Therefore isolate a policy which you think should be changed.
   2. Begin your study of the problem by analyzing the present policy in order to detect its inherent weaknesses, its impracticability, its failure to adjust to the present needs or problems. Next you must summarize the ways in which the change in policy would eradicate or modify the present problems, which result from the inadequacy of the existing policy. After a thorough study of the situation, you are prepared to outline your speech and develop your major reasons for advocating a change.
   3. In the conclusion of this speech you may be able to give final reinforcement to your presentation by contrasting the effectiveness of the new policy with the inadequacy of the one in effect. This may be reinforced further through the use of illustrations and/or quotations.

D. *Delivery:*
   Try not to antagonize your listeners. In this communicative situation, it is extremely important that you give your auditors no reason to question your credibility. Many times, the content of a message of this type is logical and sound; however, the speaker, in a special effort to sell his ideas, appears to be impatient and condescending with people who do not immediately subscribe to his point of view. This attitude is a very real detriment in this setting.

E. *Purposes of communication:* In this situation, you will attempt to achieve a behavioral objective: you will ask your listeners to demonstrate their support by working for a change in the present policy. Again, you will be concerned primarily with suasory purposes. You must relay information which has social implications with the specific purpose of upsetting your listener's complacency. But you also hope that by relaying this information you may change each individual's understanding of the problem and eventually, he will demonstrate his comprehension by some type of positive action.

APPENDIX

MODEL SPEECHES

THE LIFE OF A DIPLOMAT

PURPOSE: TO RELAY AND EXTERNALIZE

What does a diplomat do? Well—for one thing, he makes speeches. He also writes philosophical interpretations of governmental theory for scholarly quarterlies, factual analyses of trade and production data for economic weeklies, tender and pathetic accounts of courage among the war refugees (and what diplomat lacks them in these times?) for the house organs of the great charitable organizations, commentaries on the equipoise of military power as it affects his country for some of the numerous magazines specializing in ground or sea or air warfare, and forecasts concerning domestic and international politics for the elite monthlies. And he does not overlook occasional brief pieces for such special periodicals as those issued by boys' clubs, milk dealers, aluminum manufacturers, and the association of tobacco auctioneers.

And when he isn't writing, he speaks. He speaks at formal assemblies of the United Nations and at special international conferences to which his Government may appoint him a delegate. He speaks informally to small delegations that visit his office to present a gift, a petition, or a resolution of commendation on some stand recently taken by his Government. He speaks to women's clubs, to men's service luncheons, to colleges and to grade schools, to the annual banquets of labor unions and bankers, to community forums which have question

By BEN C. LIMB. Ambassador of the Republic of Korea to the United Nations. Reprinted with permission from "The Life of a Diplomat," *Quarterly Journal of Speech*, Vol. XLIII, No. 1, pp. 55-61.

periods, and on radio and television discussion panels where he is the bull's-eye in a target aimed at by several of "the nation's leading news analysts." He speaks to boys' clubs and to girls' clubs, to church groups and to investors' syndicates, to county fairs and to select dinner meetings of leading financiers. He talks to Congressmen, and State Department officials, and other Ambassadors, and Executive-Secretaries of organizations ranging from Infuriated Taxpayers Arrayed Against Foreign Aid to Aroused Citizens Militantly Marshaled to Defend International Democracy.

For several hours each day he sits at his desk writing letters. He writes to learned professors whose lifetime specialty is the interelationship of the vowel system of his national language with that of the Seminole Indians, and to returned servicemen who want to know the name and address of an orphan child photographed with a big smile while receiving a can of GI rations on a cold street corner during the terrible winter retreat. He writes to lonely and warmhearted couples who would like to adopt a child from his country, and to business opportunists who think his people ought to provide an ideal market for a newly invented gadget. He writes to the Den Mother of Cub Scouts in a South Dakota village who wants a list of eleven grade-school children in his country who can and wish to correspond with her charges (in the English language). And he writes scores of thank-you letters to the many people who express admiration for the courage of his countrymen in resisting aggression.

He also dines. He attends formal dinners given by other ambassadors on the occasion of their national holidays. (Every one of the eighty-odd nations has at least two or three holidays which merit attendance by top-ranking representatives of all the nations with which they have friendly relations.) He attends special luncheons which feature the unique dishes of various countries or of regional or cultural groups in the United States. He goes to cocktail parties and afternoon teas. He goes on picnics and excursions. He accepts invitations for breakfasts and for midnight snacks. And between times he follows a rigorous diet to keep his weight from becoming more than he can carry around.

And he travels! His secretary keeps on file the schedules of airlines, trains, buses, and ferryboats (with notations of deviations from the schedule on Sundays and holidays). He is in New England for a meeting one evening, and in Illinois (on the way to California) for another meeting the next day. He dashes through traffic in Washington and New York, and flies above storm clouds over Minnesota. And he carries a portable dictaphone so he can keep up with his correspondence while en route.

Between times he works on incoming and outgoing reports, conducts conferences, makes lavish use of the telephone, and studies endless reams of data in connection with projects assigned to him by his Government. He reads an assortment of ministerial reports and of daily newspapers from his own country, to keep up to date on what is happening and on the tenor of opinion of his own folks back home; and he reads even more newspapers of the country to which he is accredited so that he can send back summary reports of opinion for the guidance of his own Government. He administers his own staff, and he worries about the inadequacies of his own office budget.

Finally—and by no means least important—he studies. His desk is surrounded by almanacs, dictionaries, encyclopedias, histories, a selection of new books, and standard reference works. He tries not to be ignorant of cultural developments in his own country in the twelfth century or of the possible influence of new industrial techniques in affecting production of basic commodities important for his nation's trade or domestic consumption. He knows that at any moment he may be asked for an opinion concerning a little-known writer of his own homeland or about a foreign commentary on his country's political developments. He will be expected to know the status of the religious development, the figures on coal mining, the adequacy of technological training programs, and the problems of commercial fishing in his homeland. The questions sometimes will reveal an appalling ignorance which requires of him a background lecture to set the facts in perspective; and sometimes he will be queried by an expert who has just completed a scholarly treatise on some obscure facet of his national dramaturgy.

With such a program, the serious question arises as to how an ambassador lives. If he is not a bachelor, he has a wife and perhaps several children whom he loves and with whom he would like to have a certain amount of normal family life. The chances are that his children are sent away to boarding schools, where they will be relieved of the daily disappointments of home appointments broken by the demands of official duties. His wife either retreats into a lonely world of her own, or adapts herself to a round of continuously unexpected visitors and visiting. The family medicine chest accumulates a huge collection of cures for indigestion and insomnia. Since ambassadorial salaries are not large, serious family discussions are held on the clothing budget, the servant problem, and how to devise cheaper vacations. And since the ambassador (and his wife) must always be poised, pleasant, and alert in public, he (and she) very likely will be moody, irritable, and occasionally depressed in the privacy of their apartment.

Diplomacy is a mad profession. But that madness is madness with a system. Wherever he goes and whatever he does, the ambassador is the titular representative of his Government. While on duty (and he is always on duty) he is the alter ego abroad of his President. Whatever he says is official governmental policy. How he comports himself determines to a large degree the attitude of the people he meets toward his own people at home. Nor can he escape from the difficulties by saying nothing, for "no comment" on crucial issues (and what issue is not crucial these days to some segment or other of the public or of officialdom?) can often be more devastating than even a fumbled malopropism.

It follows, then, that diplomacy is above all a profession of words—written and spoken. Diplomacy should be listed among the categories of the literary and oratorical professions—somewhere midway between the serious essayists and the lyric poets, or between the commemorative orators and the after-dinner speakers. And still another sublisting should be entered under Conversation: Formal and Informal. Above all, and in multitudinous ways, the diplomat is a man of words.

He talks—and he also listens. He listens with dubious caution to earnest crusaders who seek him out to pour into his ears detailed suggestions of what they consider brilliant solutions for what they are certain are fundamental problems confronting his country. He listens with agreeable pleasure to complicated jokes—which may not be as fresh to him as they are to the narrator. He listens with educated discrimination to discussions of aesthetic influences upon the art and literature of his nation. He listens with perceptive acuity to veiled hints of policies not yet ready for public announcement—and many of which are pure fabrications of the diplomatic rumor factory. He listens to comments on international affairs heard in snatches in elevators, in restaurants, and on street corners—and tries to estimate to what extent they may represent widespread public opinion. He listens to the words of guests who have been invited so that they may meet in person the "distinguished ambassador"—or "that man who has been making all those terrible statements."

Yes, he listens, he studies, he confers. And then (frequently after midnight) he goes into his study and prepares what he shall say the next day. And at this point he becomes a literary figure with a difference. For oftentimes his main concern is not to set down in clear and simple language a statement of facts so obvious that it cannot be misunderstood (which I believe is one of the hallmarks of great writing). Quite to the contrary, his purpose often is to concoct an ambiguous composition which—no matter how carefully it may be analyzed—will add up to no real meaning whatsoever.

One of the distressing themes of which editorial writers are fond is a ringing plea that diplomats should try to master the art of plain and straightforward talk. This theme is peculiarly distressing to diplomats, for it represents a basic misunderstanding of one of their greatest contributions to humanity.

Diplomats (to use a somewhat strained analogy) are grease on the wheels of a Rube Goldbergian machine of disconnected and clashing international machinery. The clearest and most simple fact of international affairs is that they are, indeed, *inter*national. Governments are instituted to serve their own people; and every Government has a people of its own to serve. Each Government aims at the achievement of its own purposes—and sometimes these purposes clash.

Disputes between and among governments are far from uncommon, even when the relationships of the peoples involved are basically friendly and cooperative. Differences exist on all manner of policies—ranging from the recognition of Red China to the interpretation of fisheries rights on the open seas. There are varying problems and points of view on the timing of policies that are in agreement, and on the wording of minor clauses in major documents. There are disputes on questions which are imbedded in the domestic politics of one or all the nations concerned. There are disputes which could lead to temporary irritation and there are disputes which could result in war.

The diplomat, let it never be forgotten, represents a sovereign nation. And there are no nations which are not sovereign. There are treaties and alliances which represent temporary and partial surrenders of some modicum of sovereignty. There is the United Nations, where some eighty nations meet around council tables to talk about questions of common interest. There is a growing climate of internationalism and a growing sense of global interdependency. There are trans-national influences, such as religion and trade. But there remain separate governments, each, as Mark Twain might have said, with its own fish to fry.

And in the midst of this clashing dissonance of diverse purposes and methods there stands the little group of ambassadors busily (and necessarily) applying the lubricant of ambiguity.

All of the people (and their name is legion) who deliver themselves periodically of lectures to the diplomatic corps on the presumed virtues of plain speaking should be sent back to school. And when they are settled down as a captive audience in a classroom, some dispassionate professor should lecture to them, with a host of specific examples, on what the results would be if all diplomats should always express clearly and forthrightly precisely what their own governments believed and desired.

As a specific instance (and these are always dangerous!) what should be the reply of an "underdeveloped" nation's ambassador to a question asked in a public forum about some phase of the administration of American aid funds with which his Government happened to be seriously displeased? Should he describe clearly just what it is in the program that his Government dislikes—and thereby risk arousing resentment and perhaps contribute ammunition to a minority group that wants to end all foreign aid? Or, on the other hand, should he clearly and unmistakably endorse the entire program (in order to win support for it), thereby undermining the efforts of his Government to secure some revisions? Obviously, it seems to me, he should do neither. On the contrary, he should deliver himself of sentiments which will seem to be sufficiently explicit to satisfy the question, but in such circumlocutions that the sentiments expressed could not possibly be understood.

The real purpose of such ambiguities is to mask and minimize disagreements while experts are hard at work behind the scenes trying to eliminate their causes. So long as the separate sovereignty of nations is preserved, this will inevitably be a considerable part of the diplomat's job. It simply cannot be otherwise. When an occasional inexperienced or unskilled diplomat overlooks this essential fact, the consequences are immediate, most unpleasant, and often serious. Later explanations never quite catch up with the original *faux pas*.

The serious study of diplomatic speech is still, unfortunately, in its infancy. Diplomats perforce must hammer out their own rules in the midst of their day-by-day duties. Experience has to be interpreted rapidly, for the conditions and even the rules of international conferences are constantly changing.

Just a few years ago diplomacy was conducted by leisurely gentlemen who wore striped trousers and morning coats and sat in impressive offices conducting infrequent and genteel conversations. Occasional written communications (often handwritten by the ambassador himself) were exchanged between governments whose affairs seldom interlocked. As for public appearances, the old-time diplomat (and not so old as we might think) was expected to do no more than deliver polite and inconsequential after-dinner speeches composed chiefly of refurbished jokes. When international conferences were held, they were behind locked doors and the public did not expect ever to hear any more about them than the conclusions finally formulated into policies.

The global telegraphic network, radio, the movie news camera, the airplane, and television have wrought changes that are still occurring at a dizzy pace. Nowadays, "closed conferences" are about as open as a community sewing bee. Everything that is said, how it is said, and who says it are known to all who are interested within a few minutes or hours. Moreover, diplomats nowadays talk not only to one another, but to the public in the nation to which they are accredited. And the accumulation of all the instantaneous information that is now available, plus the sense of world community created by modern transportation and communication, has aroused an interest in practically anything that happens anywhere. Diplomacy in our time is conducted on an open stage.

It should not be assumed, however, that a diplomat must always be ambiguous. Occasions also frequently arise when what he must strive for above all else is to secure a clear and correct understanding of a governmental policy or of conditions within his own country. And this, too, presents problems.

For example, a delegation of labor liberals may visit his country and upon their return may secure wide publicity for views critical of the working conditions which they observed. They, of course, are not experts on the conditions in the country they have visited. And what they have to say is addressed primarily to their own home constituency, to impress upon their followers and their own Congressmen the sincerity of their determination to achieve "good" conditions for workmen. So far so good.

However, an incidental result of their publicized criticism is a lessening of respect and friendship for the nation which they have criticized. Often the facts they cite may be correct in themselves, but are decidedly out of focus in terms of the general economic, social, and political conditions within which those facts must necessarily exist. Long working hours, for instance, have always been inseparably connected with lack of machines. Low wages are correlated with low prices. Just as in the United States, advances in labor conditions have to be related to general advances of technology. The slow process of education is required to train an expert body of technicians. Laws have to be revised by legislatures which are subject to periodic election campaigns. Money has to be found for investment in new modes of productivity. Bad conditions do not exist because anyone desires them, but are inherent in complicated situations that require widespread and often gradual remedial action. All of this needs to be explained.

And it needs to be explained to a public that will read a headline charging that the work-week is too long, but will not read a three-thousand-word article explaining why. Notoriously, it is easy to criticize and difficult to educate.

The foreign correspondents of American newspapers face this same problem when they seek to write dispatches on complicated political situations (and politics are always complicated). They seek to escape from their dilemma by using catch phrases, such as "rightest," "liberal," and "leftist," which their readers will understand, but which often only dimly if at all reflect the actual conditions they are supposed to explain. Under these circumstances, the ambassador is always goaded by his own sense of righteousness and by urgent messages from his home Government to "rectify" the misunderstandings.

Under such circumstances, the plight of the diplomat is akin to that of the public school teacher who heroically attempts to explain

Einstein's quantum theory in simple terms that will be understandable to grade-school pupils. At least the teacher has a captive audience that has to listen and try to understand.

The diplomat, faced with this problem, seeks to phrase his own understanding of the essential facts in terms that will reflect conditions in his homeland accurately and at the same time will be interesting and understandable to the public of the nation to which he is accredited. He wracks his brain for a headline phrase which will be as instantly appealing as that used by his country's critics. And such phrases, under the circumstances, are not easily come by.

Now, if there are any readers left who have borne with me this far, it may seem to them that the diplomat faces an impossibly difficult job. Maybe so. It is certainly difficult enough so that no ambassador in his right mind expects to be more than partially and occasionally successful. But there also are rewards and compensations. The anterooms of national executives are seldom crowded with diplomats who are pleading to be relieved of their posts. On the contrary, most ambassadors appear to enjoy their jobs and are generally reluctant to leave them. Diplomacy, like printer's ink, gets in the blood and keeps the true professional devotedly at his tasks.

Perhaps the major appeal of the diplomatic profession is the sense it gives (partly correctly) that the ambassador is behind the scenes and on the inside in the unfolding of the great world drama of human affairs.

To a degree never before known, the ordinary lives of ordinary people are dependent upon international relations. Hot war, cold war, psychological warfare, trade, tourism, and many facets of daily living are interwoven with the relationships of nations. What decisions are made, and a portion of the processes by which these decisions are reached, are public property. Every citizen can see pictures of the great statesmen meeting together, and can read "dope" stories by skilled news analysts on how their personalities interact.

But the diplomats, nevertheless, are a special club—a group set apart. They, and only they, can assess accurately the degree to which policies are affected by personalities and, sometimes, by sheer accidents. They can appreciate one another's difficulties in phrasing statements and in dealing with public reactions. They naturally develop a "clubbable" atmosphere among themselves. They know which diplomats violate the unbreakable rules of behavior, and which ones, with skill and ofttimes personal sacrifice, keep the gears from clashing unmercifully. In their own cocktail parties and private luncheons, they (like everyone else) often let down their hair and talk shop. And this helps them keep their perspective and balance.

What should we say to a young man or young woman who would like to get into the diplomatic service? The best advice is—don't! But if you must, start young and learn everything you possibly can: about your own country, about the world at large, present and past. Study languages, and above all study human nature. Learn to say what you mean—both so it can be understood and so it couldn't possibly be understood by anyone. Develop poise and ease in all social circumstances, under all manner of unmannerly provocations. Be interested in everyone and in everything.

More seriously, diplomacy is a profession for those who not only have the skills required but above all else have a dedicated sense of public service. The great problem of our age is how to restore justice in world affairs without the cost of war. The great need is to find some way of solving problems which in the past decade have largely been postponed. What humanity desperately needs is diplomats who still stand with courage for the ideals which represent the best in civilization —and will find a way of accomplishing them peacefully if possible.

The diplomat is far indeed from being the dilettante who specializes in personal charm. He is the instrument of humanity, charged with the successful achievement of tenable solutions to the issues of life and death. If he fails, the human race may fail. It is not a profession to be taken lightly, either by those who practice it or by those who dimly and distantly observe. It is this sense of mission which keeps the real diplomats—the representatives of free people—unwearyingly at their tasks.

EDUCATION FOR LEADERSHIP:

HARDER TO TEACH MEN THAN TO TEACH A SUBJECT

PURPOSE: SUASORY

Our greatest danger in America today is the self-conscious denial of the plain fact of the differences in the intellectual capacities in our people. Political democracy and the quest for equal opportunity for all has become tinged with an intolerance of intellectual or spiritual attainments. The great athlete is made the focus of national attention. The movie star is aped by every schoolgirl. The noisiest politician gets the most newspaper space, but the great scholar or religious leader is little recognized unless he startles the world by some novel or mysterious concept.

In a lesser degree, the high school student of excelling mind and imagination withdraws to the shadows of the stage, while athletes and glamour girls receive the full play of the spotlight. Teachers dedicated to sound learning try their best to shift the balance of attention, but are themselves discouraged by the glorification of the average mind.

In the past, the respect for intellectual attainment was a strong element in the Puritan tradition in America. Waves of later immigrations brought from Europe a high respect for learning and its place in community leadership. But prosperity and easy success in a rich country have diluted this respect. The widespread distribution of the symbols of economic attainment have aroused a subtle jealousy of the less numerous evidences of intellectual attainment. Even worse, has become a sense of pity for the man who does not use his talents to make his economic status secure.

But without sustained cultivation of intellectual and spiritual talents, wherever found, the American people will not develop for themselves the leadership which a disturbed world requires. Without intellectual and spiritual leaders of great capacity, the bountiful resources of our nation will be frittered away in frustrated attempts to solve conflicts within and without.

By J. DOUGLAS BROWN, Dean of the Faculty, Princeton University, Princeton, New Jersey. Delivered at a Meeting of the Princeton University National Alumni Association, San Francisco, California, March 10, 1949.

It is the challenge of higher education to arouse anew America's latent interest in such attainments. The challenge will not be met by giving way to the urge to accept the majority's verdict of the place of learning in the world today. It will not be met by catering alone to a mass demand for education for either economic advantage or personal enjoyment, or for a technical skill divorced from understanding and responsibility.

The challenge will only be met by institutions that frankly and positively set themselves to select the highest talent of the country, from all economic and social groups, and to give that talent the intensive, individual education that high talent deserves. It will be met by institutions that foreswear bigness, public support voted on terms by the majority of our people, easy popularity by turning no student away, or athletic circuses for the sportloving voter.

But such institutions will not have clear sailing in the years to come. They are bucking the tide. They will be cheered on by their state-supported sister institutions who pray for their continuance with one breath, and offer enticing salaries to their best professors with the next.

The private endowed university will survive only if a small but significant fraction of the American people are convinced that their contribution to the flow of potential leaders is of vital importance. This fraction will be heavily weighted with those who have themselves benefited by the education which such universities afford. As a part of their lifelong contribution to the leadership of their communities, professions, and country, they will dedicate a portion of their energies and substance that such universities may survive.

If the private endowed university, with selective admissions and high academic standards, is to fulfill its proper function and gain its full support, it must declare in no uncertain terms that its task and obligation is to develop leaders for a democratic society.

This is no criticism of the great state or municipal university that must accept ever-increasing enrollments of a larger and larger segment of the young, ambitious population within its constituency.

It is no criticism of the fine, small college that rounds out the knowledge and understanding of the young people who are attracted to its halls.

Leaders arise in both of these types of institutions, but both can be satisfied if the great majority of their graduates lead happy and fruitful lives without assuming the obligation of leadership in their professions, communities, or in the nation itself.

But Princeton and institutions like it ask far more of their entrants than the satisfactory completion of secondary education. They ask far more of their students during their four years of residence than the ability to pass a certain number of specialized courses. Even more, they must expect of their graduates a sustained contribution to the leadership of the nation, state, and community, in the whole gamut of the learned professions, in government, in industry, and in essential services.

If this were not the case, we should not ask for the support, by alumni and friends, of a complex and expensive program operated within specialized and costly facilities.

Princeton was not founded two hundred years ago to do an ordinary job in education. It early proved itself a "seminary of statesmen." Its task has never changed. The need for statesmen has broadened to encompass a host of professions and enterprises. The need for statesmen —leaders—is greater than ever before.

At the heart of the private endowed university lies its emphasis on liberal education. Liberal education is the most effective means yet discovered to develop God-given talents of leadership. Leaders arise by many means. But without nurturing education, the wastage is higher than we can afford.

Liberal education augments the native qualities of mind and spirit, develops understanding and restraint, promotes inquiry and stimulates imagination, sensitizes evaluation and lays the groundwork for maturing judgment.

This type of education is intensive, personal, and costly. It involves the close interrelation of the student and the teacher. It cannot be mass-produced. It cannot be provided to all since it must ever remain at the handicraft stage. But the opportunity to have such an education should be available to all young people of talent—all potential leaders—regardless of economic or social status. In America today we need every leader we can develop.

The three great essentials of an effective liberal education for leadership are:

1. The good teacher
2. The good student and
3. A close relationship between them.

These essentials may appear simple, but they are far from easy to attain.

Why is the good teacher so vital in liberal education? Because in liberal education the teacher is not a vehicle of knowledge—a conveyor belt dumping information upon an accumulating pile—but a catalytic agent to help the student—

To know himself

To understand others

To appreciate the lasting values of our civilization

To gain a love for truth and the joy of the search for truth

To acquire wisdom and humility before God.

In liberal education the teacher primarily teaches men, not a subject. The subject is the means not the end.

Princeton stands for liberal education in depth, not a smattering of general education preliminary to vocational training. At the core of liberal education in depth lies the humanities. Without that core, the social sciences would dry up; the natural sciences would become the master and not the servant of man.

In liberal education, no teacher is a better teacher than he is a man. It is harder to teach men than to teach a subject. Therefore, it is doubly hard to find the good teacher in liberal education, because he must be a good man who can teach men well.

To teach the love of truth and the joy of the search for truth—sincerely and effectively—the teacher must continue to experience this love and joy throughout his life in both teaching and scholarship. You can fool the students for a while—but never all, nor any for long—that one has the thrill of inquiry when it is worn bare. The best teaching is joint inquiry—joint scholarship—about an idea, a value, a truth. A university-college like Princeton is a community of joint inquiries, at all levels, from freshman to professor.

Is it so difficult then to see why Princeton strives so hard to secure and retain the good teacher in the fullest sense of the term? To succeed, it needs the help of its alumni and friends, for good teachers are few and the demands for them very, very great.

But effective liberal education for leadership also requires the good student. There must be two ends to a bridge. One could take long to describe the ideal qualities of the good student—his intellect, character, imagination, industry, personality and physical vigor.

But the good student worthy of the finest of liberal education should have more than these attractive qualities. He should have a sense of responsibility for leadership, for serving his fellow men. Without that sense of dedication, we cannot afford the intensive, personal and costly education which I have described, nor should the good teacher be justified in spending his energies in enhancing the personal advantage of the student.

There are such good students by the thousands in America today—but not by the millions! Princeton needs help as never before in attracting its full share to partake of the liberal education it can provide. Its alumni and friends can help Princeton find the good student, as well as the good teacher. With this help, that great framing structure, tangible and intangible, the traditions, experience, ideals and environment, that we call Princeton will exercise its leavening powers, as it has for two hundred years, to bring teacher and student into that relationship that nurtures the God-given qualities of leadership. With this help we cannot fail to sustain Princeton's vital place in contributing to that small but significant body of men who carry forward a civilization.

INTRODUCTION OF DAG HAMMARSKJÖLD

PURPOSE: TO RELAY AND EXTERNALIZE

In the lives of men and institutions come those great events which are never forgotten. Today we at Ohio University are participating in one of those unique experiences. We are welcoming to our university the Honorable Dag Hammarskjöld from Sweden, Secretary-General of the United Nations.

The record of what I should say in introducing Mr. Hammarskjöld is endless! But we come to honor the Secretary-General, to listen to him speak, and not to hear me praise him. You all could do that from what you know of his widely heralded achievements. There are, however, four simple facts to which I would like to refer in presenting him: (1) He was Swedish Minister of State before being elected in 1953 Secretary-General of the United Nations; (2) he has won and held the respect of the nations of the world for his honesty, integrity, fairness, shrewdness, and courage; (3) his dedicated efforts for peace have helped to keep the world from bloodshed, tragedy, and chaos; and finally to support all that I have said (4) he was on September 26, 1957, unanimously—note that in a divided world I say unanimously—re-elected to a second five-year term as Secretary-General of the United Nations. This surprised no one and should give us all great hope for peace and the future of the world.

It is a great personal pleasure to present to the Ohio University trustees, faculty, and students the Honorable Dag Hammarskjöld!

President JOHN C. BAKER of Ohio University introduced the Honorable Dag Hammarskjöld at a University convocation on February 5, 1958.

FOR THE LEAGUE OF NATIONS

PURPOSE: SUASORY

MR. CHAIRMAN AND FELLOW COUNTRYMEN:

You make my heart very warm with your generous welcome, and I want to express my unaffected gratitude to your chairman for having so truly struck the note of an occasion like this. He has used almost the very words that were in my thought, that the world is inflamed and profoundly disturbed, and we are met to discuss the measures by which its spirit can be quieted and its affairs turned to the right courses of human life. My fellow countrymen, the world is desperately in need of the settled conditions of peace, and it cannot wait much longer. It is waiting upon us. That is the thought, that is the burdensome thought, upon my heart tonight, that the world is waiting for the verdict of the Nation to which it looked for leadership and which it thought would be the last that would ask the world to wait.

My fellow citizens, the world is not at peace. I suppose that it is difficult for one who has not had some touch of the hot passion of the other side of the sea to realize how all the passions that have been slumbering for ages have been uncovered and released by the tragedy of this war. We speak of the tragedy of this war, but the tragedy that lay back of it was greater than the war itself, because back of it lay long ages in which the legitimate freedom of men was suppressed. Back of it lay long ages of recurrent war in which little groups of men, closeted in capitals, determined whether the sons of the land over which they ruled should go out upon the field and shed their blood. For what? For liberty? No; not for liberty, but for the aggrandizement of those who ruled them. And this had been slumbering in the hearts of men. They had felt the suppression of it. They had felt the mastery of those whom they had not chosen as their masters. They had felt the oppression of laws which did not admit them to the equal exercise of human rights. Now, all of this is released and uncovered and men glare at one another and say, "Now we are free and what shall we do with our freedom?"

By WOODROW WILSON. Delivered in Des Moines, Iowa, September 6, 1919.

What happened in Russia was not a sudden and accidental thing. The people of Russia were maddened with the suppression of Czarism. When at last the chance came to throw off those chains, they threw them off, at first with hearts full of confidence and hope and then they found out that they had been again deceived. There was no assembly chosen to frame a constitution for them, or, rather, there was an assembly chosen to choose a constitution for them and it was suppressed and dispersed, and a little group of men just as selfish, just as ruthless, just as pitiless, as the agents of the Czar himself, assumed control and exercised their power by terror and not by right. And in other parts of Europe the poison spread—the poison of disorder, the poison of revolt, the poison of chaos. And do you honestly think, my fellow citizens, that none of that poison has got in the veins of this free people? Do you not know that the world is all now one single whispering gallery? Those antennae of the wireless telegraph are the symbols of our age. All the impulses of mankind are thrown out upon the air and reach to the ends of the earth; quietly upon steamships, silently under the cover of the Postal Service, with the tongue of the wireless and the tongue of the telegraph, all the suggestions of disorder are spread through the world. Money coming from nobody knows where is deposited by the millions in capitals like Stockholm, to be used for propaganda of disorder and discontent and dissolution throughout the world, and men look you calmly in the face in America and say they are for that sort of revolution, when that sort of revolution means government by terror, government by force, not government by vote. It is the negation of everything that is American; but it is spreading, and so long as disorder continues, so long as the world is kept waiting for the answer to the question, What kind of peace are we going to have and what kind of guarantees are there to be behind that peace, that poison will steadily spread more and more rapidly, spread until it may be that even this beloved land of ours will be distracted and distorted by it?

That is what is concerning me, my fellow countrymen. I know the splendid steadiness of the American people, but, my fellow citizens, the whole world needs that steadiness, and the American people are the make-weight in the fortunes of mankind. How long are we going to debate into which scale we will throw that magnificent equipoise that belongs to us? How long shall we be kept waiting for the answer whether the world may trust us or despise us? They have looked to us for leadership. They have looked to us for example. They have built their peace upon the basis of our suggestions. That great volume that contains the treaty of peace is drawn along the specifications laid down by the American Government, and now the world stands amazed because an authority in America hesitates whether it will indorse an American document or not.

You know what the necessity of peace is. Political liberty can exist only when there is peace. Social reform can take place only when there is peace. The settlement of every question that concerns our daily life waits for peace. I have been receiving delegations in Washington of men engaged in the service of the Government temporarily in the administration of the railways, and I have had to say to them, "My friends, I cannot tell what the railways can earn until commerce is restored to its normal courses. Until I can tell what the railroads can earn I cannot tell what the wages that the railroads can pay will be. I cannot suggest what the increase of freight and passenger rates will be to meet these increases in wages if the rates must be increased. I cannot tell yet whether it will be necessary to increase the rates or not, and I must ask you to wait." But they are not the only people that have come to see me. There are all sorts of adjustments necessary in this country. I have asked representatives of capital and labor to come to Washington next month and confer—confer about the fundamental thing of our life at present; that is to say, the conditions of labor. Do you realize, my fellow citizens, that all through the world the one central question of civilization is, "What shall be the conditions of labor?" The profound unrest in Europe is due to the doubt prevailing as to what shall be the conditions of labor, and I need not tell you that that unrest is spreading to America.

In the midst of the treaty of peace is a Magna Charta, a great guarantee for labor. It provides that labor shall have the counsels of the world devoted to the discussion of its conditions and of its betterment, and labor all over the world is waiting to know whether America is going to take part in those conferences or not. The confidence of the men who sat at Paris was such that they put it in the document that the first meeting of the labor conference under that part of the treaty should take place in Washington upon the invitation of the President of the United States. I am going to issue that invitation, whether we can attend the conference or not. But think of the mortification! Think of standing by in Washington itself and seeing the world take counsel upon the fundamental matter of civilization without us. The thing is inconceivable, but it is true. The world is waiting, waiting to see, not whether we will take part but whether we will serve and lead, for it has expected us to lead. I want to testify that the most touching and thrilling thing that has ever happened to me was what happened almost every day when I was in Paris. Delegations from all over the world came to me to solicit the friendship of America. They frankly told us that they were not sure they could trust anybody else, but that they did absolutely trust us to do them justice and to see that justice was done them. Why, some of them came from countries which I have, to my shame, to admit that I never heard of before, and I had to ask as privately as possible what language they spoke. Fortunately they always had an interpreter, but I always wanted to know at least what family of languages they were speaking. The touching thing was that from the ends of the earth, from little pocketed valleys, where I did not know that a separate people lived, there came men—men of dignity, men of intellectual parts, men entertaining in their thought and in their memories a great tradition, some of the oldest people of the world—and they came and sat at the feet of the youngest nation of the world and said, "Teach us the way to liberty."

That is the attitude of the world, and reflect, my fellow countrymen, upon the reaction, the reaction of despair, that would come if America said: "We do not want to lead you. You must do without our advice. You must shift without us." Now, are we going to bring about a peace, for which everything waits? We cannot bring it about by doing nothing. I have been very much amazed and very much amused, if I could be amused in such critical circumstances, to see that the statesmanship of some gentlemen consists in the very interesting proposition that we do nothing at all. I had heard of standing pat before, but I never had before heard of standpatism going to the length of saying it is none of our business and we do not care what happens to the rest of the world.

Your chairman made a profoundly true remark just now. The isolation of the United States is at an end, not because we chose to go into the politics of the world, but because by the sheer genius of this people and the growth of our power we have become a determining factor in the history of mankind, and after you have become a determining factor you cannot remain isolated, whether you want to or not. Isolation ended by the processes of history, not by the processes of our independent choice, and the processes of history merely fulfilled the prediction of the men who founded our Republic. Go back and read some of the immortal sentences of the men that assisted to frame this Government and see how they set up a standard to which they intended that the nations of the world should rally. They said to the people of the world, "Come to us; this is the home of liberty; this is the place where mankind can learn how to govern their own affairs and straighten out their own difficulties," and the world did come to us.

Look at your neighbor. Look at the statistics of the people of your State. Look at the statistics of the people of the United States. They have come, their hearts full of hope and confidence, from practically every nation in the world, to constitute a portion of our strength and of our hope and a contribution to our achievement. Sometimes I feel like taking off my hat to some of those immigrants. I was born an American. I could not help it, but they chose to be Americans. They were not born Americans. They saw this star in the west rising over the peoples of the world and they said, "That is the star of hope and the star of salvation.

We will set our footsteps towards the west and join that great body of men whom God has blessed with the vision of liberty." I honor those men. I say, "You made a deliberate choice which showed that you saw what the drift and history of mankind was." I am very grateful, I may say in parentheses, that I did not have to make that choice. I am grateful that ever since I can remember I have breathed this blessed air of freedom. I am grateful that every instinct in me, every drop of blood in me remembers and stands up and shouts at the traditions of the United States. But some gentlemen are not shouting now about that. They are saying, "Yes; we made a great promise to mankind, but it will cost too much to redeem it." My fellow citizens, that is not the spirit of America, and you cannot have peace, you cannot have even your legitimate part in the business of the world unless you are partners with the rest. If you are going to say to the world, "We will stand off and see what we can get out of this," the world will see to it that you do not get anything out of it. If it is your deliberate choice that instead of being friends you will be rivals and antagonists, then you will get exactly what rivals and antagonists always get, just as little as can be grudgingly vouchsafed you.

Yet you must keep the world on its feet. Is there any business man here who would be willing to see the world go bankrupt and the business of the world stop? Is there any man here who does not know that America is the only nation left by the war in a position to see that the world does go on with its business? And is it your idea that if we lend our money, as we must, to men whom we have bitterly disappointed, that money will bring back to us the largess to which we are entitled? I do not like to argue this thing on this basis, but if you want to talk business, I am ready to talk business. If it is a matter of how much you are going to get from your money, I say you will not get half as much as antagonists as you will get as partners. Think that over, if you have none of that thing that is so lightly spoken of, known as altruism. And, believe me, my fellow countrymen, the only people in the world who are going to reap the harvest of the future are the people who can entertain ideals, who can follow ideals to the death.

I was saying to another audience today that one of the most beautiful stories I know is the story that we heard in France about the first effect of the American soldiers when they got over there. The French did not believe at first, the British did not believe, that we could finally get 2,000,000 men over there. The most that they hoped at first was that a few American soldiers would restore their morale, for let me say that their morale was gone. The beautiful story to which I referred is this, the testimony that all of them rendered that they got their morale back the minute they saw the eyes of those boys. Here were not only soldiers. There was no curtain in front of the retina of those eyes. They were American eyes. They were eyes that had seen visions. They were eyes the possessors of which had brought with them a great ardor for a supreme cause, and the reason those boys never stopped was that their eyes were lifted to the horizon. They saw a city not built with hands. They saw a citadel towards which their steps were bent where dwelt the oracles of God himself. And on the battlefield were found German orders to commanders here and there to see to it that the Americans did not get lodgment in particular places, because if they ever did you never could get them out. They had gone to Europe to go the whole way towards the realization of the teaching which their fathers had handed down to them. There never were crusaders that went to the Holy Land in the old ages that we read about that were more truly devoted to a holy cause than these gallant, incomparable sons of America.

My fellow citizens, you have got to make up your minds, because, after all, it is you who are going to make up the minds of this country. I do not owe a report or the slightest responsibility to anybody but you. I do not mean only you in this hall, though I am free to admit that this is just as good a sample of America as you can find anywhere, and the sample looks mighty good to me. I mean you and the millions besides you, thoughtful, responsible American men and women all over this country. They are my bosses, and I am mighty glad to be their servant. I have come out upon this journey not to fight anybody, but to report to you, and I am free to predict that if you credit the report there will be no fighting. It is not only necessary that we should make peace with Germany and make peace with Austria, and see that a reasonable peace is made with Turkey and Bulgaria—that is not only all of it, but it is a very dangerous beginning if you do not add something to it. I said just now that the peace with Germany, and the same is true of the pending peace with Austria, was made upon American specifications, not unwillingly. Do not let me leave the impression on your mind that the representatives of America in Paris had to insist and force their principles upon the rest. That is not true. Those principles were accepted before we got over there, and the men I dealt with carried them out in absolute good faith; but they were our principles, and at the heart of them lay this, that there must be a free Poland, for example.

I wonder if you realize what that means. We had to collect the pieces of Poland. For a long time one piece had belonged to Russia, and we cannot get a clear title to that yet. Another part belonged to Austria. We got a title to that. Another part belonged to Germany and we have settled the title to that. But we found Germany also in possession of other pieces of territory occupied predominately or exclusively by patriotic Poles, and we said to Germany, "You will have to give that up, too; that belongs to Poland." Not because it is ground, but because those people there are Poles and want to be parts of Poland, and it is not our business to force any sovereignty upon anybody who does not want to live under it. When we had determined the boundaries of Poland we set it up and recognized it as an independent Republic. There is a minister, a diplomatic representative, of the United States at Warsaw right now in virtue of our formal recognition of the Republic of Poland.

But upon Poland center some of the dangers of the future. South of Poland is Bohemia, which we cut away from the Austrian combination. Below Bohemia is Hungary, which can no longer rely upon the assistant strength of Austria, and below her is an enlarged Rumania. Alongside of Rumania is the new Slavic Kingdom, that never could have won its own independence, which had chafed under the chains of Austria-Hungary, but never could throw them off. We have said, "The fundamental wrongs of history center in these regions. These people have the right to govern their own Government and control their own fortunes." That is at the heart of the treaty, but, my fellow citizens, this is at the heart of the future: The business men of Germany did not want the war that we have passed through. The bankers and the manufacturers and the merchants knew that it was unspeakable folly. Why? Because Germany by her industrial genius was beginning to dominate the world economically, and all she had to do was to wait for about two more generations when her credit, her merchandise, her enterprise, would have covered all the parts of the world that the great fighting nations did not control. The formula of pan-Germanism, you remember, was Bremen to Bagdad—Bremen on the North Sea to Bagdad in Persia. These countries that we have set up as the new home of liberty lie right along that road. If we leave them there without the guarantee that the combined force of the world will assure their independence and their territorial integrity, we have only to wait a short generation when our recent experience will be repeated. We did not let Germany dominate the world this time. Are we then? If Germany had known then that all the other fighting nations of the world would combine to prevent her action, she never would have dreamed of attempting it. If Germany had known—this is the common verdict of every man familiar with the politics of Europe—if Germany had known that England would go in, she never would have started it. If she had known that America would come in, she never would have dreamed of it. And now the only way to make it certain that there never will be another world war like that is that we should assist in guaranteeing the peace and its settlement.

It is a very interesting circumstance, my fellow countrymen, that the League of Nations will contain all the nations of the world, great and small, except Germany, and Germany is merely put on probation. We have practically said to Germany, "If it turns out that you really have had a change of heart and have gotten nonsense out of your system; if it really does turn out that you have substituted a genuine self-governing Republic for a Kingdom where a few men on Wilhelmstrasse plotted the destiny of the world, then we will let you in as partners, because then you will be respectable." In the meantime, accepting the treaty, Germany's army is reduced to 100,000 men, and she has promised to give up all the war material over and above what is necessary for 100,000 men. For a nation of 60,000,000! She has surrendered to the world. She has said, "Our fate is in your hands. We are ready to do what you tell us to do." The rest of the world is combined, and the interesting circumstance is that the rest of the world, excluding us, will continue combined if we do not go into it. Some gentlemen seem to think they can break up this treaty and prevent this League by not going into it. Not at all.

I can give you an interesting circumstance. There is the settlement, which you have heard so much discussed, about that rich and ancient Province of Shantung in China. I do not like that settlement any better than you do, but these were the circumstances: In order to induce Japan to cooperate in the war and clear the Pacific of the German power England, and subsequently France, bound themselves without any qualification to see to it that Japan got anything in China that Germany had, and that Japan would take it away from her, upon the strength of which promise Japan proceeded to take Kiauchau and occupy the portions of Shantung Province, which had been ceded by China for a term of years to Germany. The most that could be got out of it was that, in view of the fact that America had nothing to do with it, the Japanese were ready to promise that they would give up every item of sovereignty which Germany would otherwise have enjoyed in Shantung Province and return it without restriction to China, and that they would retain in the Province only the economic concessions such as other nations already had elsewhere in China—though you do not hear anything about that—concessions in the railway and the mines which had become attached to the railway for operative purposes. But suppose that you say that is not enough. Very well, then, stay out of the treaty, and how will that accomplish anything? England and France are bound and cannot escape their obligation. Are you going to institute a war against Japan and France and England to get Shantung back for China? That is an enterprise which does not commend itself to the present generation.

I am putting it in brutal terms, my fellow citizens, but that is the fact. By disagreeing to that provision, we accomplish nothing for China. On the contrary, we stay out of the only combination of the counsels of nations in which we can be of service to China. With China as a member of the League of Nations, and Japan as a member of the League of Nations, and America as a member of the League of Nations, there confronts every one of them that now famous Article X, by which every member of the League agrees to respect and preserve the territorial integrity and existing political independence of all the other member States. Do not let anybody persuade you that you can take that article out and have a peaceful world. That cuts at the root of the German war. That cuts at the root of the outrage against Belgium. That cuts at the root of the outrage against France. That pulls that vile, unwholesome Upas tree of Pan-Germanism up by the roots, and it pulls all other "pans" up, too. Every land-grabbing nation is served notice: "Keep on your own territory. Mind your own business. That territory belongs to those people and they can do with it what they please, provided they do not invade other people's rights by the use they make of it." My fellow citizens, the thing is going to be done whether we are in it or not. If we are in it, then we are going to be the determining factor in the development of civilization. If we are out of it, we ourselves are going to watch every other nation with suspicion, and we will be justified too; and we are going to be watched with suspicion. Every movement of trade, every relationship of manufacture, every question of raw materials, every matter that affects the intercourse of the world, will be impeded by the consciousness that America wants to hold off and get something which she is not willing to share with the rest of mankind. I am painting the picture for you, because I know that it is as tolerable to you as it is to me. But do not go away with the impression, I beg you, that I think there is any doubt about the issue. The only thing that can be accomplished is delay. The ultimate outcome will be the triumphant acceptance of the treaty and the League.

Let me pay the tribute which it is only just that I should pay to some of the men who have been, I believe, misunderstood in this business. It is only a handful of men, my fellow citizens, who are trying to defeat the treaty or to prevent the League. The great majority, in official bodies and out, are scrutinizing it, as it is perfectly legitimate that they should scrutinize it, to see if it is necessary that they should qualify it in any way, and my knowledge of their conscience, my knowledge of their public principle, makes me certain that they will sooner or later see that it is safest, since it is all expressed in the plainest English that the English dictionary affords, not to qualify it—to accept it as it is. I have been a student of the English language all my life and I do not see a single obscure sentence in the whole document. Some gentlemen either have not read it or do not understand the English language; but, fortunately, on the right-hand page it is printed in English and on the left-hand page it is printed in French. Now, if they do not understand English, I hope they will get a French dictionary and dig out the meaning on that side. French is a very precise language, more precise than the English language, I am told. I am not on a speaking acquaintance with it, but I am told that it is the most precise language in Europe, and that any given phrase in French always means the same thing. That cannot be said of English. In order to satisfy themselves, I hope these gentlemen will master the French version and then be reassured that there are no lurking monsters in that document; that there are no sinister purposes; that everything is said in the frankest way.

For example, they have been very much worried at the phrase that nothing in the document shall be taken as impairing in any way the validity of such regional understandings as the Monroe Doctrine. They say: "Why put in 'such regional understandings as'? What other understandings are there? Have you got something up your sleeve? Is there going to be a Monroe Doctrine in Asia? Is there going to be a Monroe Doctrine in China?" Why, my fellow citizens, the phrase was written in perfect innocence. The men that I was associated with said, "It is not wise to put a specific thing that belongs only to one nation in a document like this. We do not know of any other regional understanding like it, we never heard of any other; we never expect to hear of any other, but there might some day be some other, and so we will say 'such regional understandings as the Monroe Doctrine'," and their phrase was intended to give right of way to the Monroe Doctrine in the Western Hemisphere. I reminded the Committee on Foreign Relations of the Senate the other day that the conference I held with them was not the first conference I had held about the League of Nations. When I came back to this our own dear country in March last I held a conference at the White House with the Senate Committee on Foreign Relations, and they made various suggestions as to how the Covenant should be altered in phraseology. I carried those suggestions back to Paris, and every one of them was accepted. I think that is a sufficient guarantee that no mischief was intended. The whole document is of the same plain, practical, explicit sort, and it secures peace, my fellow citizens, in the only way in which peace can be secured.

I remember, if I may illustrate a very great thing with a very trivial thing, I had two acquaintances who were very much addicted to profanity. Their friends were distressed about it. It subordinated a rich vocabulary which they might otherwise have cultivated, and so we induced them to agree that they never would swear inside the corporate limits, that if they wanted to swear they would go out of town. The first time the passion of anger came upon them they rather sheepishly got in a street car and went out of town to swear, and by the time they got out of town they did not want to swear. That very homely illustration illustrates in my mind the value of discussion. Let me remind you that every fighting nation in the world is going to belong to this League, because we are going to belong to it, and they all make this solemn engagement with each other, that they will not resort to war in the case of any controversy until they have done one or other of two things, until they have either submitted the question at issue to arbitration, in which case they promise to abide by the verdict whatever it may be, or, if they do not want to submit it to arbitration, have submitted it to discussion by the council of the League.

They agree to give the council six months to discuss the matter, to supply the council with all the pertinent facts regarding it, and that, after the opinion of the council is rendered, they will not then go to war if they are dissatisfied with the opinion until three more months have elapsed. They give nine months in which to spread the whole matter before the judgment of mankind, and if they violate this promise, if any one of them violate it, the Covenant prescribes that that violation shall in itself constitute an act of war against the other members of the League. It does not provide that there shall be war. On the contrary, it provides for something very much more effective than war. It provides that that nation, that covenant-breaking nation, shall be absolutely cut off from intercourse of every kind with the other nations of the world; that no merchandise shall be shipped out of it or into it; that no postal messages shall go into it or come out of it; that no telegraphic messages shall cross its borders; and that the citizens of the other member States shall not be permitted to have any intercourse or transactions whatever with its citizens or its citizens with them. There is not a single nation in Europe that can stand that boycott for six months. There is not a single nation in Europe that is self-sufficing in its resources of food or anything else that can stand that for six months. And in those circumstances we are told that this Covenant is a covenant of war. It is the most drastic covenant of peace that was ever conceived, and its processes are the processes of peace. The nation that does not abide by its covenants is sent to coventry, is taboo, is put out of the society of covenant-respecting nations.

This is a covenant of compulsory arbitration or discussion, and just as soon as you discuss matters, my fellow citizens, peace looks in at the window. Did you ever really sit down and discuss matters with your neighbor when you had a difference and come away in the same temper that you went in? One of the difficulties in our labor situation is that there are some employers who will not meet their employees face to face and talk with them. I have never known an instance in which such a meeting and discussion took place that both sides did not come away in a softened temper and with an excess of respect for the other side. The processes of frank discussion are the processes of peace not only, but the processes of settlement, and those are the processes which are set up for all the powerful nations of the world.

I want to say that this is an unparalleled achievement of thoughtful civilization. To my dying day I shall esteem it the crowning privilege of my life to have been permitted to put my name to a document like that; and in my judgment, my fellow citizens, when passion is cooled and men take a sober, second thought, they are all going to feel that the supreme thing that America did was to help bring this about and then put her shoulder to the great chariot of justice and of peace which was going to lead men along in that slow and toilsome march, toilsome and full of the kind of agony that brings bloody sweat, but nevertheless going up a slow incline to those distant heights upon which will shine at the last the serene light of justice, suffusing a whole world in blissful peace.

INDEX

INDEX

INDEX

Anderson, Delmar C., 145
Articulating mechanism, 179–189
Articulation, definition of, 180
Articulation, as message conveyor, 163
Articulation, problems of, 181–184
  addition of sounds, 182–183
  omission of sounds, 182
  sound distortions, 181–182
  sound substitutions, 181
Ashley, Annabelle, 188–189
Assignment outline, 235–236
Attitude
  change through balance, 160
  components of, 141–142
    affective, 141
    behavioral, 141
    cognitive, 141
  definition of, 140–142
  and set for listening, 208
Attitudinal communications, 152–153
Audience, characteristics of, 50–51
  age, 50
  occupation, 50
  other factors, 50–51
  sex, 50

Baker, John C., 284
Balance, theory of, 159
Barnard, Chester I., 11
Barnes, Duane Clayton, 121
Becker, Samuel L., 38
Behavioral theory, 69–70

Berlo, David, 5, 16, 19
Bettinghaus, Erwin P., 162
Bitzer, Lloyd F., 153
Body, use of, in speaking, 194–197
  eye contact, 194–195
  facial expression, 195
  gestures, 195–196
  movement, 196–197
Body of speech, 85–92
  development of, 89–92
  examples of, 106–111
  information sources, 90–92
  kinds of arrangement in, 87
    chronological, 87
    derived from cognitive imbalance, 89
    logical, 88–89
    place, 88
  major points in, 86–87
  purpose of, 87
Bowers, John Waite, 125
Brack, Harold, 133
Breathing, 166–167
Brehm, Jack W., 160
Brockreide, Wayne, 156
Brown, J. Douglas, 280
Bryant, Donald C., 140–141
Buckley, William F., 155–156

Campbell, James H., 21
Carnegie, Dale, 11
Cathcart, Robert S., 145
Cherry, Colin, 4
Churchill, Winston, 130–131

Civil disobedience, 228-229
"Clear and present danger" decision, 225-227
Clevenger, Theodore, 51
Cohen, Arthur R., 160
Communication
  attitude changes in, 158-162
  cultural diffusion, 9-10
  definition of, 4-17
    Berlo, David, 16
    Goyer, Robert, 15
    Hartman, Frank, 14
    Miller, Gerald, 15
  breakdown in, 7-9
  federal regulation of, 228-229
  interpersonal relationships in, 11-12
  invention in, 49-50
  learning and, 12-13
  limitations of, 225-229
    clear and present danger, 225-229
    civil disobedience, 228-229
    minority reactions, 228
    obscenity in, 227-228
  needs for, 6
  occupational demands, 10-11
  as persuasive or informative, 25-26
  professional use of, 5
  purpose, 3-4
  forms of, 28-34, 140-143
    esthetic, 32-34
    externalizing, 29-30
    mands, 30-31
    relays, 30
    suasory, 34, 140, 143
Communication models of, 18-24
  basic processes of, 22-24
  Berlo, 19
  and percept of, 22
  Shannon-Weaver, 18
  Westley-McLean, 19-20
Communicative skill, 38-39

Communicator, 229-230
  obligation to all levels of government, 230
  responsibility of, 224-225
Conclusion, 92-95
  examples of, 111
  purpose of, 92
  types of, 92-95
    summary, 92
    personal, 93
    illustrative, 94
    stimulative, 94-95
Conclusion identification, drill, 240-242
Cory, Elsie, 132

Darnell, Donald K., 112
Dashiell, J., 164
Delivery
  conversational style of, 192
Dialect, 188
Dickens, Charles, 20
Dissonance, cognitive, 159-160
Doob, Leonard, 139-140
Dresser, William R., 145
Drills, 254-267
  advocacy of change of policy, 266-267
  book, play, movie, TV review, 259
  defense of status quo, 265-266
  demonstration, 254-255
  explanation of a process, 257
  explanation of abstract idea, 262
  externalizing an idea, 261
  introduction, 258-259
  presentation of a problem, 263-264
  sales talk, 264-265
  using chalkboard, 255-256
Duker, Sam, 201

Ehninger, Douglas, 156
Enthymeme, 153

Esthetic communication, 32–34
Evaluation, criteria for, 210–219
Evaluation form, 234
Evidence
  audience reaction to, 146
  definition of, 144
  effectiveness of, 145
  example as, 149
  facts as, 146
  in Toulmin's model, 154–158
  statistics as, 150–152
  testimony as, 150
Eye contact, 194–195
Externalizing, 29–30

Facial expression, 195
Festinger, Leon, 159–160
Field theory, 68–69
Fishbein, Martin, 162
Fotheringham, Wallace, 162
Francis, W. Nelson, 128–129

Gestures, use of, 195–196
Government, obligation to by communicator, 229–230
Goyer, Robert, 15
Grammar, problems of, 126–127
Greenberg, Bradley S., 37
Group discussion, 248–249
Gwynn, Fredrick L., 8

Hall, Edward, 14
Halsey, William F., 7
Hartman, Frank, 14
Heider, Fritz, 159
Heinberg, Paul, 186–187
Hepler, Hal W., 21
Hildreth, R. A., 145
Hovland, Carl, 141–143
Huxley, Aldous, 218

Information sources, 90–92
  card catalog, 90
  indexes, 91
  people as, 90
  reading as, 90
  reference works, 91
Institute for Propaganda Analysis, Inc., 216–217
Introduction, 81–84
  examples of, 106
  purpose of, 81
    attention in, 81
    key idea in, 81–82
  types of, 82–84
    historical, 83
    illustration, 82–83
    quotation, 84
    personal, 84
    statement or question, 83
  identification drill, 242–245
Invention, in communication, 49–50

Jones, H. E., 205–206

Kantner, Claude E., 113
Key idea, definition of, 84
  evaluation drill, 237
  use of, 85

Laird, Charlton, 125
Langer, Susanne, 6
Language, 113–138
  attitude change and, 124–125
  attitude toward, 114
  grammar and better usage of, 128–136
  tools of, 114
  vividness in, 130–134
  vocabulary, 135–136
  vocalization, 179–180
Lee, Irving J., 124
Leyte Gulf, 7
Limb, Ben C., 271
Limitations in communications, 225–229
Lindsay, John, 11

Listeners, 206-222
  criteria for, 210
  evaluation of by speaker, 211-219
  model for, 206
Listening
  attitude toward, 208
  distractions, and, 210
  hearing and, 207-208
  importance of, 204-205, 221-222
  improvement devices, 252-254
  learning and, 202
  note-taking and, 209
  preoccupation and, 209
  time differential, and, 209
  vocabulary in, 209
Locke, John, 3
Logic, 153-158
  definition of, 153
  symbolic, 153
  Toulmin's model of, 154
Loudness, as voice variable, 177-179

MacLean, Malcolm, 19
Mands, 30-31
Malmstrom, Jean, 188-189
McLuhan, Marshall, 5
Meaning, 120
  abstraction, 122-123
  connotative, 122
  denotative, 121-122
Miller, Gerald R., 15, 37, 144
Model speeches, 271-296
Movement of body of speaker, 196-197

Nichols, Ralph G., 203, 208-209
Nimitz, Admiral Chester, 7

Obscenity, use of, 227-228
Offensive matter and communications, 228

Ogden, Charles K., 122
O'Neill, Robert M., 225, 227
Osgood, Charles B., 159
Ostermeier, Jerry N., 145
Outline
  assignments in, 235-236
  examples of, 102-111
  expanding of, 96-99
  need for, 80-81
  purpose of, 81
  supports for, 101-102
    analogy or comparison of, 101
    explanation of, 101
    illustration of, 102
    statistics for, 102
  testimony in, 102
    specific instance of, 102

Performances
  communication breakdowns, 249
  group discussion, 248-249
  introduction of a classmate, 247-248
  three-minute oral communications, 249-250
  voice and articulation, 250
Pitch
  problems of, 173
  use of, 173-174
  of voice, 170-174
Projects, 245-246
  emphasis on physical reinforcement, 246
  group interaction, 245
  observation of formal speaking situation, 245
  propaganda analysis, 245-246
  vocal effectiveness, 246
Pronunciation, 184-189
  problems of, 184-185
  regional influence on, 185-187
  standard for, 186-187
  use of, 180

Propaganda, techniques of, 214–218
  distortions of truth, 215
  bandwagon, 218
  German Fascism, 215, 216, 218
  glittering generalities, 216
  half-truths, 214–215
  hasty generalizations, 215
  plain folks device, 217–218
  testimonial, 217
  transfer device, 217–218
Psychoanalytic view of communicative situation, 68

Quality of voice, 174–177

Rankin, Paul, 204
Rate of speaking, 189–192
  control of, 190–191
  techniques in, 190
  use of, 189–190, 191–192
Relays, 30
Rhythm in speaking, 191–192
Richards, I. A., 122
Rogers, Carl, 6
Rosenberg, Milton, 141–143, 162

Scheidel, Thomas, 162
Shannon, Claude, 18
Scrambled outlines drill, 239
Skinner, B. F., 30
Sound
  articulation, formation in, 180
  elements of
    air conductor, 169–170
    energy as, 166–167
    resonator as, 168
    vibrator as, 167–169
  pronunciation as tool, 180
Source
  as beginning of communication, 48–75
  control of, 70–75
  imbalance and, 160–161
  responsibility of, 75
  speaker-centered approach in analysis of, 71–72
  objectivity in, 72–73
  release of, 72
  topic-centered approach to, 73–74
Speech
  appropriateness of, 193
  conversational style in, 192–193
  expanding outline of 96–99
  freedom of, 223–224
  outline supports of, 101–102
Stage fright, 67–68
Statistics, 150–152
Stimuli
  change and contrast as, 164
  duration and repetition of, 164
  extensity of, 164
  habits of attention as, 165
  intensity of, 164
  movement of, 164
Structuring message, 76–112
  application of principles, 99–112
  expanding outline, 96–99
  outlining, 81
  body, 85–92
    examples of, 107–111
  conclusion, 92–95
    examples of, 111
  introduction, 81–84
    examples of, 106
  key idea, 84–85
    example of, 106
Suasory communication, 34, 140, 143
Supreme Court, 225–228

Tannebaum, Percy, 159
Testimony, 150
Thinking, 52–62
  communication source, 52–53
  to define a purpose, 62–66
  exposure to stimuli, 54–56

Thinking (*continued*)
  isolating topics, other characteristics of, 66–70
    adjustment in, 67
    behavioral theory of, 69–70
    field theorists in, 68–69
    psychoanalytic view of, 68
  to limit extent of communication, 62–66
Topic, approach to, 73–75
  guides for, 64–66
Toulmin, Stephen, 154
Toussaint, Isabella H., 205
Tuchow, Seymour, 132–133
Transitions, 136–138

Visual aids
  as stimuli, 198
  types of, 198–199
  use of, 197–200
Vocabulary, 135–136
Voice
  and articulation, 163
  mechanism of, 165–170
  variables of, 170–179
    loudness as, 177–179
    pitch as, 170–174
    quality as, 174–177
Von Koenigswald, G. H. R., 3

Weaver, Warren, 18
Webster's *Seventh New Collegiate Dictionary*, 187, 188, 189
Westley, Bruce, 19
Wilson, Woodrow, 285
Words, choice of, 125